The historic Belgian cities of Bruges, Ghent, Antwerp, Mechelen, Brussels and Leuven have become increasingly popular tourist destinations in recent years. The remarkable blossoming of Flemish art and architecture in the 15th century, and the cultural influences of other European countries brought by trade, have created a rich diversity of fascinating sights in a relatively small region - and an appetite for enjoyment that is revealed in some of the best cooking, brewing and general joie de vivre in Europe.

Flemish Cities Explored guides the visitor authoritatively through six cities on a series of walks that cover everything of interest from art galleries and museums to secret convents and convivial cafés. A clear and informative map accompanies each of the walks, together with some 60 illustrations of paintings and architecture. There is practical advice on choosing restaurants and hotels, and information on museum and gallery opening times.

For both the casual visitor and the serious art lover, *Flemish Cities Explored* is the ideal travelling companion.

ABOUT THE AUTHOR: A chance encounter with the Ghent Altarpiece more than twenty years ago sparked off Derek Blyth's exploration of Flemish cities and art. He now lives in Brussels with his wife and four children, working as a writer and translator. He has written a guidebook to Amsterdam, where he lived for six years, and a book on Berlin, Potsdam and Dresden. Amsterdam Explored, a companion to this volume, will be published by Pallas Athene in Spring 1997.

SECOND EDITION. FULLY REVISED.

D0601496

FLEMISH CITIES EXPLORED

BRUGES, GHENT, ANTWERP, MECHELEN, BRUSSELS & LEUVEN

DEREK BLYTH

PALLAS ATHENE

ACKNOWLEDGEMENTS

My main debt is to Guido Waldman, who as editor at The Bodley Head in 1988 responded enthusiastically to the original manuscript, at a time when no other publisher in London appeared remotely interested in a book on Belgium. His departure from The Bodley Head was an inestimable blow, though both Jill Black and Corrine Hall provided support in the latter stages of the project. Much that I discovered in Brussels in 1988 was due to the writers on The Bulletin magazine, in particular Cleveland Moffett. I owe other insights to John Chalker, who hunted out a 1905 Baedeker guide to Holland and Belgium, in which I continue to delve for the occasional insight. Help and encouragement in various other forms came from Helen Bannatyne, Jane Hedley-Prole, C.M. Maclure, Menno Spiering and Deborah Whitworth. Finally, I would like to thank my wife Mary Maclure, who deserves a medal for putting up with my frequent trips to Bruges, Ghent and all the other cities.

TO THE READER:

Cities do not stand still for long. Though I have tried to check every fact in this book, it can sometimes happen that a museum will move, an established restaurant lose its flair, a fashionable neighbourhood fall out of favour. It is always helpful when readers who discover such changes note down their observations on a postcard and send them to the publisher.

ISBN 1 873429 61 4
© Derek Blyth 1990 Revised edition © Derek Blyth 1996
Series editor: Alexander Fyjis-Walker Editorial Assistants: Lynette Quinlan and Barbara Fyjis-Walker
Printed through World Print, Hong Kong for
Pallas Athene, 59 Linden Gardens, London W2 4HJ
First published 1990
Second revised edition 1996

CONTENTS

Appendices, p 332

ILLUSTRATIONS

MAPS
drawn by Ted Hammond

Preface to the Second Edition

I have good news from Ghent. And better news still from Antwerp. The cities of Flanders are becoming increasingly fashionable. People are beginning to discover the eccentric allure of Antwerp fashion design, the excitement of Ghent theatre, the superb quality of Flemish cooking and the extraordinary range of beers brewed in Belgium.

Back in 1988, when I first wrote this book, I was often struck by the tragic neglect of Flemish architecture and art. Since then, I have watched the restoration of the Place des Martyrs in Brussels, wandered through the renovated Patershol district in Ghent and admired the freshly-restored interior of Antwerp's Bourla theatre. A few things have inevitably changed for the worse - the wonderful 19th-century wooden house behind the cloth hall in Bruges has gone for ever, and the Brouwershuis in Antwerp is no longer open - but the main developments in recent years have been enormously encouraging for anyone with an interest in Flanders.

It is now more than twenty years since I first set foot in a Flemish city. Bound for Austria on a family holiday, I assured my father that a detour to Ghent would take no time at all. The aim of this subterfuge was to see the van Eyck altarpiece in Ghent cathedral, which I had read about in a newspaper travel article. I can still recall the extraordinary experience as we stood in a tiny chapel and the custodian opened the two folding wings of the altarpiece to reveal the painting of the Adoration of the Mystic Lamb (a ceremony regrettably no longer performed). From that day on, I took every available opportunity to seek out Flemish paintings in art galleries and explore the city streets of Flanders.

This book is devoted to my parents, who introduced me to the pleasures of travel and remained in good humour when I occasionally took them to unplanned destinations.

Derek Blyth
Ixelles, 1996

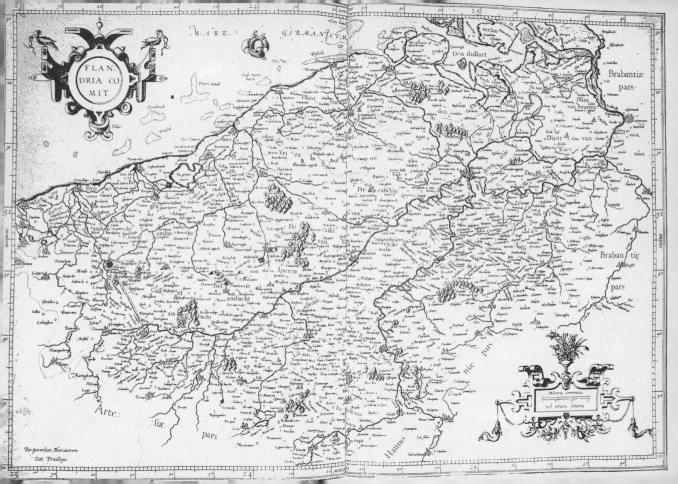

Introduction

Bruges, Ghent, Antwerp, Mechelen, Leuven, Brussels are cities that we sometimes glimpse in the background of Flemish paintings. Through an open window behind a Virgin and Child we may see a street of Flemish houses, like the detail in our frontispiece from the painting by the Master of Flémalle in London's National Gallery. At other times we gain only a tantalising glimpse of a city, such as the street that is reflected in a tiny convex mirror in the foreground of Quinten Metsys' *The Money Changer and his Wife* in the Louvre. Or it may be a distant view of spires and gables that we see, as in Roger van der Weyden's *Bladelin Altarpiece* (reproduced on page 49) in Berlin's Dahlem Museum. These paintings may tempt us to visit the Flemish cities, just as van Gogh's landscapes draw us to Provence, or Canaletto's take us to Venice.

We may be disappointed, on arrival, to find that the cities have aged and weathered since they were proudly built of brick and stone many centuries ago. Only in Bruges, and parts of Mechelen and Ghent, do we still find scenes reminiscent of medieval Flemish paintings. The cities of Flanders are still beautiful, yet they seem somehow tinged with sadness. They look back wistfully upon the distant golden age when great fortunes were amassed within their walls, and majestic spires and belfries soared above the flat countryside. Bruges, to me, dwells on its 15th-century glories, while Antwerp remembers its heyday in the 19th century. This romantic nostalgia gives the cities of Flanders a mellow mood; they are particularly attractive, I think, on misty

13

autumn days, or in winter when the streets are hushed by a blanket of snow. The bright sunshine of a summer's day tends to draw attention to their imperfections, like the wrinkles on the aged face of a once-beautiful film star.

Flanders has been a region of vague and shifting boundaries since it was first settled. It originally encompassed the area of northern Europe ruled by the counts of Flanders, whose power eventually extended over the territory shown on the 16th-century map on page 12, which was published in Duisburg in Mercator's famous atlas. On this map, Flanders extends from northern France to Zeeland, now part of the Netherlands. Ghent and Bruges are clearly Flemish, but Antwerp, Mechelen and Brussels seem not to be. It would be fickle, however, to exclude them from this book, as the boundary of Flanders ceased to exist politically in 1384, and the term Flemish now refers to all the Dutch-speaking provinces of Belgium. Bruges in the province of West Flanders, Ghent in East Flanders, and Antwerp and Mechelen in the province of Antwerp are all Flemish cities by this definition.

Brussels is still a borderline case, as its nineteen *communes* form a separate bilingual enclave within the province of Flemish Brabant. Though now predominantly French-speaking, Brussels has been included in this guide because of its Flemish past, and its museums and galleries filled with treasures of Flemish art.

According to one school of etymology, Flanders (Vlaanderen in Dutch) means 'the flooded land' - an apt description for this low-lying area at the delta of the River Scheldt. Like neighbouring Holland, Flanders had to be drained and diked to make it habitable. Holland and Flanders are alike in other ways, too; for example, the architectural traditions in both regions are based on brick, as stone is so scarce. However, Flanders straddles the frontier between French and German civilisations, and so has endured a much more turbulent and tragic history. If Flemish culture sometimes seems to have an edginess and anxiety compared to that of Holland, it is perhaps because Flanders has been, as Collins English Dictionary puts it, the 'scene of many battles in many wars'.

As long ago as 1640, James Howell described Flanders as 'the cockpit of Europe'. Looking again at our 16th-century map, we see numerous place names evoking bleak images of war. Outside the walls of Kortrijk (spelt Cortrycke on this map), a Flemish army crushed the French at the Battle of the Golden Spurs in 1302. The *Chronicles of Froissart* tell of a battle 80 years later on a hill near Roosbeke, at which Charles VI of France defeated the Flemish weavers. Not far from Roosbeke, we see the names of many other small Flemish towns that were the scene of horrifying battles in the First World War, such as Passendale, Diksmuide, Poperinge and Ypres (Ieper in Dutch and corrupted to Wipers by the British troops).

The tragic history of Flanders began during the waning years of the Roman Empire, when German tribes poured into the northern area of Gallia Belgica, but failed to penetrate the region to the south. This remained populated by the Romanised Wala, who were protected by a vast forest, the Silva Carbonaria, which at that time extended from the Rhine to the North Sea.

Although now much reduced in extent, some of this forest still stands south of Brussels, where it is known as the Forêt de Soignes in French and the Zonienwoud in Dutch. The invisible language frontier that divides present-day Belgium into French-speaking Wallonia and Dutch-speaking Flanders runs through the middle of this thick forest. If we head south of Brussels through the woods, we may notice that the names on signs change from Dutch to French: Brussel becomes Bruxelles, Leuven becomes Louvain. At that point we have crossed the frontier from Flemish Brabant to French Brabant, from German to French civilisation.

A new frontier was drawn across this region by the Treaty of Verdun in 843, under which the empire of Charlemagne was divided into the Western, Middle and Eastern Kingdoms. The River Scheldt formed the boundary in northern Europe between the Western Kingdom and the Middle Kingdom. The nascent cities of Bruges and Ghent lay to the west of the Scheldt, in the Middle Kingdom, and so became subject to the French king, whereas the cities of Antwerp, Brus-

15

sels and Mechelen lay to the east, and so were in German territory.

In the early middle ages the counts of Flanders gave a distinctive identity to the area of French civilisation west of the Scheldt. To defend the land against the Vikings, Baldwin of the Iron Arm, the first Count of Flanders, built a castle at Bruges in 865 and one at Ghent a few years later. His successor, Baldwin II, added to the defences by building city walls around Bruges and Ypres. In the 11th century, the counts of Flanders gradually conquered the lands to the east of the Scheldt.

At the turn of the 11th century, the Flemish rulers turned their energies to the Crusades. Count Robert II of Flanders earned himself the title of 'Lance and Sword of Christendom' in the Holy Land, while Count Baldwin IX of Flanders was appointed Emperor of Constantinople in 1204. By the 13th century the counts of Flanders had exhausted their military ambitions, and devoted themselves to a more peaceful struggle against the North Sea, building dikes to reclaim the marshes and bogs of their flooded land.

In the 13th century the Flemish cities of Ypres, Ghent and Bruges grew enormously wealthy from the production of cloth. It was then that the proud belfries, cloth halls, meat markets and town halls were built. The Flemish cities at this time developed close ties with England: 'All the nations of the world are kept warm by the wool of England made into cloth by the men of Flanders,' wrote Matthew of Westminster. But the wool trade led to a conflict of loyalties during the Hundred Years War. The aristocracy of Flanders remained feudally bound to the French king, whereas the guilds pragmatically supported the English king to safeguard the supply of high quality wool. In the late 13th century, Edward I of England attempted to protect the Flemish trade by sending an army to repel Philip the Fair of France. But when Edward was forced to withdraw this army to deal with the Scots, the French promptly marched back to reclaim their territories. They were again driven out in 1302 by a Flemish uprising known as the Matins of Bruges. Attempting to regain Flanders soon afterwards, the French knights suffered their humiliating defeat at the Battle of the Golden Spurs.

On the death in 1384 of Count Louis de Male, Flanders passed to Philip the Bold, Duke of Burgundy, who had married Louis' daughter, Margaret of Flanders in Ghent in 1369. The dukes of Burgundy thereby inherited the great cities of Flanders and Brabant, including Ghent, Bruges, Antwerp and Brussels. This meant the end of Flanders as a political entity, and the beginning of the language problem, for the dukes and the nobles at their court spoke only French, whereas the craftsmen and shopkeepers of the Flemish cities spoke Dutch. Hence, in 15th-century Flemish portraits, the mottos of the nobles and clergymen are invariably in French.

The Burgundian period was a golden age for Bruges, Brussels and Ghent. The patronage of the highly cultured dukes and nobles of Burgundy led to an extraordinary blossoming of Flemish art and architecture, exemplified by the 15th-century altarpieces of the Flemish Primitives and the soaring late gothic spires of the churches and cathedrals.

Philip the Bold's grandson, Duke Philip the Good, skilfully expanded the territories of Burgundy by ceremonies, contracts and cunning rather than by military conquest. Having succeeded to Flanders in 1419, he bought Namur in 1421, inherited Brabant, Limburg and Antwerp in 1430, and plotted the fall of Jacqueline of Hainaut in 1433 to acquire Hainaut, Holland and Zeeland. He then bought Luxembourg ten years later, had his nephew elected Bishop of Liège and, finally, saw his son installed as Bishop of Utrecht. The prosperous feudal states, counties, duchies and lordships acquired in this way formed the Burgundian Netherlands, an area which corresponds roughly to the present-day states of Belgium, the Netherlands and Luxembourg.

Our knowledge of the Burgundian Netherlands is extremely vivid because the art of painting was then so precise and factual. Works were commissioned by cloth merchants, bankers, jewellers, mariners, butchers, fishmongers, burgomasters and judges. They were hard-headed practical people, interested in cloth, bills, nails, meat, iron, fruit, jewels, spices and shoes. The 15th-century Flemish Primitives produced paintings that were as satisfying and well-made as a doll's house. When we look at the works of Jan van Eyck, for example, we hardly notice their form, for we are captivated by the *things* they represent. We notice the grain of the wooden floorboards in the *Arnolfini Wedding Portrait* in London, the individual threads of a frayed carpet in the *Madonna with Canon van der Paele* in Bruges, the hedgerows in the *Adoration of the Mystic Lamb* in Ghent. We are enthralled by the Flemish Primitives' child-like delight in illusion, deception, ceremonies and hidden secrets.

The death in 1477 of Charles the Bold, the son of Philip the Good, brought an end to the brief and brilliant period of Burgundian rule in the Netherlands. His daughter, Mary of Burgundy, married Maximilian of Austria, later Emperor of Germany. Maximilian's grandson, Charles V, became Emperor of Germany through his father, Philip the Fair, and King of Spain through his mother, Joanna the Mad. The Flemish cities were favourably placed to benefit from the vast wealth generated by this vast empire. But there was a nagging doubt, a rumour of dissent, at the heart of 16th-century Flanders. We see it in the paint-ings of Hieronymus Bosch, in the crowded renaissance studies of the Antwerp Mannerists, and even in some of Pieter Bruegel the Elder's works. These artists were no longer at ease with the world; their paintings were a protest, a prophecy of doom, anticipating the religious torments of the 16th century. Under Charles V a few unfortunate heretics were burnt; under his son Philip II entire cities were set alight.

The Dutch Revolt against Philip II of Spain split the Burgundian Netherlands in two. The southern Netherlands (now Belgium) remained staunchly Catholic, whereas the northern Netherlands (now the Netherlands) turned vehemently Protestant. We may nowadays scarcely be aware of this difference as we travel between Belgium and the Netherlands, for the boundary does not correspond to any natural division. Like the frontier that once split Germany, it was a purely military demarcation, following the front in 1648, when the Dutch and Spanish signed the Treaty of Münster.

Yet though there may be no visible frontier, there are still fundamental cultural differences.

From 1579 (when the northern provinces banded themselves together to resist Spanish oppression) until 1713, the Spanish Netherlands were a remote territory of the Spanish Hapsburgs. The great cloth cities and trading ports of Flanders declined into provincial backwaters. Cities that had once astonished travellers such as John Evelyn and Albrecht Dürer with their wealth and their art, were now depopulated, ageing and enervated. The Protestant weavers, diamond cutters, merchants, bankers and printers had almost all fled to Holland or to England.

The role of the Spanish Netherlands in the 17th century was as a bulwark of Catholicism. In the former northern Netherlands, the Dutch were rapidly establishing a maritime empire, constructing ships, warehouses, banks, exchanges, weigh houses and arsenals. But in the Spanish Netherlands whatever money was available was devoted to constructing baroque churches and filling them with paintings, statues, confessionals and pulpits.

In 1713 the Spanish Netherlands passed into the hands of the Austrian Hapsburgs; a remote government in Madrid was replaced by a remote government in Vienna. Initially the Austrians were indifferent to the Netherlands, provoking riots in Brussels, but under the Empress Maria Theresa the economy of the Austrian Netherlands gradually improved.

In 1795 Napoleon's army invaded; a remote government in Vienna was then replaced by a somewhat less remote government in Paris. In the nineteen years of French administration that followed, the churches and monasteries of Flanders were sacked, and art treasures carried off to Paris. French became the official language of the administration, and the population became more strongly divided than ever into a French-speaking upper class, and a Dutch-speaking lower class.

After the final defeat of Napoleon at Waterloo in 1815, the Treaty of Vienna created the new state of the United Kingdom of the Netherlands, which briefly reunited the northern and southern Netherlands. This was something of a marriage of convenience, intended to create a strong state to the north-east of France, but the allies had not realised just how incompatible these two countries had become after 236 years of separation. The southern part of the new kingdom was now Catholic and French-speaking, whereas the northern part was Protestant and Dutch-speaking. Fifteen years later the inevitable split occurred. The south rebelled against the north and, after a brief and relatively bloodless revolution, the state of Belgium was born. In 1831 Prince Léopold of Saxe-Coburg, a favourite uncle of Queen Victoria's, was invited to be King.

The reign of Léopold II, his son (photograph page 234), was a period of extraordinary growth and prosperity, fuelled by industrialisation and rampant colonialism. The difference between Belgium and the Netherlands became even more pronounced in this period. Whereas the cities of Holland even today possess a modest quality, with their neat little houses and precise details, the cities of Belgium, particularly Brussels and Antwerp, were rebuilt on a colossal scale, with echoes of 19th-century Paris or even ancient Egypt. If you take a coach tour in Brussels, you will probably be shown one of the largest buildings in the world, the Palais de Justice, whereas on a tour of Amsterdam you are more likely to be shown the smallest house in the city.

The First World War marked the end of a golden age in Belgium as it did everywhere else in Europe. In 1914 the German army swept through Belgium from the Ardennes. Liège fell six days after the invasion, soon followed by Charleroi, where the French army was defeated, and Mons, where the British army fell back. A few days later Leuven and Brussels were taken, and the government fled to Antwerp. The Belgian army made a final stand behind Antwerp's massive ramparts and advanced forts, supported by a detachment of British troops commanded by Winston Churchill, who had gallantly rushed to the aid of 'plucky little Belgium'. But after twelve days of bombardment Antwerp fell, and the Belgian army retreated to defend a last tiny corner in the north-west of the country, beyond the River Yser. The opposing armies then dug a line of trenches across Flanders and, in the years of heavy shelling that followed, many of the mediaeval dikes built by the counts of Flanders were destroyed, turning Flanders once again into

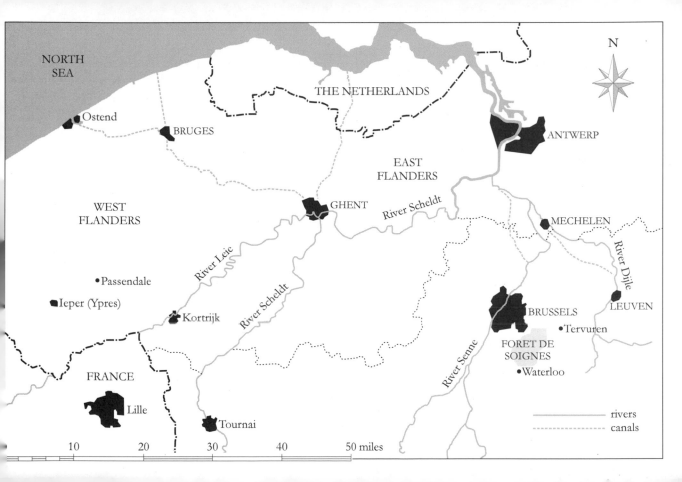

'the flooded land'.

Because of this war, the names of many Flemish towns such as Passendale and Ypres are laden with sadness, and to talk of Flanders today is to evoke images of war and misery, rather than beautiful gothic paintings or soaring medieval spires. It is unlikely that these painful associations will ever be erased, for the landscape of Flanders is too crowded with regimented military cemeteries. There is even an American military cemetery called 'Flanders Field'; it is at Waregem, not far from the site of the Battle of the Golden Spurs, and its name comes from John McCrae's elegiac poem that begins, 'In Flanders Field the poppies blow,/Between the crosses, row on row'.

The wars may be over, but Belgium is still plagued by the old conflict between German and French civilisations. Its population is divided into Flemings, Walloons and a tiny, almost forgotten, enclave of German speakers in the eastern Ardennes. The Flemings, concentrated on the plain of the River Scheldt in the north of the country, are Dutch-speaking, although their language is old-fashioned compared to the Dutch spoken in the Netherlands. The Walloons, who inhabit the valley of the Meuse to the south, speak French, although it too is archaic and quaint. Whether travelling in Flanders, the Dutch-speaking area of Belgium, or in Wallonia, the French-speaking area, it is probably advisable to speak English, which serves as a neutral language.

Many of the institutions of the European Communities are now based in Belgium. The significance of a united Europe can best be appreciated in Brussels by visiting the Musée de l'Armée, where one vast hall is filled with the relics of the First World War. A five-minute walk through the Parc du Cinquantenaire then brings you to the European Quarter, where the fifteen states of the European Union now work together in a sort of harmony which would have seemed unimaginable to a soldier in the First World War. The country once described as the cockpit might now be said to be the crucible of Europe.

Bruges

Bruges

The beautiful old town of Bruges is the ideal starting point for a tour of Flemish cities. Almost nothing disturbs the medieval atmosphere of this decayed maritime city, where crumbling brick houses are mirrored in placid canals, and narrow streets gently meander past old almshouses. Exploring Bruges we come upon many picturesque spots reminiscent of old Flemish paintings, such as the marvellous view of distant spires from the eastern ramparts above Kruisvest. Bruges is a profoundly medieval city, even down to tiny details such as the gothic letter *b*, the symbol of the city, which appears on everything from museum guard uniforms to the carpets in the town hall. Many of the street corners are watched over by a statue of the Virgin and Child, of which there are about 500 in the old city. Some are very elaborate indeed, such as the wonderful 18th-century wooden calvary at the corner of Carmerstraat and Korte Speelmansstraat.

This compact town of some 118,000 inhabitants has a charm that is almost impossible to resist. Even in the 16th century, when Bruges had passed its prime, Hadrianus Borlandus, Professor of Rhetoric at Leuven University, wrote: 'The cities of Ghent, Antwerp, Brussels, Leuven and Mechelen are beautiful, but they are nothing in comparison to Bruges.' Disillusioned by the 'air-conditioned nightmare' of American life, Henry Miller was delighted, on a visit to Bruges in 1953, 'to see the world afresh with the eyes of a child'. Much of the joy in visiting Bruges is indeed to rediscover forgotten pleasures, such as wandering down a cobbled lane, listening to the tinkling of a distant carillon, or watching the reflection of a swan on the ruffled surface of a canal.

But a word of warning; not every visitor has been captivated. In 1896 Arnold Bennett complained: 'The difference between Bruges and other cities is that in the latter you look about for the picturesque, while in Bruges, assailed on every side by the picturesque, you look curiously for the unpicturesque, and don't find it easily.' Having seen so many of our cities ruined by the 'unpicturesque', we are unlikely to be as pernickety as Bennett, but we may well find that the narrow streets of Bruges are too crowded in the summer months. It is advisable to avoid this season if possible, and to visit Bruges in the spring, when the precincts of the Begijnhof are carpeted with daffodils. Better still, visit in the autumn, for the mellow browns and golds of the autumnal trees lining the canals are perfectly in keeping with the sad crumbling beauty of the town.

A settlement existed at Bruges as early as the 7th century, and in 865 Baldwin of the Iron Arm, the first Count of Flanders, built a castle here as protection against Viking raids from the coast. The prosperity of Bruges was founded upon commerce, and from the 13th to the 15th centuries it was the principal trading city of northern Europe. Merchants from seventeen different European countries settled here, conducting their business from splendid gothic buildings in the northern quarter of the city.

Wool was the chief commodity traded here. It formed the basis of the Flemish cloth industry, upon which the prosperity of the whole region depended. Cloth-making had been important in Flanders since Roman times, when flocks of sheep were introduced to the Scheldt and Leie valleys, and Flemish weavers had become renowned throughout Europe for the exceptionally fine quality of their work. As demand increased in the 11th century, wool was imported from England, Scotland and Ireland. The lime soils of the Cotswolds and Yorkshire produced a particularly high quality wool with long silky fibres ideally suited for weaving the luxury cloth of Flanders. A regulation introduced in Bruges in 1282 stipulated that only cloth made from English wool could be stamped as first class. Scottish wool was stamped second class, while Flemish wool was deemed third class. For many years Bruges was the exclusive market on the Continent for the export of English and Scottish wool, and the merchants who traded here took home Flemish pantiles to roof their houses and Flemish paintings to hang in their chapels. That is why buildings in the Cotswolds and the east coast of Scotland often have such a strong Flemish character to this day.

Bruges also had a large community of Italian merchants from Venice, Lombardy and Tuscany, who shipped fruit, spices and silks. These commodities gave the burghers of this damp northern city a dazzling splendour, causing a French queen visiting Bruges in 1302 to exclaim: 'I imagined myself alone to be queen, but I see hundreds of persons here whose attire vies with my own.'

In the 15th century Bruges became an important artistic centre, to which Flemish painters and sculptors flocked in search of commissions. Jan van Eyck settled in Bruges in about 1425, and was later appointed court painter by Philip the Good, which entitled him to a regular salary. His work for the Duke included several diplomatic missions, as well as two secret assignments whose purpose remains an intriguing mystery. In 1428 Philip the Good commissioned van Eyck to paint a portrait of Isabella, the daughter of the King of Portugal, whom he intended to marry provided that her looks were satisfactory. They apparently were, and in 1430 Philip married Isabella in a ceremony of unprecedented Burgundian splendour. Fourteen ships brought the Portuguese guests to the port of Sluis and a gargantuan feast was held in the Prinsenhof in Bruges. As part of the wedding celebrations Philip the Good founded the Order of the Golden Fleece. The collar worn by members of this chivalric order was decorated with a pendant modelled as a fleece, symbolising the vital importance of the wool trade to Flanders. This chain appears frequently in 15th-century portraits, on memorial tablets in churches and even on the façade of a building on Jan van Eyckplein.

The last Burgundian festivity in Bruges was

the marriage in 1468 of Duke Charles the Bold, son of Philip the Good, to his third wife Margaret of York, sister of Edward IV of England. The fountains of Bruges ran with Burgundian wine shipped north in massive barrels for the occasion, and the streets were decked with decorations designed by the great Flemish artists of the day, including Hans Memling and Hugo van der Goes. After the procession had passed through the streets of Bruges, a lavish banquet was held in the Prinsenhof, at which bizarre entertainments were staged, including a motet of singing goats and a model whale which opened to reveal some forty performers within.

One of the guests in 1468 was William Caxton, who had been a member of the English Nation in Bruges since about 1441. At the time of the wedding he was Governor of the English Merchant Adventurers in the Burgundian Netherlands. Caxton resigned in 1470 to enter the service of Margaret of York, and was sent to Cologne, where he learned the art of printing. On his return to Bruges, he set up a printing press with the help of a local manuscript illuminator named Collaert Mansion. Using type founts probably obtained from a printer in Leuven, Caxton printed *The Recuyell of the Historyes of Troye* at Bruges in 1475, the first printed book in the English language. Caxton produced several other English books in Bruges before returning to London to set up the first printing press there the following year.

Towards the end of the 15th century, Bruges slowly began to decline. The main cause was the silting-up of the River Zwin, which led to Bruges being cut off from the sea. The city failed to respond to this catastrophe, and in 1505 the Fuggers of Augsburg, the important German banking family, prudently moved their business to Antwerp.

Most of the other trading nations followed the Fuggers and Bruges eventually became a moribund city, so much so indeed that Baedeker's 1905 guide has nothing to say about its history after the 16th century. But an episode in the 17th century suggests that Bruges cannot have been entirely dead; the young Charles II spent three years of his exile here during the rule of Cromwell and the Commonwealth. Together with his brothers Henry and James, and some 200 loyal followers, Charles II lived in Bruges from 1656 to 1659. An entire block of houses on the Hoogstraat was put at the disposal of the exiled king and his retinue. Charles spent much of his time in the company of the military guilds, and it was at Bruges that he founded the Grenadier Guards.

The rot does seem to have set in by 1786, however, when the British traveller Philip Thicknesse wrote of Bruges: 'When you have seen what this town offers to the notice of a stranger, you will be, as I was, glad to quit it, for the inhabitants (quite the reverse of their neighbours the French) are all shut up within their houses, and a stranger is apt at Bruges, to think himself in a city just depopulated by the plague.'

Frozen in the middle ages, Bruges was rediscovered in the 19th century by British travellers on their way to view the battlefield of Waterloo. In his *Memorials of a Tour on the Continent* William Wordsworth found in Bruges 'a deeper peace than in deserts found'. Accompanying her brother on this tour in 1820, Dorothy Wordsworth noted in her journal that at Bruges: 'The race of the Great and Powerful by whom the noble public edifices were raised has passed away, yet the attire, the staid motions and the demeanour of the present inhabitants are accordant with the stateliness of former ages.'

The Victorians admired Bruges, as they admired Venice, because of its medieval architecture. The High Victorian architect A.W.N. Pugin even sent his son to Bruges to study the Burgundian gothic style. Gradually, a curious colony of British expatriates formed in Bruges; they had their own school in the Engelse Klooster (a convent founded by several British nuns in 1629), they attended services in the Anglican church on Ezelstraat, and could even peruse English newspapers in a reading room established in the former trading house of the Genoese merchants on Vlamingstraat. With typical Victorian zeal, the British expatriates set about rescuing gothic Bruges from centuries of neglect. When the cathedral tower burned down in 1839, a British resident even provided the necessary funds to construct a new one. Encouraged by the British, local architects in Bruges studiously began to design every new building in neo-gothic style. Numerous statues were also erected on the main squares to celebrate illustrious citizens, such as Jan Breydel and Pieter de Coninck, who led the successful uprising against the French in 1302, and are commemorated by a statue on Markt.

The publication in 1892 of Georges Rodenbach's novel *Bruges-la-Morte* brought a new type of visitor to Bruges, quite different from the gothic-minded High Victorians. Set in the silent and deserted streets of Bruges in the dead of winter, this elegiac novel describes the melancholy wanderings of Hughes, a British exile who had come here not to admire the gothic, but to recover from the untimely death of his wife Ophelia. 'In the silent setting of the water and the deserted streets, the suffering of his heart weighed less heavily on Hughes, the thought of death became more endurable.' The idea of a dead city had an immense appeal to world-weary Europeans, and travellers flocked here from the fashionable coastal resorts of Ostend and Blankenberge to savour its mood of languid decay. The strange symbolic paintings of Bruges by Fernand Khnopff also capture its melancholy atmosphere. There is even a hint of this in Pamela Hansford Johnson's novel *The Unspeakable Skipton*, which recounts the adventures of a decadent British exile in Bruges in the 1950's.

Finally the authorities of Bruges decided that the epithet *la-Morte* had to go and they embarked on various imaginative schemes to revitalise the city. In 1958, for example, the city inaugurated a procession to commemorate the marriage of Charles the Bold to Margaret of York. This event, which takes place every five years in August, features splendid Burgundian costumes, although sadly the fountains do not gush Burgundian wine as they did in 1468.

The canals of Bruges have also been purged of weeds, an operation that was concluded by the Burgomaster drinking a glass of canal water. As a result of this municipal élan, Bruges is now a booming tourist centre, with numerous new hotels situated in beautiful historic buildings, an abundance of good restaurants, elegant boutiques along Steenstraat, and lively cafés on many of the squares. Since 1949 Bruges has also been home to the College of Europe, which has helped to restore the cosmopolitan atmosphere of the 15th century. Nevertheless, if you visit Bruges in the autumn or winter, when most of the tourists have gone home, and many of the hotels and restaurants are closed, you can still savour something of the atmosphere of Bruges-la-Morte, the town which reminded Hughes of Ophelia, 'it, too, being entombed by its stone quays, with the arteries of its canals turning cold as they ceased to beat with the sea's strong pulse'.

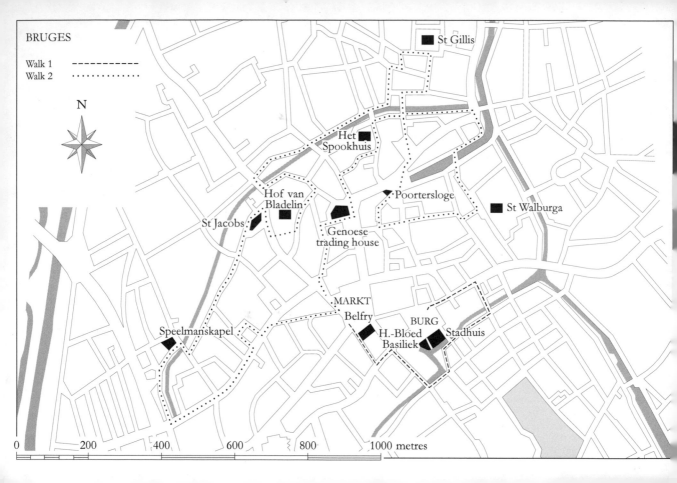

BRUGES

Walk 1 -----------
Walk 2 ....

N

St Gillis

Het
Spookhuis

Hof van
Bladelin

Poortersloge

St Jacobs

St Walburga

Genoese
trading house

Speelmanskapel

MARKT
Belfry

BURG

Stadhuis

H.-Bloed
Basiliek

0   200   400   600   800   1000 metres

WALK 1

The Buildings on Markt and Burg

On this walk we will look at the two great squares of Bruges, admire a 17th-century windvane and meet the patron saint of bureaucrats. We begin on **Markt**, the great market square overlooked by the belfry. It is probably unnecessary to provide directions for getting to Markt, for we are ineluctably drawn towards it by the white stone lantern of the belfry rising above the mossy brick walls and red roofs of Bruges.

Of the many cafés where we might read our way through this walk before setting off, my favourite is **Craenenburg** at Markt 16, a pleasant old fashioned place with neo-gothic stained-glass windows and gleaming brass chandeliers. It stands on the site of a medieval house called Craenenburg where in 1488 the citizens of Bruges imprisoned the Archduke Maximilian for four months. To console the Archduke, the captors commissioned the painter Gerard David to paint scenes on the window shutters of the prison. Finally, Maximilian was released, having promised to respect the rights of the Netherlands Estates, but a few weeks later his father, the Emperor Frederick III, marched into Ghent to wreak vengeance on the rebellious Flemings.

'In the market place of Bruges,' begins Longfellow's poem *The Belfry of Bruges*, 'Stands the Belfry old and brown/ Thrice consumed and thrice rebuilt/ Still it watches o'er the town.' Begun in the 13th century as part of the cloth hall, the **Belfry** rises from the flat, featureless polders of West Flanders as a potent and omnipresent symbol of medieval civic pride. Soaring to a height of 83 metres, it is still the first building we see when approaching Bruges by road or rail. Its impact on medieval travellers must have been

33

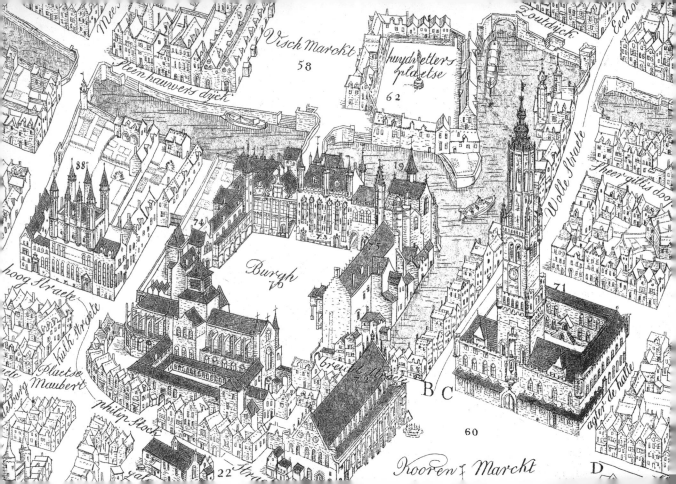

even greater, and its graceful octagonal lantern inspired architects throughout Europe.

But was the belfry perhaps also a symbol of human arrogance and folly? G. K. Chesterton was not enthralled with the edifice, which he described as 'an unnaturally long-necked animal, like a giraffe', built 'in defiance of all decencies of architecture'. This sounds like the familiar sour tone of the irascible Englishman abroad, yet perhaps Chesterton was right, for, as Longfellow's poem recalls, the belfry has burned down three times in its history. The original wooden edifice was destroyed after being struck by lightning in 1280 and a new belfry, built of stone, was erected in 1282-96. This is the building we see in the background of paintings by the Master of the Legend of St Lucy in the Groeningemuseum and the St Jacobskerk. In 1483-7 it was crowned with a tall octagonal lantern in Brabant late gothic style, which in turn was surmounted by an ornate wooden spire. Six years later, however, the wooden spire burned down after being struck by lightning. It was rebuilt soon afterwards, but was consumed by fire again in 1741, and never rebuilt.

The belfry remained flat-topped, and in 1822 was surmounted by the present stone parapet, like a trimming of Bruges lace. We do, however, know how the second spire looked, since it appears in a map of Bruges engraved by Marcus Gerards in 1562. Gerards, a Protestant, later fled to England, where his son, also Marcus, painted the famous 'Ditchley' portrait of Elizabeth I. His father continued to paint, and made the first etchings in England, but it could be argued that his greatest achievement was this spectacularly detailed map, rivalled technically only by de Barbari's great map of Venice drawn in 1500. We will be able to follow the whole of this walk from the detail reproduced opposite, and, as with the belfry, compare Bruges at the height of its wealth with the city we see today.

When we climb the 366 remaining steps of the belfry - ideally at the end of our time in Bruges, as then many of the buildings will be recognisable - we will see a room within the tower known as the *secreet comptoir* where the privileges of the city were kept. These documents, in which the counts of Flanders granted certain rights to the city, were so precious that they were kept in a sturdy chest fitted with seven locks. The chest - now displayed in the Stadhuis - was originally kept in the belfry behind an ornate double iron grille made in 1290-2. This was secured by an elaborate lock that could only be opened using nine separate keys, each of which was held by a different official.

The 13th-century **Halle** (Cloth Hall) at the foot of the belfry was modelled on the great cloth hall at Ypres. The wing facing Markt was built first in an early gothic style, the long side wings were then added in 1363-5, and finally the rear wing on Oude Burg was built in 1561-6. This last wing has an arcade on the street side that recreates the atmosphere of an Italian renaissance city, as do the two renaissance galleries overlooking the courtyard. In the middle ages the cloth hall was occupied by stalls piled high with lengths of vivid red and blue cloth, and the courtyard was filled with the smells of exotic spices sold here by Venetian merchants.

The row of buildings opposite Craenenburg stands on the site of a second cloth hall, the Waterhalle, built in the 13th century on a bridge over the canal so as to permit boats to unload bales of wool directly into the hall. It was demolished in 1786, and all that now remains are two stone columns standing in the Arentspark. Again we can get some idea of its appearance from the Gerards map detail.

The three public buildings erected on the site of the Waterhalle are interesting examples of neo-gothic design. The dazzling white stone edifice in the centre was designed by Louis Delacenserie for the Provincial Government of West Flanders. Delacenserie borrowed several motifs from the 15th-century Gruuthuse mansion, such as the parapet and the dormer windows, and modelled the four slender turrets on those of the town hall on Burg. The building to the left was added in the 1920's in the delicate style of Burgundian gothic. We may nowadays tend to disapprove of architects who slavishly imitate historic styles, but in Bruges (as in Venice) the neo-gothic style has played an essential role in preserving the impression of a medieval city.

Let us now leave Markt and look at Burg, the

other large square in Bruges. On leaving Crae-nenburg, we turn right past a curious old house on the corner of St Amandsstraat. Dating from 1480, it has an octagonal compass which was once attached to a windvane on the roof. This curiosity was added by the city fathers in 1682 as a civic convenience for the merchants of Bruges. Like many medieval buildings in Bruges, the house has a crenellated curtain wall at the top, which is purely decorative, as we will clearly see when we look down from the top of the belfry. This feature was added - in defiance of all decencies of architecture - to give a common dwelling house the appearance of a lofty castellated mansion.

We now walk through the courtyard of the cloth hall and leave by the rear portal. Turning left along Oude Burg and then right down Wollestraat, we come upon two delightful curiosities. The first, at **Wollestraat 9**, is a neo-gothic building now occupied by a lace shop. The ornate loggia has been decorated in the style of an old Bruges house, and inside there is an eerie mechanical model of an aged lace-maker at work.

Further down the street, at **Wollestraat 28**, is a house dating from 1634 with three polychrome reliefs illustrating the siege of Bruges in 1631 by the Protestant army of Frederick Henry of Nassau. A little lane on the opposite side of the street, at Wollestraat 35, leads into a small square with a beautiful view across an old canal to the historic buildings on Burg.

Then we cross a bridge with a statue of St John of Nepomuk, the patron saint of bridges, and turn left along Rozenhoedkaai (seen in the photograph overleaf). In the novel *Bruges-la-Morte*, Hughes rented a room overlooking this quay after the death of his young wife. We turn left from here into an intimate square, Huidenvettersplein, once an enclosed courtyard where the guild of tanners carried on their messy trade. Just beyond the square, a little bridge crosses the Dijver, to the right of which we see the gothic gables of the 15th-century **Brugse Vrije**, designed by Jan van den Poele in 1520-32 (and seen in the background of the photograph of the Vismarkt on page 93). A lane, Blinde Ezelstraat (Blind Donkey Street), leads directly to Burg from here, passing beneath

the attractive renaissance archway that we see in the photograph on this page. Tempting though it is to walk down the lane, I propose that we take a slightly longer route to Burg, continuing along Steenhouwersdijk, an attractive canal, then turning left to stand on an old stone bridge dating from 1392. Few people ever cross this bridge, yet it offers one of the most enticing views in Bruges. We now continue straight ahead down Meestraat and left on Hoogstraat past the mouldering vestiges of the **Huis de Zeven Torens** (House of the Seven Towers) at no. 7, built in 1320 for Wouter Bonin van den Gapere, an official at the court of the Count of Flanders. The house now looks forlorn, its seven towers having been lopped off in the 18th century, but its glory can be glimpsed in Gerards' map.

Burg is the site of a castle built in the 9th century by Baldwin of the Iron Arm. All evidence of this fortress has vanished, apart from the plaques marking the sites of its former gates, and the square is now a harmonious ensemble of buildings in romanesque, gothic, renaissance, baroque and neo-gothic styles.

A small park on the north side of Burg contains a few benches where, if the weather is fine, we can sit beneath the chestnut trees to read about the buildings before us. This little park was once the site of the great Carolingian cathedral of St Donaas, which was demolished in 1799 by the French Republicans, leaving in its wake a sad empty space. All that now remains of St Donaaskathedraal is a fragment of the choir, apparently marking the spot where in 1127 Count Charles the Good was murdered. A 19th-century statue of Jan van Eyck nearby reminds us that he was buried in the cathedral in 1441.

The oldest building on Burg is the **Heilig Bloed Basiliek** (Basilica of the Holy Blood). Tucked away in a corner on the right of the square, the basilica comprises a lower and upper chapel, both originally romanesque buildings erected in 1139-49, although the upper chapel was totally rebuilt in a 19th-century neo-gothic style. The two oriental towers that rise above the chapel are also late gothic details. The basilica is entered by a bluestone portal designed in 1529-34 by Willem Aerts, which looks late gothic from afar, but incorporates some renaissance details.

Entering the lower chapel, we are plunged unexpectedly into a gloomy romanesque building with massive columns supporting a low vaulted roof, and thick walls pierced by tiny windows. The only decoration in the chapel is a 12th-century baptism scene on the tympanum of the former entrance. The lower chapel was founded to house a relic of St Basil, the patron saint of masons, that was seized in the Holy Land during the First Crusade by Count Robert II of Flanders.

A beautiful late gothic staircase built in 1523 ascends to the upper chapel. Here we find a riot of neo-gothic murals which contrast strikingly with the sobriety of the chapel we have just left. The bizarre pulpit, carved in the form of a globe, dates from 1728.

Behind the altar in this chapel is housed a phial said to contain some drops of the blood of Christ. This relic was presented in 1150 by the King of Jerusalem to Dirk of Alsace, Count of Flanders, as a reward for his bravery during the ill-fated Second Crusade; every year on Ascension Day, it is paraded through the streets of Bruges.

The **Stadhuis** (Town Hall) stands to the left of the Basilica. This dazzling white sandstone building constructed in 1376-1420 inspired many other Flemish gothic town halls, including those of Ghent, Brussels and Leuven. Among its novel features, the most striking is the display of statues on the façade. Representing Biblical figures, counts, countesses and dukes, the statues were originally gilded and polychromed. A few may even have been coloured by Jan van Eyck. Disapproving of such symbols of aristocratic and religious authority, the French Republicans destroyed all 40 statues in 1792. The lost works were replaced in the 19th century, but the stone that was employed weathered so rapidly that a new set had to be carved in the 1960's. A plan to insert modern sculptures was proposed, but the prototypes provoked such a deluge of complaints that the idea was quickly abandoned.

A bluestone staircase ascends to the magnificent gothic hall on the first floor of the Stadhuis. This was the setting of many spectacular Burgundian ceremonies, including the first meeting of the States General of the Netherlands in 1464. The hall still has its original timber roof with a double vault. The outer ribs of the two vaults spring from corbels decorated with figures representing the twelve months and the four seasons, while the inner ribs meet in a row of pendants bearing bosses decorated with scenes from the Old Testament. The frescoes in this hall are romantic 19th-century representations of episodes in the medieval history of Bruges.

An adjoining room contains historical relics, including some of the original 14th-century consoles carved by Jean de Valenciennes for the façade of the Stadhuis. We also see the original copper plates engraved 400 years ago by Marcus Gerards for the map we have been following with such ease today. A fascinating view of the Burg painted by Jan Baptist van Meunincxhove shows the scene in the 17th century, when several bookshops stood against the wall of the cathedral, and an iron cage on the corner of the Stadhuis protected the statue of *Our Lady of the Inkwell*, the patron saint of clerks, and hence of bureaucrats.

The Stadhuis is linked by a bridge to the

delightful **Oude Griffie**. Designed by Jean Wallot in 1535-7 to house the municipal records office, the Oude Griffie is like a chrysalis struggling to shed the old gothic style and become a truly renaissance building. Vestiges of the gothic, such as the gables and the vertical lines of the building, are combined with renaissance elements such as Corinthian columns and friezes of arabesques. The gilded statues atop the three gables represent Justice, flanked by Moses and Aaron.

The final building before us is the **Gerechtshof** (Court of Justice), a stately baroque edifice of weathered sandstone on the east side of Burg. It was built in the 1720's on the site of the 15th-century county hall of the Brugse Vrije (Liberty of Bruges), a body which exercised jurisdiction over an area of Flanders between the Rivers Yser and Scheldt, with the exception of Bruges itself. All that remains of the hall are the three rooms that make up the **Museum van het Brugse Vrije**, reached through a little doorway in the corner between the Gerechtshof and the Oude Griffie. The former courtroom contains a magnificent chimneypiece carved from dark oak and black marble. Occupying almost the length of a wall, it was commissioned to celebrate the Battle of Pavia in 1525 and the Treaty of Cambrai in 1529, two events which together brought an end to French interference in Flanders.

Various sculptors and carpenters laboured on the work between 1529 and 1531 under the supervision of the Bruges painter Lancelot Blondeel. Like the later Oude Griffie, it is executed in a tentative renaissance style that retains some hints of the gothic. The heavy sensuality and robust figures are very much in the spirit of the Flemish renaissance, but the heraldic emblems still seem medieval.

The five virtually life-size figures were carved from oak by Guyot de Beaugrant. The central figure in the composition is Charles V, whose forceful policies finally persuaded François I of France to renounce his claims on Flanders. The two figures to the left of Charles V are his paternal grandparents, Maximilian of Austria (the Archduke imprisoned in Craenenburg), and Mary of Burgundy (who is buried in Onze-Lieve-

Vrouwekerk in Bruges). To the right of Charles V are his maternal grandparents, Ferdinand of Aragon and Isabella of Castile. Partly concealed by Charles V's cloak are portrait medallions of his parents, Philip the Fair and Joanna the Mad. Above, but virtually invisible, are two other medallions. One honours Charles de Lannoy, the general who led Charles V's army to victory at the Battle of Pavia; the other shows Margaret of Austria, Charles V's aunt, whose efforts led to the Treaty of Cambrai (we can compare the picture of her on page 223). A further two medallions, borne aloft by putti, contain portraits of François I of France and Eleonora of Austria, a sister of Charles V who married François under the terms of the Treaty of Cambrai.

The alabaster frieze on the mantelpiece is decorated with four scenes from the story of Susanna. While bathing in her garden, the naked Susanna (in the first scene) is surprised by two old men who threaten to bring a charge of adultery against her if she refuses their advances. Susanna does refuse and in the second scene we see her in the courtroom facing the false accusation. In the third scene, just before she is sentenced to death, the old men are cross-examined by Daniel, and proved to be lying. Susanna is acquitted and, in the final scene, the two old men are stoned to death.

The Merchants' City

Now that we know a little more about the buildings on Burg, let us explore some or all of them. Afterwards, we might stop in a café, such as Garre, an attractive old Flemish tavern hidden down a narrow passage between two lace shops on Breidelstraat. For lunch or dinner in this neighbourhood, I recommend 't Dreveken at Huidenvettersplein 10, overlooking the canal. The restaurant occupies the former guild house of the tanners, which was rebuilt in baroque style in 1680. The menu lists several tempting Flemish dishes, such as rabbit with plums, Flemish stew, and chicken in Rodenbach beer. In the afternoons 't Dreveken also serves coffee, homemade cakes, and excellent pancakes. Another reliable restaurant nearby is Malpertuus at Eiermarkt 9, a traditional Flemish restaurant with a fine cellar that once belonged to the 16th-century

monastery whose tower has just made it onto our second detail from Gerards' map on page 52.

In the 14th and 15th centuries Bruges teemed with foreign merchants who congregated in the dense tangle of narrow streets and interconnected squares to the north of Markt. Some seventeen different nations were once represented in Bruges, each with its own ornate gothic trading house. Most traces of this early European Union have vanished and often all that remains to remind us of a nation's presence in Bruges is the name of a street or a square. Engelsestraat, for example, was where the English Merchant Adventurers built a weigh house, and Biskajersplein recalls the Basque merchants' trading house which once stood here. Only a handful of mercantile buildings survive, such as the inn on Vlamingstraat where Spanish and Italian merchants met, the trading house of the Genoese merchants nearby, the Medici representative's house on Naaldenstraat, and the remnants of the trading houses of the Spanish merchants and the Hanseatic League. Yet although most of the buildings have disappeared, the street pattern is still much as it was when Caxton, Arnolfini and Portinari traded here in the 15th century. The warren of narrow, crooked lanes is strikingly similar to that of the City of London, though the scale of London's mercantile quarter has changed utterly, whereas that of Bruges has remained constant, so that here we gain a rare glimpse of the urban environment in which the modern European economy developed.

Our walk (*see page 32 for map*) in the medieval mercantile quarter of Bruges is not a lengthy one, and three hours should suffice to see all the sights. In the course of the walk, we will discover the origin of the word Bourse, meet a man who was rich enough to build a medieval town, and pause to admire a gothic cinema. The irregular street plan of this quarter forces us to trace a winding peregrination, which may be rather difficult to follow, but to lose one's way in this area is not entirely undesirable, as almost every lane contains an interesting detail or an unexpected glimpse of a distant tower.

Let us begin by setting off down St Amandsstraat, where we pass several convivial bistros. In the 15th century many splendid processions passed down this street, for it lay on the route between the Prinsenhof and the old cathedral on Burg. Turning left along Noordzandstraat, we soon pass on the right a street bearing the name Prinsenhof. The small, drab square to which this leads was once the courtyard of a magnificent palace, begun by Philip the Good in 1429. The **Prinsenhof** was the scene of two extraordinary Burgundian banquets; the first at the wedding of Philip the Good and Isabella of Portugal in 1430, and the second 38 years later at the wedding of Charles the Bold and Margaret of York. It was also here that Philip the Fair was born to Mary of Burgundy in 1479. The age of the Burgundians came to a sad symbolic end in the Prinsenhof in 1482, when Mary died here after falling from her horse in the woods near Wijnendaele.

45

Thomas More twice lodged in the Prinsenhof while on diplomatic missions to the court of Charles V on behalf of Henry VIII. On his first visit here in 1515, he met his old friend Erasmus and took time off from his duties to travel with him to Antwerp. Inspired partly by conversations with Erasmus and other Flemish humanists, More began writing *Utopia*. Six years later, he met Erasmus again in Bruges, where they parted for the last time.

Following Noordzandstraat, then turning right along Speelmansrei, we come upon a delightful little chapel, the **Speelmanskapel** (Minstrels' Chapel), founded in 1421 by the guild of minstrels, whose members enjoyed the exclusive right to play at weddings and feasts in the city.

Standing on the nearby bridge and looking northwards along the canal, we see the squat tower of the **St Jacobskerk**, which can be reached by turning down Moerstraat. The St Jacobskerk was originally a plain structure built in the 13th century. Serving as the parish church of the mercantile community, it expanded rapidly in the 15th century, when its two late gothic aisles were added.

So many paintings are hung on the walls of St Jacobs that it now looks more like an art gallery than a church. Look out in particular for the triptych of the *Legend of St Lucy*, painted in 1480 by the anonymous Bruges artist known as the Master of the Legend of St Lucy. We see Lucy in the left panel giving away her possessions to the poor, while a group of lean beggars look on. In the middle panel, her fiancé, enraged at being cheated of Lucy's dowry, accuses her before the Roman magistrate of being a Christian. Lucy is sentenced to a life of prostitution, but divine intervention comes to her aid and in the final panel we see the brothel-keepers attempting unsuccessfully to drag her away using two oxen. In the background of this panel, we see the familiar spires of Bruges, including the belfry which at the date of this painting was still without its late gothic lantern.

The loveliest chapel in Bruges is found in St Jacobs, tucked into a corner to the right of the choir. It was built in 1516-18 by Ferry de Gros, Treasurer of the Order of the Golden Fleece.

The polychrome mausoleum in this chapel was probably commissioned by Ferry de Gros after the death in 1521 of his first wife. Her recumbent effigy lies on the top tier next to his. A difficult problem of etiquette was posed in 1530 when de Gros' second wife predeceased him. Simply to have forgotten her would have been unthinkably disloyal for a knight whose motto, repeated many times in the chapel, was *Tout pour estre toujours lealle*. The chivalrous de Gros therefore had a lower shelf added to the mausoleum, which bears the reclining figure of his second wife. What better demonstrations could there be of his pledge 'All to be always loyal'? The chapel also contains a small enamelled terracotta medallion of the Virgin and Child; this attractive renaissance work attributed to the Della Robbia workshop was probably brought to Bruges in the 15th century by a Florentine banker.

The St Jacobskerk also contains mementos of the Spanish mercantile community in Bruges. A chapel off the south aisle contains a brass memorial dated 1577 to the memory of Don Francisco de Lapuebla and his wife, and a chapel in the south aisle contains a memorial of 1616 to Don Pedro de Valencia and his wife, both looking rather stout and warmly wrapped in furs.

On leaving St Jacobs, we will find a lane on the north side of the church, at Moerstraat 6-16. At the foot of the lane is an unexpected little group of 15th-century almshouses overlooking the placid canal. From this delightful spot, we now proceed into the heart of the old commercial quarter by turning right along St Jacobsstraat, and left down a lane called Botermarkt (Butter Market). It faces the Hotel Navarra, a handsome town house built in the 17th century by Juan de Peralta, consul of Navarre. The attractive round tower we glimpse as we walk down Botermarkt is a relic of the Hof van Gistel, a grand town house built in 1444 by Antoine de Bourbon, Duke of Vendôme. It was later owned by Jean de Matance of Burgos, who headed the Spanish community in Bruges.

Our next destination is the **Hof van Bladelin**, a magnificent town house at Naaldenstraat 16, which we reach by turning left beyond the gothic arch at the end of Botermarkt. The house was built in 1451 for Pieter Bladelin, who is portrayed kneeling before the Virgin in a striking neo-gothic polychrome sculpture above the entrance. This decoration, which relieves an otherwise blank wall, was the happy invention of Louis Delacenserie in 1892.

Pieter Bladelin was Philip the Good's counsellor, and treasurer of the Order of the Golden Fleece. Within the courtyard is an arcade with two interesting carved stone consoles on which the ribs rest. They are decorated with scenes alluding to Bladelin's duties: one has the figures of a woman and a dog, the latter a conventional symbol of fidelity; the other illustrates the story of St Alphège of Canterbury. Kidnapped by the Danes in 1011, Alphège refused to pay the ransom demanded by his captors because it would have depleted funds set aside for the needy. He was finally killed by the Danes in 1012 during a drunken feast when they pelted him to death with animal bones.

Bladelin was one of the richest men in the Burgundian Netherlands, and in 1448 he and his wife, Margaret van Vagewiere, embarked on an ambitious project to establish a new town on reclaimed land to the northeast of Bruges. Called Middelburg after the Cistercian abbey of Middelburg on whose lands it was built, it is the only example in the Low Countries of a medieval town created by private wealth. Bladelin built the castle in 1448 and the town was completed a mere six years later. Middelburg had its own walls and was even granted privileges, but today all that remains of it is the church. The silting of the River Zwin was as disastrous for Bladelin's settlement as for Bruges, and the site is now occupied only by a cluster of farmhouses.

The *Bladelin Altarpiece* (now in Berlin's Dahlem Museum and reproduced opposite) offers an intriguing glimpse of this vanished Flemish town. Pieter Bladelin commissioned the painting from Roger van der Weyden to hang in the new church at Middelburg. Painted in 1452, it includes a distant view of Middelburg in the centre panel, and an attractive portrait of Pieter Bladelin at prayer.

Bladelin's house in Bruges was later owned by the Medicis, the powerful Florentine banking family. Cosimo the Elder sent a bank agent to

Bruges in 1439, and in 1466 his son, the afflicted Piero the Gouty, bought the Hof van Bladelin to serve as a bank and residence for the Medici's agent. Beneath the arcade on the street side of the courtyard are several tiny details added to the house while it was in the hands of the Medicis. The ribs spring from consoles bearing the symbol of three feathers passing through a ring - the emblem of Lorenzo the Magnificent, Piero's son. Following the ribs upwards, we come upon bosses decorated with seven red balls surrounded by a garland adorned with feathers and rings, another Medici device. But the most interesting features are the two renaissance medallions attached to the wall facing into the courtyard. Decorated with the busts of Lorenzo the Magnificent and Clarice Orsini, they were probably carved to celebrate their marriage in 1469.

Tommaso Portinari represented the Medicis in Bruges from 1473-97, almost bankrupting his principals at one point by rashly lending money to Charles the Bold to finance military adventures. True to the Medici spirit, Portinari was also a generous patron of the arts; in about 1474

he commissioned Hugo van der Goes to paint an altarpiece of the Nativity to hang in the Portinari family's chapel in the church of Santa Maria Novella in Florence. This extraordinary work is now in the Uffizi. Portinari also commissioned Memling to paint a portrait of himself and his wife, which is now in New York's Metropolitan Museum of Art.

A remarkable swashbuckling adventure befell an altarpiece which a previous Medici agent, Angelo Tani, had commissioned from Hans Memling. In 1473 the altarpiece was taken to the port of Damme and loaded into the hold of a ship belonging to Portinari, and bound for Tuscany. But the ship was attacked and captured by the pirate Paul Benecke off the coast of England and taken to Benecke's home town of Danzig (now Gdansk), where the booty of cloth, furs and spices was unloaded. Memling's painting - an uncharacteristically gloomy depiction of the Last Judgement - apparently caused quite a stir in the northern seaport because of its numerous naked figures. The altarpiece never did reach its destination, and it still stands in St. Mary's Church in Gdansk.

If we now continue along Naaldenstraat and turn left up Grauwwerkersstraat, we come out again on the quayside. Crossing the bridge and turning right down Pottenmakersstraat we lose sight of the canal briefly, but meet it again at the **Vlamingbrug**. Standing on this ancient bridge, we can see a charming oriel window overlooking the canal, at Vlamingstraat 100. This ornate detail, an intricate example of Flemish late gothic brickwork, was commissioned in 1514 by the goldsmith Herman van Oudvelde. During a recent restoration, four tiny chimneys were discovered in the ceiling, suggesting that the bay also served as the goldsmith's workshop.

Augustijnenrei, down which we now walk, is one of the most attractive quays in Bruges. On the far side of the canal are fragments of the first city wall, built in the 12th century. Ahead of us lies the oldest bridge in Bruges, a handsome three-arched stone bridge known as the **Augustijnenbrug**, built in 1391 to provide the friars from a nearby Augustinian monastery with a convenient crossing into the city. It is one of several old bridges in Bruges with stone benches set into the parapet, where medieval merchants displayed their goods on fine days.

The quay we have been following comes to an end at the idyllically-situated Hotel Ter Brughe and we have to turn left up Oost Gistelhof. A confusing tangle of quiet lanes leads us now to the **St Gilliskerk**. Turning right at the end of Oost Gistelhof along Sterstraat, left down Schottinnenstraat and then right along Lange Raamstraat is the simplest route to follow. The parish church of St Gillis has a similar history to St Jacobs. Begun in the 13th century as a simple aisleless church, it was converted in 1462-79 to a hall church by the addition of two aisles equal in height to the nave. This church is the only one in Bruges still roofed with a wooden barrel vault.

Several Flemish painters lived in the parish of St Gillis in the 15th and 16th centuries. Hans Memling, who owned three houses in the neighbourhood, and an atelier on Jan Miraelstraat, was buried in St Gillis in 1494. The renaissance artist Lancelot Blondeel was also buried here in 1561, though the tombs of both artists have vanished.

If we now walk down Gilliskerkstraat we come to Gouden Handstraat, where Jan van Eyck lived with his wife Margaretha. Turning right here, then left down Torenbrug, we return to the canal we have been following since the Speelmanskapel. Once over the bridge, we turn left and follow Gouden Handrei, a beautiful cobbled quay that leads to the broad main canal of Bruges. This canal once flowed from the Dampoort to Markt, but now disappears underground at Jan van Eyckplein.

Spiegelrei, which bends around to the right, brings us to the imposing 14th-century Koningsbrug. From this stone humpback bridge we obtain an impressive view down to Jan van Eyckplein. Perhaps we recognise there the **Poortersloge**, a late gothic building with a beautiful slender spire, which appears in the background of several paintings in the museums of Bruges, such as Gerard David's *Judgement of Cambyses* in the Groeninge. The neoclassical school overlooking the bridge, at Spiegelrei 13, stands on the site of the trading house of the English Merchant Adventurers. The

stone foundations are all that survive of the building where William Caxton worked for 35 years.

Let us now cross the bridge and venture down St Koningstraat to the **St Walburgakerk**. Begun in 1619, this is one of several baroque churches in Flanders built by the Jesuit architect Peter Huyssens in the style of the Gesù church in Rome; there are others in Ghent and Antwerp. The interior of St Walburga illustrates the Jesuit fondness for opulent baroque furnishings. The pulpit, designed by Artus Quellin of Antwerp in 1667-9, is particularly spectacular.

By now following Korte Ridderstraat, then St Jansstraat, we come to St Jansplein, the first of a series of small squares which we will now explore. Dominating the square is the **Huis de Crone**, at Wijnzakstraat 2, a tall late gothic house built at the end of the 15th century. The four bays of the façade are defined by very tall gothic niches which exaggerate its height. The lofty and precarious chimney stacks continue this upward movement yet further.

A few steps further brings us to **Kraanplaats**, where a large municipal crane stood in the middle ages (which we can just make out in our detail from Gerards opposite, hoisting a bale just below the words *Craene Plaetse*, and similar to the one we see in the map of Antwerp on page 149). This square appears in the background of Memling's *Altarpiece of St John the Baptist and St John the Evangelist* in the Memlingmuseum. Kraanrei, which we follow as it curves northwards, was once a canalside quay, and leads into Biskajersplein, where the trading house of the Basque merchants once stood; this again we can make out in Gerards' map, a large building with an ornamental entrance crowned by statues.

At Jan van Eyckplein 1, just north of here, is the **Tolhuis**, an impressive late gothic sandstone building erected in 1477. Tolls were collected here on goods shipped inland from Bruges. Above the entrance, we see the splendid heraldry of Peter of Luxembourg, who inherited the right to levy tolls, probably through marriage. Notice the chain of the Order of the Golden Fleece, which Peter has proudly added to his coat of arms.

The very narrow late gothic building to the left

DOMUS
OSTERLNGO-
RUM
Brugæ

of the toll house belonged to the guild of steve-
dores. Its ornate sandstone decoration is
influenced by the flamboyant gothic architecture of Brabant.

Passing a statue of Jan van Eyck erected in
1879, we head up Genthof and left into **Woens-
dagmarkt**, where a statue of Memling was placed
in 1871. Crossing this quiet square and continuing north, we enter the small **Oosterlingenplein**.
In 1478, the Hanseatic merchants commissioned
Jan van der Poele to build a trading house on this
square. The 17th-century engraving reproduced
here shows the grand late gothic building occupied by the energetic German merchants, who
shipped fur and grain from the Baltic, beer from
Bremen and Hamburg, and wines from the
Rhineland. The crenellated main building is still
standing, although it has been drastically altered
over the centuries. The small building to the
rear has also survived in a modified form. We
may indeed be staying in this building, as German
merchants once did, for it now houses the attractive Hotel Bryghia. Above the hotel entrance, we
can still see a double-headed eagle, the sign

under which the German merchants traded.

If we turn left along Spaanse Loskaai and left again down Spanjaardstraat, we come upon the last vestiges of the Spanish mercantile community. The main goods unloaded on **Spaanse Loskaai**, the Spanish Quay, were wool, hides and fruit. Spanish merchants remained in Bruges long after the Germans, English and Italians had resettled in Antwerp, which is why at Spanjaardstraat 16 we find a 17th-century renaissance portal built for the Spanish merchant de la Torre. The house on the opposite side of the street at no. 17 has two names: **Den Noodt Gods** (Divine Providence) and **Het Spookhuis** (The Haunted House). It was built in 1616 by the Spanish merchant Francisco de Peralta, who opted for an outmoded late gothic town house, albeit with a renaissance portal to rival de la Torre's.

The house at **Spanjaardstraat 9** was owned in the 16th century by Gonzalez d'Aguilera. Ignatius Loyola, the founder of the Jesuit order, spent his summer vacations here between 1528 and 1530 while studying at the Sorbonne in Paris. On his visits to Bruges, Loyola befriended the Span-

ish humanist Juan Luis Vives, whose statue stands behind the Gruuthusemuseum.

Let us now walk down Kipstraat, an attractive lane below the walls of a Jesuit church built in the 19th century. As we near the end of the lane, we see the peculiar façade of a late gothic house at **Vlamingstraat 51**. It was built for the goldsmith Jacob Cnoop, whose daughter married the painter Gerard David. Cnoop's house has perhaps the most eccentric top in Bruges, consisting of a bulbous protuberance decorated with eight crockets and a pinnacle, and flanked by two tiny triangular gables.

We now head left down Vlamingstraat towards Markt, crossing a square called Beursplein, which once formed the heart of Bruges' mercantile quarter. If we stand roughly opposite the **Stadsschouwburg** (Municipal Theatre) and look north, we will see what remains of the square depicted in the 17th-century engraving by Sanderus (reproduced overleaf). The square is named by Sanderus the *Byrsa Brugensis*, from which is derived *bourse* in French and *beurs* in Dutch as the name for a stock exchange. The usage, based

on the Latin *bursa* (a purse), originated in Bruges in the 13th century, when Spanish and Italian merchants met to carry on business here at an inn with a sign showing three purses. The family that ran the inn later assumed the name van den Beurse.

Nothing now remains of the original inn, but a later building, known as the **Huize ter Buerze**, was built in 1453 as a bank and dwelling house, and has been recently restored by the Bank van Roeselare en West Vlaanderen. We see it on the engraving to the left of the house with the step gable; it has storks nesting on its chimney.

The medieval Italian merchants conducted much of their business on this square. Venetian merchants were the first to establish a trading house here, buying a house named Ten Ouder Buerze in 1379, where they dealt in exotic and costly goods such as silk, velvet, spices and fruit. Their trading house - the building with the step gable in the engraving - was demolished in 1965 when Vlamingstraat was widened.

The merchants of Florence later erected a splendid turreted trading house next to the Venetians. This building, identified on the engraving as the *Domus Florentinorum* (House of the Florentines), and visible on Gerards' map but with more and fatter turrets, has also vanished, and all there is to remind us of the Florentine merchants is a plaque on the side wall of Academiestraat 1, which quotes a verse from Dante's Inferno comparing a topographical detail of Hell to the dike erected by the Flemings between Bruges and Wissant (a town to the west of Calais). The plaque was presented to the city by the Dante Society of Rome in 1976.

A third trading house was built on this square in 1399 by the merchants of Genoa, who shipped fruit, spices, silver, gold, gems, furs and alum to Bruges. Alum was an important compound used in Flanders to dye cloth and dress leather. The Genoese house is the only medieval trading house in Bruges to have survived intact, although it has been somewhat modified over the centuries, as we can see if we compare the crenellated building labelled Domus Genuensium (House of the Genoese) on the engraving, with the façade at Vlamingstraat 33. The **Genoese trading**

house is, as we can see, a most extraordinary building, faced with a beautiful and costly honey-coloured sandstone from the Balegem quarries near Ghent. The house is entered by an ornate late gothic portal with a relief above depicting St George, the patron saint of Genoa, slaying the dragon. The first floor had pointed gothic windows rather like a chapel, while the upper floor was originally a crenellated curtain wall of no particular thickness, as we see on Gerards.

After the Genoese merchants moved their business to Antwerp in 1516, the building was used as the cloth hall of the serge weavers. The iron sign we see bearing the name 'Saaihalle' (Serge Hall) is a reminder of this. In 1720 the Genoese trading house assumed a bizarre appearance when its crenellated curtain wall was replaced by a bell gable, proving how inessential the former decoration had been. To add to the strangeness of this building, the bell gable was pierced by a pointed gothic window.

In the early 20th century, the Genoese trading house attained a zenith of eccentricity, as we see in the photograph on this page. The building, now with a door and window added at street level, was occupied by a café and hotel. The walls were plastered with miscellaneous advertisements offering 'Rooms', 'Steaks at all Hours' and 'Fish and Herring Stew'. When Baedeker's 1905 guide was published, the English Reading Room was here, and in the early days of silent films a cinema too. Now the building has been fastidiously restored, and all traces of these former uses have, alas, been erased.

We now turn right down Adriaan Willaertstraat, then left into Kuipersstraat, there coming upon another gothic curiosity. No. 23, known as the **Zwart Huis** (Black House), has a tall, gothic gable built at the end of the 15th century. The first time I passed this way, the façade was caked with black soot, but the yellowish brickwork has now been scrubbed clean, and the old name is now thoroughly misleading. The Zwart Huis is now occupied by a small three-screen cinema complex named Gulden Vlies (Golden Fleece). An evocative tavern furnished with heavy wooden tables and glinting brass lamps is sometimes open on the first floor.

This area of Bruges is well supplied with restaurants selling pots of mussels and chips, or thick steaks drowned in creamy sauces. For a lighter lunch, I recommend a couple of places that tend not to be crammed with tourists. Lotus in Wapenmakersstraat is a quiet, friendly restaurant offering excellent salads, and Het Dagelijks Brood at 21 Philipstockstraat is a fashionable bakery where customers sit around a big farmhouse table eating sandwiches made with Italian hams and Flemish cheeses.

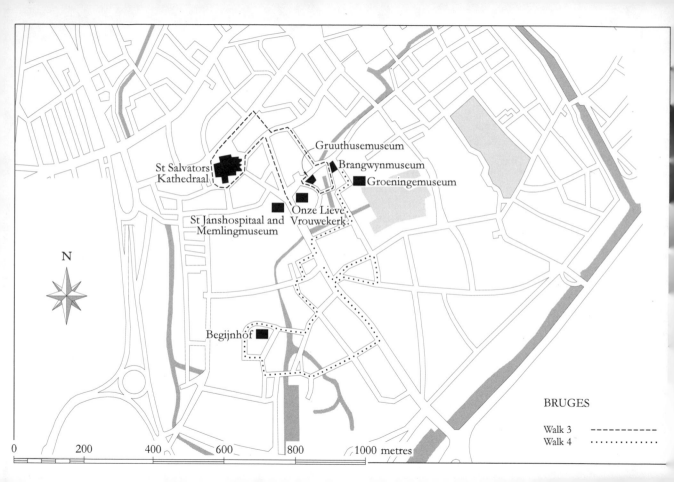

St Salvators
Kathedraal

Gruuthusemuseum

Brangwynmuseum

Groeningemuseum

St Janshospitaal and
Memlingmuseum

Onze Lieve
Vrouwekerk

N

Begijnhof

BRUGES

Walk 3 ------------
Walk 4 ··············

0   200   400   600   800   1000 metres

The Groeninge and Memling Museums

The object of this walk is to explore the two magnificent collections of paintings at the Groeningemuseum and the Memlingmuseum. These museums contain splendid medieval works by Flemish Primitives such as Jan van Eyck, Hans Memling, Petrus Christus and Gerard David. These artists worked in medieval Bruges for wealthy patrons such as city officials, hospice governors and foreign merchants, and their works depict in astonishing detail the magnificent buildings and sumptuous costumes of the Burgundian age. As each of the collections is worth at least two hours of our time, an entire day should be set aside for the walk.

Try to be at the Groeningemuseum when it opens in the morning, for only then is it possible to enjoy the extraordinary impact of the *Madonna with Canon van der Paele* by Jan van Eyck, which catches our eye immediately we enter room 1. We may have seen reproductions before coming to Bruges, but no photograph can ever convey the remarkable depth and texture of objects in the painting. Van Eyck achieved this result by a painstaking technique of painting with oil and varnish in multiple layers.

The altarpiece was commissioned in about 1436 by Canon van der Paele and originally hung in van der Paele's chapel in the old cathedral on Burg. It is now displayed against a wall of white Flemish stone to recreate as far as possible its original setting. The painting depicts the Virgin and Child in the choir of an unidentified romanesque church. They are flanked by Canon van der Paele with his patron, St George, to the right, and St Donatian, the patron saint of the old cathedral, to the left. The composition is fairly-conventional and the Madonna not particularly beautiful, but the truly thrilling quality of this work is the flawless realism of details such as the tiled floor of the church, the folds of the Madonna's vivid red cloak, and the slightly frayed edge of the thick carpet in the foreground. The portrait of the aged Canon van der Paele, then in his sixties, is so realistic that doctors, dermatologists and dentists have diagnosed the various ailments that afflicted him.

Jan van Eyck was not only one of the first painters to sign his works, but he would sometimes even include a hidden self-portrait, as in the *Arnolfini Wedding Portrait* in London's National Gallery, where his blurred reflection can be seen in a convex mirror. In the van der Paele altarpiece a mysterious figure, perhaps the artist, is reflected in the shield strapped to St George's back. This detail is so well concealed that it was only recently discovered by an attentive critic.

Two years before his death, van Eyck painted a portrait of his wife, Margaretha, which is also hanging in room 1. The Dutch inscriptions on the frame relate: 'My husband Jan completed me on 17 June in the year 1439' and 'My age was 33 years.' The artist's ambiguous device *Als ik kan* ('As I am able') also appears on the frame. Van Eyck was also one of the first artists to paint a portrait of his wife, and he depicted Margaretha with such a masterly and uncompromising realism that we feel almost in the presence of this severe woman.

Another fascinating portrait, by an anonymous master, is that of Lodewijk van Gruuthuse, whose fine 15th-century mansion is still standing in Bruges. Van Gruuthuse was a fabulously wealthy Burgundian noble who belonged, as the chain around his neck reveals, to the Order of the Golden Fleece. As well as being a politician, diplomat and patron of the arts, van Gruuthuse was a military leader. Carved on the oak frame of the picture is his device *Plus est en vous* ('there is more within you'), an allusion to the superior firepower of his artillery.

Petrus Christus was to some extent Jan van Eyck's successor in Bruges; he softened the Eyckian style and introduced sweeping views of landscapes. Although he worked in Bruges, no complete work by Petrus Christus survives in this city. What we see at the Groeninge are merely fragments of larger works: the *Annunciation* and the *Nativity* are two panels from a lost triptych painted in 1452, and the *Portrait of a Donor with St Elizabeth* perhaps formed the left wing of a triptych. The kneeling woman attired in sumptuous Burgundian clothes in this lovely work may be Isabella of Portugal, the wife of Philip the Good.

Gerard David, another follower of Jan van Eyck, painted the marvellous *Baptism of Christ* in about 1508. It is set in a beautiful landscape with lovingly rendered details such as flowers and rippling water. The left wing has a portrait of the donor, Jan des Trompes, with his patron saint John the Baptist, while the right wing shows his first wife, Elisabeth van der Meersch, under the protection of her patron saint, Elizabeth of Hungary. David also painted the work that no visitor to the Groeninge ever forgets. The *Judgement of Cambyses* is a diptych commissioned in 1498 to hang in the Stadhuis on Burg; it illustrates the story of a corrupt judge put to death by Cambyses, king of the Persians. The left panel shows the arrest of the judge, while the right panel depicts him being flayed alive. Although illustrating a 6th-century legend, the setting is unmistakably 15th-century Bruges, for the left panel includes a view of the Poortersloge on Jan van Eyckplein and the trading house of the Florentine merchants (which we saw in the print on page 56). The judge is apparently modelled upon Pieter Lanchals who, ten years before, had been beheaded during the uprising against Maximilian of Austria.

A painting of *St Nicholas* by the Master of the Legend of St Lucy shows us this popular Christmas saint attired in luxurious bishop's vestments. Through the windows we see familiar features of Bruges, including the Minnewater, the belfry, the Poortersloge, the spire of Onze-Lieve-Vrouwekerk and, on the far right, the strange tower of the Jeruzalemkerk. The belfry at the time of this painting was still without its octagonal lantern.

Stepping into room 6, we enter the rather different world of the 16th-century Flemish

Mannerists. Many of the works by these artists are Last Judgments, an indication of the melancholy world view of the time . Jan Provoost's *Last Judgement* was painted in 1525 to hang in the Aldermen's Room of the Stadhuis. This room was already gloomy, for it was here that the *Judgement of Cambyses* hung, to remind the aldermen of the consequences of corruption. The scene of Hell in the lower corner of Provoost's work, in which several church officials appear among the damned, was overpainted in the mid-16th century after Charles V issued a decree banning defamatory representations of the clergy. Another *Last Judgement* in the Groeninge is by Hieronymus Bosch, whose vision of burning cities and warring armies was eerily prophetic of Philip II's reign of terror.

The rooms that follow contain some likeable 18th-century works, such as *Afternoon Tea*, painted by Jan Garemyn in 1778, which reveals the thoroughly English tenor of life in 18th-century Bruges, and *The Invention of Drawing*, a striking neoclassical work by Joseph Suvée, reminiscent of the style of David. Also here is Fernand Khnopff's *Secret-reflet*, an ambiguous work of 1902 that depicts the side wall of the St Janshospitaal (which we will see later) and its reflection in the waters of the canal, while a panel above shows a mysterious woman gazing at a mask.

The last room of the Groeninge is devoted to Belgian Surrealism. Paul Delvaux's *Serenity*, painted in 1970, illustrates the mystical peace of his later works. There is also a cabinet of curiosities filled with works by Marcel Broodthaers, whose quirky Surrealism dwells on typical Belgian themes such as overflowing pots of mussels.

On leaving the museum, we might pause for coffee in the Taverne Groeninge at Dijver 13, an attractive café decorated with gritty expressionist works by Frank Brangwyn. From here we turn down Groeninge, right along Kastanjeboomstraat, left on Mariastraat and then right into Stoofstraat, a narrow, secret lane. It emerges on Walplein, one of many lovely squares in Bruges. Crossing it, we pass what used to be the Henri Maes brewery, discreetly concealed behind a 19th-century house at Walplein 23. Established in 1564 in a house named 'The Half Moon', from which it derived its trade mark, it is now one of the last two breweries in Bruges. The brewing process can be followed in the museum, and the final product, Staffe Hendrik, sampled in the café.

We now turn right at a corner overlooked by a statue of St Roch, the patron saint of plague victims. He wears the shell sported by pilgrims and is accompanied by his dog, carrying a loaf of bread in its mouth to feed its plague-stricken master. On the corner of the house opposite is a Virgin in a grotto. Wijngaardstraat leads into a quaint little square where carriages congregate and horses snort and stamp their hooves impatiently on the grey cobblestones.

A neoclassical portal dated 1776 leads us into the precincts of the **Begijnhof**, a delightful experience like entering a secret garden. All that can be seen from the outside is a brick wall with a few red tiled roofs poking above, but on pushing open the door we enter an enchanting little community of whitewashed houses, each with its own gate and wrought iron bell-pull (photograph overleaf). The houses are grouped around a broad green which is particularly attractive in spring when it is carpeted with daffodils.

A priest in Liège named Lambert le Bègue is credited with establishing the order of Beguines in about 1189. Its aim was to provide a semi-religious retreat for the widows of Crusaders, or women who had no prospect of finding a husband after the carnage of the Crusades.

Inspired by the Béguinage at Liège, of which no trace remains, the daughters of Baldwin the First of Constantinople, Margaret and Joanna, founded a number of similar institutions in Flemish cities in the 13th century. Presumably the crusading zeal of the Flemings had left numerous widows and spinsters in Flanders. The movement spread throughout the Low Countries and up the Rhine, though the only Begijnhofs to survive are in Holland and Flanders. There are beautiful examples of intact Begijnhofs in quiet corners of Ghent, Antwerp, Leuven, Kortrijk, Lier and Amsterdam. Sometimes the houses overlook a courtyard or green, as in Bruges, Ghent and Amsterdam; elsewhere they are reached by a warren of narrow cobbled lanes, as

in Antwerp, Leuven and Kortrijk. These villages of women, as they essentially were, usually contained a church and infirmary. The Beguines lived and dressed like nuns, although they took no formal vows and continued to live in separate dwelling houses. They devoted themselves to caring for the sick, or lace-making. The Begijnhofs in Holland were disbanded by the Protestants, and in Flanders the order has almost died out, though we will still occasionally see sisters in the precincts of the Begijnhof in Bruges.

Bruges' Begijnhof was founded in about 1245 by Margaret of Constantinople, Countess of Flanders. Although most of the houses now standing date from the 17th and 18th centuries, they still cling tightly to the conventions of medieval architecture. No. 4, for example, was built in the 17th century, but it still has medieval trefoils and pointed arches. The 18th-century houses at Nos. 8 and 28 only betray their relatively late date by ornate baroque doors and fanlights.

We leave the Begijnhof, perhaps with a pang of regret, by its southern entrance, emerging on the water's edge of the picturesque **Minnewater**.

The boatmen who ferry you to this corner of Bruges by motor launch claim that Minnewater means 'Lake of Love'; on seeing the swans gliding on the placid stretch of water, you may well consider the name apt, and imagine romantic trysts by moonlight on its shore. But the etymological truth is that Minnewater means simply 'inner harbour', though I doubt whether this scholarly quibble will persuade the boatmen and coachmen of Bruges to alter their patter. This inlet of water was created in the 13th century as a small harbour for boats bound for Ghent along the Lieve canal. Two tall round towers that once defended the harbour mouth were built by Jan van Oudenaerde at the same time as the Kruispoort and Gentpoort. The Poertoren on the west side of the Minnewater is still standing, but its counterpart was demolished long ago.

Kasteel Minnewater, a 19th-century mock castle, stands in a small park on the far side of the water. It contains a pleasant café and restaurant, where we might pause for coffee or lunch, either on the quayside terrace if the weather is good, or within its opulent Victorian interior.

We then leave the park and turn right along Arsenaalstraat, past a 16th-century chimney, now incorporated into the 19th-century Academy of Fine Arts and supported by a 20th-century buttress. Turning left along Katelijnestraat we pass the **Godshuis De Generaliteit**, at Nos. 79-83, an almshouse founded, according to the numerals on the wrought iron wall braces, in 1572. The lovely *Godshuis Onze-Lieve-Vrouw der Zeven Weeën* (Almshouse of the Virgin of the Seven Sorrows) can be found by turning right down Oude Gentweg, then left into Drie Kroezenstraat. A foundation stone on the baroque portal reveals that this almshouse was established in 1654. It originally comprised seven tiny dwelling houses, which explains its name. Turning left on Nieuwe Gentweg takes us past the late gothic portal of the **Godshuis St Jozef**, at No. 24-32, founded in 1634, and the baroque portal of the **Godshuis de Meulenare**, at Nos. 8-22, founded in 1613.

If we now turn right up Mariastraat, we come to the **St Janshospitaal**. This magnificent medieval hospice now houses the **Memling-museum**, a small, but exceptional collection of paintings by the 15th-century artist Hans Memling. The hospice, built of weathered dark brown brick, is one of the oldest in Europe, and served as a model for similar institutions in Ghent, Ypres and Lübeck. The Heiligen Geist Hospital in Lübeck, which is still standing, is designed in a style strikingly similar to the St Janshospitaal.

Entering the hospice beneath the squat romanesque tower on the right of the photograph opposite, we reach a quiet courtyard down a narrow cobbled lane flanked by dusky brick walls. If the weather is mild, we might sit on a bench here to read about the hospital.

Dedicated to St John the Evangelist and St John the Baptist, the St Janshospitaal was founded in about 1150 on the north bank of the canal which then marked the city boundary. Of the original hospice only a few fragments remain. The present building consists of three immense wards built in the 13th and 14th centuries (all clearly visible on Gerards' map on page 78). The middle ward, the oldest of the three, was erected in the early 13th century in a sober romanesque style.

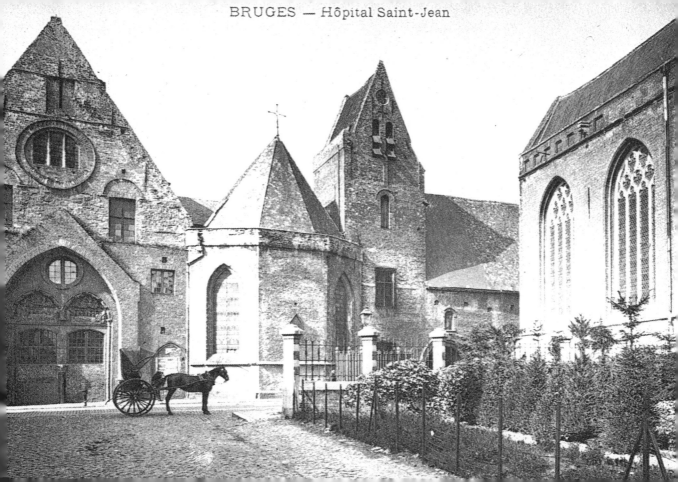

BRUGES — Hôpital Saint-Jean

It looks very like the nave of a church, and even has a splendid portal in northern French gothic style, whose tympanum is decorated with scenes of the Death of the Virgin, and the Last Judgement. A second ward, parallel to the first, was added on the north side in about 1290, and a third to the south in 1310-15. To make the hospice more church-like still, the side walls of the middle ward were subsequently pierced with large arches. The three vast and chilly wards were used for some 700 years, up until the early 20th century - that is, even after our photograph was taken. A fascinating painting by Jan Beerblock hanging in one of the old wards shows the hospital in about 1778, the sick arriving in sedan chairs and the beds arranged into separated rows for men, women, surgery cases and the terminally ill.

Situated in a partitioned corner of the north wing, the former hospital chapel is decorated with handsome renaissance carvings and a large baroque altar. It is here that the six paintings by Hans Memling are hung. Of these works four were commissioned for the St Janshospitaal, while the other two, displayed in a room off the chapel, were brought here from a hospice dedicated to St Julian when it closed in 1815.

Memling was born in a village near Frankfurt in about 1435 and, after spending some years working in Roger van der Weyden's atelier in Brussels, he moved to Bruges in about 1465. Memling eventually became one of the richest men in the city, owning three houses on the St Jorisstraat. His clients were often foreign merchants or diplomats, so that many of his works are now located in far-flung places; there is the *Last Judgement* by him in Gdansk that was seized by pirates as it was being shipped to Tuscany, and an altarpiece in London's National Gallery commissioned by Sir John Donne of Kidwelly when he visited Bruges in 1468 for the wedding of Margaret of York.

The most remarkable work in the museum is the *St Ursula Shrine*. Two sisters who worked in the hospice commissioned this work in about 1480 to hold certain relics of St Ursula. The shrine is made of gilded wood and decorated with pinnacles and finials so that it looks rather like a little gothic chapel. The sloping roofs, as it were, are decorated with six miniature medallions, while the figures at the four corners represent St John the Evangelist bearing a chalice, St Agnes with a lamb at her feet, St Elizabeth wearing a crown, and St James with a pilgrim's staff. A small painting at one end shows the two sisters who donated the shrine kneeling before the Virgin, while at the other end St Ursula is sheltering ten maidens with her cloak.

The two long sides of the shrine are decorated with six small panels depicting the legend of St Ursula. The panels are separated by arches so that we have the impression of looking out of a window as the scenes unfold from left to right. The story of Ursula is rarely depicted in paintings, and it may therefore be worth recounting this curious Rhineland tale found in the Golden Legend, a 13th-century compilation by Jacob of Voragine. The story tells of a princess born in a hairy coat, and so named Ursula, the little bear. She was the daughter of a Christian king, and lived 'in partibus Britanniae'. This might mean either Britain or Brittany. If Britain, then the episode must have taken place after AD 600,

when Britain was converted to Christianity. But other aspects in the narrative suggest that the events described took place at a much earlier date, and so it seems more likely that Ursula was a princess of Brittany. She was renowned for her beauty and a pagan king wished her to marry his son. Ursula said that she would consent on two conditions. First, her suitor had to convert to Christianity and, secondly, he must send 11,000 virgins to accompany Ursula on a pilgrimage to Rome. Or was it merely 11 virgins? The 13th-century manuscript used the Latin shorthand *XI.M.V*, which medieval readers took to mean eleven *(XI)* thousand *(M)* virgins *(V)*. But punctilious critics have pointed out that the cryptic description might equally be decoded as 11 Martyred Virgins, which would make the tale more plausible, if less moving.

After receiving the Pope's blessing in Rome, Ursula and her 11,000 (or merely 11) companions returned home to Brittany (or Britain), accompanied by the Pope. After crossing the Alps, they sailed up the Rhine to Cologne, which during their absence had fallen to the Huns (suggesting

71

that the story took place long before the conversion of Britain). The maidens were captured and, after refusing to renounce Christianity, martyred outside the city walls. The son of the king of the Huns, we are told, was saddened to see Ursula put to death, having fallen in love with her.

Memling illustrates the later episodes of this legend, beginning with the virgins arriving in Cologne on their way to Rome. We see Ursula, who is identified throughout the narrative by her blue robe and white cloak, inside a house, where an angel forewarns her of her death. Memling had spent some time in Cologne before moving to Brussels, and the view of the city is topographically accurate. Several of the buildings are still standing, such as the romanesque tower of Gross St Martin and the gothic cathedral. At the time Memling saw the cathedral, the unfinished south tower was surmounted by a crane. Work on it had come to a standstill in 1437 and in fact was not resumed until the 19th century.

The other scenes on this side show the arrival of the fleet of ships in Basel and the blessing of the virgins in Rome. These two episodes are linked together by a long procession of pilgrims, seen setting off for the Alps in one panel and entering the gates of Rome in the next.

The first scene on the opposite side depicts the pilgrims' return to Basel, while the two final scenes show their massacre in Cologne. There is another panoramic view of the city, including two other churches and the Bayenturm, a medieval tower still standing on the waterfront. The final scene shows Ursula about to be shot by an arrow, with a dog at her feet to symbolise her fidelity. If we examine this scene closely, we will see that Ursula and the king are reflected in the breastplate of the love-struck prince, while a soldier is likewise mirrored in the king's back-plate.

Another work by Memling in the hospice chapel is the large *Altarpiece of St John the Baptist and St John the Evangelist*, painted in 1479 for the high altar of the chapel. The work is sometimes referred to as *The Mystic Marriage of St Catherine* because of the scene in the middle panel showing the Christ Child giving a ring to St Catherine, who is identified by the broken wheel on which she was bound, and the sword with which she was executed. The beautiful St Catherine is possibly a likeness of Mary of Burgundy, while St Barbara (identified by a miniature tower) may, according to some critics, be modelled on her stepmother, Margaret of York.

The other principal figures in the middle panel are the patron saints of the hospice, St John the Baptist (identified by a lamb) and St John the Evangelist (identified by a chalice). The wings are decorated with scenes from the lives of these two saints. The left wing, depicting the life of John the Baptist, contains a beautiful landscape with the Baptism of Christ, Salome dancing rather stiffly before Herod in a Burgundian interior and, to the fore, Salome averting her eyes coyly as the head of John the Baptist is delivered to her on a plate. The right panel, devoted to John the Evangelist, shows his vision of the Apocalypse, including the four horsemen, the seven-headed dragons and several fiery rocks tumbling from the heavens. But Memling's vision of the Apocalypse is somehow unconvincing when compared with, say, Bosch's *Last Judgement* in the Groeningemuseum. His sky seems too blue, his sea too placid, and even his monsters look tame.

Beyond the columns in the centre panel are yet more miniature episodes from the lives of the two saints. Behind John the Baptist are scenes depicting him preaching in the desert, his arrest, and the burning of his body. The tiny scenes behind the figure of John the Evangelist show him being plunged in boiling oil, and his departure for the island of Patmos. The latter episodes are set on the Kraanplaats in Bruges, where the great wooden crane once stood that we saw in Gerards' map. The figure in the foreground wearing a black gown was probably the person employed by the St Janshospitaal to gauge imported wine here. In the 14th century the St Janshospitaal was granted the privilege of testing and taxing wine as a means of raising revenue.

On the backs of the wings we see the two brothers and two sisters who jointly donated this altarpiece to the hospice. Following gothic convention, the donors are shown kneeling before their patron saints: St James of Compostella, St Anthony Abbot (identified by a pig with a long snout), St Agnes with her lamb, and St Clare.

Memling adopted a subtler method of portraying the donor's patron saint in the exquisite *Diptych with the Virgin and Martin van Nieuwenhove*, painted in 1487 when Martin van Nieuwenhove was 23 (opposite). If we look at the top left-hand corner of the panel with Martin van Nieuwenhove, we will see a stained glass window with a tiny figure of St Martin, the donor's patron saint, cutting off a length of his cloak to clothe a beggar.

This work is a rare example of a complete Flemish diptych with both wings still joined together. Most diptychs have been divided and the wings have ended up in different collections, as in the case of the twin portraits of Erasmus and Gilles (reproduced on page 187). The van Nieuwenhove diptych contains an intriguing detail which might never have been noticed had the two panels parted company. Behind the Virgin is a convex mirror in which appears both her reflection and that of Martin van Nieuwenhove. By this variation on an Eyckian technique, Memling reveals that the two figures are seated in the corner of a room. The two panels are bound together further by the ornately patterned carpet covering the table in both scenes, and the length of the Virgin's scarlet cloak that appears beneath the book that the young man is reading.

This diptych, which was once owned by St Julian's hospice, is one of Memling's most attractive works. He has copied van Eyck's intense inner world of jewels, mirrors and symbols, but he has also learnt from van der Weyden to throw open the window shutters and reveal beguiling landscapes with winding roads and pale blue distant hills. This felicitous style appealed immensely to the 19th-century German Romantics, who discovered in their fellow countryman's paintings an appealing world of innocent maidens and arcadian landscapes.

The other painting brought here from St Julian's hospice is a portrait of a woman called the *Sibylla Sambetha*. This strange title comes from the inscription in the top left-hand corner, which must have been added by a later hand, as it is set in a renaissance frame. The inscription on the flowing banderole at the bottom of the frame, quoting the Persian Sibyl's prophecy of Christ's coming, was probably added at the same time,

presumably by a renaissance artist who thought that the mysterious and pensive young woman resembled an Old Testament prophet. She may in fact have been a daughter of Willem Moreel, Burgomaster of Bruges.

In 1479, one year before the Sibylla Sambetha, Memling was commissioned by Jan Floreins, another brother at the hospice, to paint the small *Triptych of the Adoration of the Magi*. The donor of this altarpiece is seen kneeling on the far left of the middle panel. He was 36 at the time, as we discover from tiny numerals that look as if they have been chiselled in the wall alongside. The king kneeling to the left of the Virgin may be a likeness of Charles the Bold, who fell at the siege of Nancy in 1477, and was eaten by wolves. It has also been suggested that the figure peering through the window to the right is Memling himself, wearing the yellow cap of convalescents at the hospice. According to an old legend, the artist was admitted to the hospice on returning wounded and exhausted, but in one piece, from the battle of Nancy, where he had fought on Charles' side.

Another small triptych, the *Lamentation over Christ*, was commissioned one year after that of Jan Floreins by his brother Adriaan Reins. Based on a painting by van der Weyden now in the Mauritshuis in The Hague, it is an unsatisfactory work, revealing Memling's inability to deal with tragedy and suffering. The left panel has a portrait of the donor with his saint, the right panel an attractive St Barbara.

Before leaving, we should glance into the 17th-century dispensary, which contains several magnificent oak chests, one with a bas relief of a hospital ward, revealing that patients more often than not slept two to a bed. It also boasts a magnificent collection of Delftware dispensers' jars. A series of portraits of hospital governors hanging in the dispensary provides an insight into the development of dress, beards and hairstyles in Bruges from the 17th to the 20th centuries.

Among the restaurants nearby, it is worth investigating the menu outside De Koetse at Oude Burg 31. A 17th-century house furnished in Old Flemish style, it offers fish grilled on skewers as an alternative to the ubiquitous steak.

Onze-Lieve-Vrouwekerk, St Salvatorskathedraal and the Gruuthusemuseum

This is a short walk *(see page 60 for map)*, easily accomplished in an afternoon, taking in the two great gothic churches of Bruges and a museum of decorative arts situated in the splendid Burgundian mansion of Lodewijk van Gruuthuse. We begin in **Onze-Lieve-Vrouwekerk** (Church of Our Lady), which stands opposite the Memlingmuseum. Begun in the 13th century on a site previously occupied by two successive romanesque churches, Onze-Lieve-Vrouwekerk has an impressive west front, flanked by two round towers, a typical feature of the austere early medieval style known as Tournai gothic. But as Gerards shows us overleaf, the spire is the thing: a thrilling structure soaring to a height of 122 metres, it is constructed entirely of brick, the natural building material of West Flanders. The base dates from the 13th century, while the top was added in the 15th century. It remained the tallest building in the Burgundian Netherlands until the completion, in 1518, of the north spire of Antwerp Cathedral, a mere one metre higher, and it is still, I believe, the tallest brick tower in the world.

Onze-Lieve-Vrouwekerk contains several major works of art, including a *Virgin and Child* by Michelangelo. It is easy to overlook this small statue, which is displayed in a black marble niche set in an overbearing altar at the end of the south aisle. Carved soon after the famous *Pietà* in Rome,

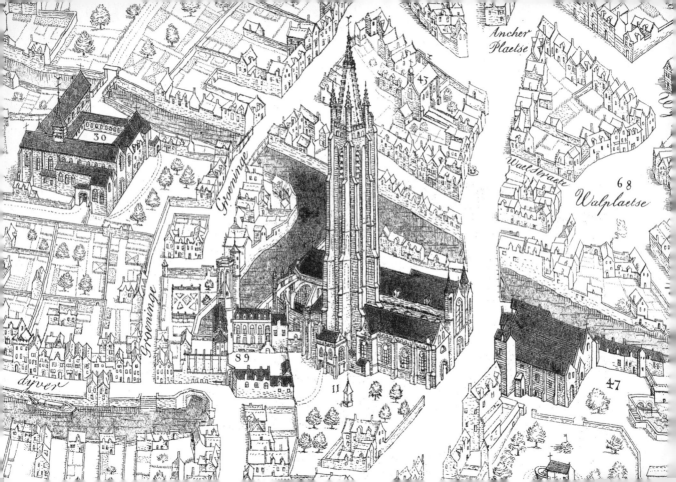

this work illustrates Michelangelo's soft and serene early style. It was bought in 1506 and brought back to Bruges by Jan Mouscron, a merchant of Italian descent. Dürer was one of the first to admire this statue when he visited Bruges in 1521.

The choir of Onze-Lieve-Vrouwekerk was the scene in 1468 of a splendid meeting of the Order of the Golden Fleece, convened to celebrate the marriage of Charles the Bold to his third wife Margaret of York. The coats of arms of the knights who attended this sumptuous wedding are still hanging in the choir.

The choir also contains the **mausoleums of Charles the Bold and Mary of Burgundy**. Both father and daughter died in tragic circumstances. Charles the Bold met his end while laying siege to Nancy in 1477, as we saw in the last walk. His mutilated body was discovered in a frozen pond a few days after the battle and buried at Nancy. Deciding that his great-grandfather deserved a more magnificent memorial, Charles V ordered the body to be exhumed and taken to Bruges. It was not entirely certain that the mutilated body found in the ice outside Nancy in 1477 had been that of the duke and by the time the skeleton was exhumed in 1550 it was of course impossible to identify. But the remains were sent back back to Bruges anyway. The journey went very slowly, partly due to a three-year halt in Luxembourg and, by the time the shipment arrived in Bruges, Charles V had abdicated. It therefore fell to his son Philip II to build the mausoleum. Designed in 1559-62 by an Antwerp sculptor, Jacob Jonghelinck, it is inscribed with Charles the Bold's device, 'I have made the venture; may it prosper.'

The work was meant to imitate the beautiful mausoleum of Mary of Burgundy, who had died five years after her father, in 1482, after falling from her horse while hunting in the Wijnendaele woods. Her husband, Maximilian, commissioned the tomb in 1495; it is surmounted by a recumbent bronze figure of Mary cast by Renier van Thienen and gilded by Pieter de Beckere, a Brussels jeweller.

In one chapel off the choir we come upon another sad relic of the late middle ages: the

ornate tomb of Pieter Lanchals. This is decorated with his emblem, a swan - alluding to his
name, which in Dutch means 'long neck'. After
the uprising against the Emperor Maximilian in
1488, Lanchals, a city official, was beheaded on
Markt for allegedly betraying the interests of
Bruges, that is, for siding with Maximilian. The
unjust judge in Gerard David's *Judgement of
Cambyses* was apparently modelled on this unfortunate man. The story has a strange, typically
medieval ending, for the townspeople were later
required to atone for the murder by introducing
the emblematic swans to the canals of Bruges.

While in the choir, be sure not to miss the
beautiful late gothic bay window set into the
north wall of the ambulatory. It bears the device,
Plus est en vous, which we may remember having
seen on the frame of the portrait of Lodewijk van
Gruuthuse at the Groeningemuseum. The
mystery of this intriguing bay window will be
revealed before the day is over.

After exploring Onze-Lieve-Vrouwekerk, we
continue to **St Salvatorskathedraal**, which in
1834 became Bruges Cathedral. A striking way

of approaching this church is to head up Mariastraat, then turn left into St Salvatorskoorstraat.
This quiet lane is terminated by the choir of the
church, which is surrounded by an attractive
cluster of radiating chapels added in 1480 by
Jan van den Poele. The tower at the west end rests
on stone foundations dating back to the 12th
century. After a fire in 1853, the upper tier was
rebuilt with British funding and by a British
architect, Robert Chantrell, in a dull neo-
romanesque style.

The gothic choir, transepts and nave were built
almost entirely of brick in the 13th century. The
choir contains misericords carved to commemorate the foundation of the Order of the Golden
Fleece in 1430, and the proud coats of arms of the
knights who attended the wedding in 1468,
including those of Edward IV of England.

The transepts and choir of the cathedral are
particularly interesting to explore. Off the north
transept is a chapel built for the guild of shoe-
makers in 1372, and enlarged in 1424. A large
baroque altar placed here in 1667 is decorated
with the guild's emblem, a fashionable high-

heeled leather boot surmounted by a crown. This motif also appears on the gable of the shoe-makers' guild house built in 1527 at Steenstraat 40.

The radiating chapels in the ambulatory were built, as we have already noted, by Jan van der Poele in a beautiful late gothic style. The first chapel on the north side has a screen dated 1513 with a mysterious monogram, while the next chapel, commissioned by the guild of wheel-wrights, is closed off by a screen dating from 1517 with reliefs illustrating aspects of the wheel-wright's trade.

St Salvatorskathedraal is now overcrowded with paintings, sculptures, reliquaries and relics, most of which once hung in the old cathedral on Burg. The most important works of art are now kept in the **Cathedral Museum**, situated in a neo-gothic cloister with an adjoining chapter house strangely lit by round neon lights in the shape of haloes. One of the highlights of the collection is the *Martyrdom of St Hippolytus*. The centre panel, painted by Dirk Bouts, shows the saint being torn apart by four wild horses after refusing to renounce his faith. The donors'

portraits on the left wing were added later by Hugo van der Goes.

Six monumental brasses from the old cathedral are also displayed in the cloister, including that of Jacob Schille-Waert, who died in 1483; he taught theology at the Sorbonne, and is depicted in the midst of his students. Another charming work is a 15th-century wooden figure of a solemn-looking Daniel in the lions' den. There is also an unusual altarpiece with a hinged door, commis-sioned in the 14th century by the guild of tanners.

The Virgin between St Eloi and St Luke was painted in Bruges in 1545 by the eccentric renaissance artist Lancelot Blondeel. St Eloi, a 7th-century Frankish metalworker who later became a missionary, is the patron saint of goldsmiths, silversmiths and blacksmiths. In the same room we see a silver reliquary of St Eloi made by Jan Crabbe in about 1616. But perhaps the most curious relic in this museum is a lead tablet with an inscription in Latin found in the grave of Gunhilde, sister of Harold, last Anglo-Saxon king of England. After the Battle of Hastings Gunhilde fled to Bruges, where she died in 1087.

There are numerous attractive restaurants for lunch in the neighbourhood of the cathedral. One of these, Vasquez, is situated in a beautiful late gothic town house overgrown with ivy at Zilverstraat 38. It was built in 1468 for Juan Vasquez, Isabella of Portugal's Spanish secretary, who accompanied her to Bruges in 1430 when she married Philip the Good. There are also restaurants and cafés grouped around the quiet courtyards of the Zilverpand, a shopping centre reached down a passage next to Vasquez.

After lunch we head down Steenstraat and then right on Simon Stevinplein, a square named after the Bruges mathematician who invented the decimal system. Straight ahead, the 15th-century **Hof van Watervliet**, at Oude Burg 27, was once the home of the unfortunate Pieter Lanchals. In 1567 it was bought by Marcus Laurinus, dean of the cathedral and a friend of many Flemish humanists. Erasmus, Pieter Gilles, Thomas More and Guy Morillon were all guests in this house.

Turning left on Oude Burg, then right down Nieuwstraat, we reach Dijver. The **Brangwyn-museum** at No. 16 is a small museum situated in an 18th-century house, the Arentshuis, built astride the Dijver canal. It contains a collection of some 400 drawings and paintings by Frank Brangwyn, born in Bruges in 1867. His father, William Brangwyn, was a British Victorian architect who settled in Bruges; he campaigned vigorously for the restoration of Flemish gothic architecture, and even designed a number of buildings in Flanders in neo-gothic style. Frank Brangwyn shared his father's enthusiasm for Bruges and in 1936 presented the city with a collection of his works 'as a memorial of my love for your great city'. Many of the works are sombre, such as *Last Boat from Antwerp*, an engraving sold during World War I to support Belgian refugees in Britain. The museum also has some views of Bruges by various artists, and a bizarre collection of objects made of mother-of-pearl.

A lane beside the museum leads into an attractive little park, the **Arentspark**, once the garden of the Gruuthuse mansion, but on the opposite side of the river to the house. Gerards gives us an idea of how it was planted in 1562. Notice the two squat columns standing forlornly in this park. The little iron signs attached to them have become illegible with rust, giving them a delectable air of mystery; they are in fact the last vestiges of the Waterhalle that once stood on Markt.

Pausing for a moment by the water's edge, we can look across the canal to the great brick gothic gable rising from the water. This is the oldest wing of the **Gruuthuse mansion**, built in 1425 by Jan van Gruuthuse, whose coat of arms, and that of his wife, appear on the gable. The design of the façade is based on twelve gothic trefoils of different sizes, including one that ingeniously embraces all the others.

Let us now stroll to the little hump-backed bridge called the **Bonifaciusbrug** that spans the canal at this point. This is one of the loveliest spots in Bruges, with the water gently lapping at the crumbling brick foundations of aged ivy-covered houses. It comes as a disappointment to discover that the bridge was placed here only in 1910. Attached to a wall is a stone tablet decorated with a boat, which once served as a sign for a waterside inn at Nieuwpoort.

Thanks to the bridge, we can now have a good view of the early gothic choir of Onze-Lieve-Vrouwekerk. The choir is modelled on that of Tournai Cathedral, which in turn was inspired by the great cathedrals of northern France. Rising dramatically to our right is the south wing of the Gruuthuse mansion, added by Lodewijk van Gruuthuse in 1465-70. Looking closely at the high brick walls, you might be able to spot a tiny gothic window. This provides one of the most delightful, and least familiar, views in Bruges, as we will soon discover.

Once across the bridge we pass a bust of a 16th-century humanist, Juan Luis Vives from Valencia, who spent much of his life in Bruges. We now head down a lane squeezed between the mossy buttresses of the church and the lofty walls of the Gruuthuse mansion. After passing under a bridge (about which more later), we come upon a building of gleaming white stone attached to Onze-Lieve-Vrouwekerk. This is the **Paradijsportaal** (Gate to Paradise), although it is now not a portal but a baptistery. It was added to the church in 1465 in the ornate style characteristic of Brabant late gothic architecture. Like the Stadhuis on Burg, it seems out of place in this windswept northern port, where most of the buildings are old and crumbling brick edifices.

We turn right now to enter the courtyard of the **Gruuthusemuseum**. The Gruuthuse family owed their extraordinary wealth to a right granted in the 13th century to levy tolls on *gruut* (grout), a mixture of herbs used by medieval brewers to flavour ales. Most beers are now seasoned with hops, but *gruut* is still used in the production of at least one Belgian beer, *Stropken Grand Cru*, an amber-coloured brew with a pleasant taste hovering between a *Duvel* and a *Bière Blanche*. This beer was launched some years ago by the Hopduivel café in Ghent. Its name *Stropken* (a noose) sounds ominous, as do other Belgian beers, such as *Duvel* (Devil), *Lucifer* and *Verboden Vrucht* (Forbidden Fruit). However, *Stropken* merely recalls the episode in the 15th century when the leading citizens of Ghent were forced to humble themselves before Philip the Good wearing hangman's nooses around their necks.

Despite appearing somewhat diffident in the portrait in the Groeningemuseum, Lodewijk van Gruuthuse was one of the most powerful nobles in the Burgundian Netherlands. He was a knight of the Order of the Golden Fleece, Governor of Bruges and Oudenaarde, Governor of Holland, Zeeland and West Friesland, and Commander of the Burgundian armies and fleets. His friends included King Edward IV of England, who stayed here with his brother Richard from October 1470 to April 1471 during their exile from England. Van Gruuthuse lent money to Edward IV to help him to regain his throne, and in return was granted the title of Earl of Winchester to add to his long list of honours.

Lodewijk van Gruuthuse was also a great patron of the arts, and built up a library of illuminated manuscripts that was considered the finest private collection in the Burgundian Netherlands. After his death in 1492, however, his son defected to the side of the French and moved to Abbeville. The famous library was sold, and now forms part of the Bibliothèque Nationale in Paris.

The Gruuthuse mansion then lay empty until

1628, when a charitable lending bank known as the *Mons Pietas* or *Berg van Barmhartigheid* was established here. This was modelled on the *Monte di Pietà*, an institution that existed in many Italian cities. The Dutch name, which means literally 'Mountain of Charity', derives from an erroneous translation of the Italian term *monte*, which in this context means a sum of money, or a loan, but not a mountain. These new banks lent money at a very low rate of interest, and sometimes charged nothing at all, thus breaking the monopoly of the bankers of Lombardy, who allegedly caused much suffering in Flanders by the extortionate rate of interest they charged on loans. The first charitable bank in Flanders was established at Ypres in 1534, followed by one at Bruges in 1573. The bank in the Gruuthuse mansion was one of several founded by the Archduchess Isabella. There are similar lending banks in Ghent, Antwerp and Mechelen.

The former lending bank now contains a captivating collection of Flemish sculpture, furniture, altarpieces, musicial instruments, paintings, tapestries and lace. This collection was begun in 1865 by a society of local antiquarians, whose members included William Brangwyn, the Victorian architect, and James Weale, an expert on the Flemish Primitives. A third British expatriate in Bruges, John Steinmetz, presented the museum with his extensive collection of Flemish drawings, engravings, etchings and woodcuts. Steinmetz had arrived in Bruges in 1819 bound for Venice, but this northern gothic city so captivated him that he abandoned his plans and settled here.

The antiquarian society originally displayed its collection in a room on the first floor of the belfry, but in 1900 the museum was moved to the Gruuthuse mansion, which had just emerged from an eight-year-long restoration by Louis Delacenserie. Having piously removed everything that did not belong to the 15th-century fabric, Delacenserie then went on to add certain neo-gothic features of his own, with the result that the building is now a baffling mixture of 15th- and 19th-century elements. The equestrian statue of Lodewijk van Gruuthuse above the entrance, for example, is a pure 19th-century invention, and so is the magnificent ceiling in the entrance hall.

The extraordinary mantelpiece in room 1, another 19th-century caprice, is adorned with a scene of a walled city and trumpeters blasting from the battlements. This is not entirely fanciful, however, for the heraldic devices and symbolic motifs here are culled from authentic 15th-century windows, ceilings and mantelpieces in the house. It is therefore a catalogue, of sorts, of the mottos and motifs of Lodewijk van Gruuthuse, including his ubiquitous device *Plus est en vous*, and the symbol of a blasting mortar, both alluding to the superiority of his artillery. A more romantic device shows the initials of Lodewijk and his wife Margaretha united by a cord.

The most striking object in room 1 is a terracotta and wood bust of Charles V, probably carved by the German renaissance artist Konrad Meit in about 1520. Charles, aged about twenty, is wearing the collar of the Golden Fleece, and has a removable wooden hat.

Room 4 is an enticing gothic interior reminiscent of paintings by the Master of Flémalle. The mantelpiece dates from the early 15th century, and once stood in a house in the nearby Mariastraat. The two stained glass windows decorated with St George and St Michael were made in about 1500 for the chapel of the guild of painters.

In room 6 we should note particularly the attractive sculpture of *The Madonna Reading* by Adriaen van Wezel of Utrecht. This lovely figure formed part of a retable carved in 1477 for the Brotherhood of Our Lady at 's-Hertogenbosch. Hieronymus Bosch, who was a member of this Brotherhood, was asked in 1508 to advise on the polychroming of the work. The retable is now split into many parts; museums in 's-Hertogenbosch, Amsterdam, Cologne and Berlin all possess fragments.

Room 13, often overlooked, is where we discover that tiny gothic window we spied from the Bonifaciusbrug. Looking through it, we obtain a captivating view reminiscent of the landscapes of Memling. Continuing to room 16, another mystery is finally solved, for here we come upon a bridge leading to a late gothic oratory with a bay window. This is the curious window that we saw from the choir of Onze-Lieve-Vrouwekerk. In

1472, after protracted negotiations with the church authorities, Lodewijk van Gruuthuse finally obtained permission to construct this small private chapel overlooking the choir, so that he and his family could attend Mass without the inconvenience of having to leave the mansion. The oratory contains some delightful features, such as the gilded paper flowers that bespangle the vaulted wooden roof, and the ingenious skylight windows to admit daylight to the chapel.

Another feature of the mansion is the loggia reached from room 18, which offers a magnificent view of the choir and spire of Onze-Lieve-Vrouwekerk. Standing here, we can see another tiny gothic window on a nearby wall. Room 22 contains some unusual mementos of the young Charles II, who spent three years of his exile here. It seems that Charles and his two brothers whiled away the days in the shooting butts of the three guilds of civic guards. The guilds were delighted to have such distinguished members, and each commissioned splendid baroque paintings or sculptures of the royal Englishmen to decorate their banqueting halls. A magnificent memorial to Charles II still hangs above the fireplace in the guild house of the archers on Carmerstraat. The other two guild houses were demolished in the 19th century and their Caroline memorabilia found its way into the Gruuthuse collection. A portrait of Henry, Duke of Gloucester, was brought here from the guild house of the cross-bowmen, while the painting of a shooting competition came from the guild house of the arquebusiers.

On leaving the museum, we should glance at the small lapidary museum in the arcade opposite. This contains a baffling miscellany of gothic gravestones, architectural fragments and 15th-century cannon. Hanging from the gatehouse is an ornate wrought iron sign bearing a crescent moon, the trade mark of the Henri Maes brewery. Notice, too, the fascinating stone frieze embedded in the outside wall of the mansion, depicting a 15th-century military campaign.

If we now turn right on Gruuthusestraat we can walk back to Markt along Dijver, a lovely stretch of water shaded by elm trees.

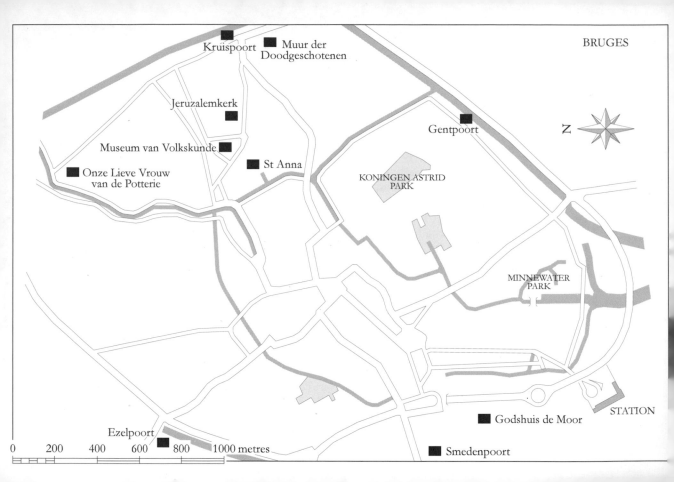

Bruges Explored Further

For anyone with time to spare there is still much to be seen in Bruges. On summer days, we can head out to the ramparts, and walk along landscaped paths laid out in the 19th century, as the locals with their rollicking dogs tend to do on Sundays after church. Although the city walls, built in 1297-1300, are no more, four magnificent medieval gates are still standing: **Kruispoort**, **Gentpoort**, **Smedenpoort** and **Ezelpoort**. The Ezelpoort is a particularly beautiful weathered edifice of dark red brick that has been guarding the northern approach to Bruges since 1367. The finest walks are around the Smedenpoort, a contemporary of the Ezelpoort, and the Kruispoort, the sturdy white sandstone gate shown on page 91, which was built, together with the Gentpoort, in 1401 by Jan van Oudenaerde and Maarten van Leuven. Not far from the Kruispoort is a sad and almost forgotten spot, the **Muur der Doodgeschotenen** (Wall of the Executed Prisoners). Still pock-marked with bullet holes, this brick wall is preserved as a memorial to twelve Belgians and a British soldier executed here by the Germans in the First World War.

When the centre of Bruges becomes unbearably crowded, we might spend time exploring the quiet streets in the neighbourhood of the St Annakerk. Here we come upon the strangest church in Bruges, the **Jeruzalemkerk** at Peperstraat 3. It is a private church built in 1428 by Pieter and Jacob Adorno, descendants of a 13th-century Genoese merchant named Oppicino

Adorno who joined the crusading army of Guy de Dampierre and later settled in Bruges. According to a local legend the two brothers modelled the church in Bruges on the Church of the Holy Sepulchre in Jerusalem, which they had seen on a pilgrimage to the Holy Land. It is certainly an unusual design, consisting of three separate chapels. We enter by a lower chapel, in which are several family tombs. A steep flight of stairs ascends to an upper chapel, situated within the tower. Below this, there is yet another chapel, with a tiny crypt off it containing an imitation of the Holy Sepulchre, complete with the figure of Christ.

Of the many family tombs in the church, the most striking is the black marble mausoleum with the recumbent figures of Anselm Adorno, son of Pieter, and his wife Margaretha van der Back. Anselm Adorno served the Duke of Burgundy on several diplomatic missions, including one to the court of James III of Scotland. As a result of this contact with Scotland, Anselm Adorno was appointed by James III as keeper of the privileges of the Scottish mercantile commu-nity in Bruges. He was murdered on a visit to Scotland in 1483 and his body buried at Linlithgow Palace, although later his heart was returned to Bruges in a lead casket to be buried here.

Heading north along Potterierei, once a busy waterway, we eventually come to **Onze-Lieve-Vrouw van de Potterie** at No. 79, a hospice for elderly women founded in 1276 on the site of an ancient pottery. Standing on the quayside, we will see three dusty old brick gables. They look as if they all date from roughly the same period, but in fact each belongs to a different century. The middle gable, the oldest, is the hospice chapel, which dates back to 1359. The gable to the left is the hospital ward, built in 1529, while to the right is another chapel added in 1623. The architecture is thoroughly Brugean in its sober piety, the only decorative element being the late gothic chimney of the hospital ward.

This old hospice, like the St Janshospitaal, owns a collection of paintings and sculpture donated by benefactors. The collection at the Potteriemuseum is disappointing, however, as the works here mainly date from the 16th and

17th centuries, when artistic creativity in Bruges was at a low ebb. Nevertheless, we do see some interesting paintings in the style of the Antwerp Mannerists, and an attractive 14th-century statue known as the Madonna of the Pevelenberg. The 17th-century baroque chapel is marvellous, crammed with curiosities including a striking neo-gothic mausoleum erected in memory of St Idesbald, an abbot of the Cistercian abbey of Ter Duinen who died in 1167.

Some time might also be spent in Bruges looking at almshouses, of which there are 48 still standing, many of them simple and dignified medieval buildings with whitewashed walls and intimate courtyards. Known in Dutch as *godshuizen*, they were established by wealthy citizens to accommodate the poor and elderly. My favourite is the **Godshuis de Moor** at Boeveriestraat 52-76, founded in 1480 by Donaas de Moor, a city official, and his wife Adriana de Vos. The thirteen simple houses of de Moor were allocated to the guilds of carpenters, masons and coopers, each of which was given three, while the remaining four went to a hospice dedicated to St Julian the Hospitaller. The first nine houses in the row bear the coats of arms of the different guilds to which they belonged, while the others have the hospice's coat of arms. Depicting a boat, it recalls the legend of St Julian, who atoned for the accidental murder of his parents by setting up a hospice by a ford. Eight years after the foundation of this *godshuis*, Donaas de Moor was forced to flee Bruges because of his association with the imprisoned Emperor Maximilian, and he died in exile in Middelburg.

Another fine row of whitewashed almshouses, the Schoenmakersrente at Rolweg 40, once accommodated retired shoemakers. It now houses the **Museum van Volkskunde**, a small folk museum containing a reconstructed school classroom, a shop interior and an old tavern.

Before leaving Bruges, I recommend taking a final short stroll from the **Vismarkt** (pictured opposite on a quiet day in around 1900). The neoclassical covered fish market, built in 1821, is still in use today; prawns and sole fresh from Zeebrugge harbour are laid out dripping wet on the cold stone slabs (on mornings from Tuesday

Bruges. Marché aux poissons.

to Saturday). We continue along Steenhouwers-dijk, past the **Godshuis de Pelikaan** at Groenerei 8-12. This almshouse, founded in 1634 for seven elderly women, is called 'The Pelican'. A relief above the door shows a pelican feeding its young with its own blood, a conventional Christian symbol of Charity. Following the canal as it bends around to the right, then crossing the bridge and turning left, we come to a quiet quay with one of the finest views in Bruges.

We cannot leave Bruges without looking at one last café. Café Vlissinghe at 2 Blekerstraat is the oldest tavern in the city. It may well be the oldest café in Flanders. It is a short stroll away, along the Verversdijk and right across the second bridge. Founded in 1515, Vlissinghe still has most of its old furnishings, including a wooden counter carved in the 16th century and an iron stove from the days when Bruges was *la-morte*.

The café was described in Baedeker's 1905 guidebook as 'a resort of artists, with quaint fittings.' The artists who gathered here at the turn of the century liked to trick gullible British tourists by telling them that the armchair next to the stove belonged to van Dyck. Don't believe a word of it.

Not many artists come here now. In fact the café tends to be full of tourists in the summer. Even the Chinese have heard about it, so Vlissinghe is no secret. Yet in the winter, when the old iron stove is burning and the locals are hunched over their Trappist beers, this seems like the perfect old Flemish tavern in which to end our time in this beautiful city.

Ghent

Ghent

Ghent, the capital of East Flanders, is a bustling and industrious old city, with a port and a university. Our first impression may be one of utter exasperation, as it was for the Victorian writer Martin F. Tupper who, on a visit here in 1856, lamented: 'A trifle of time in such a town as this is bewildering; it is like having to describe a curiosity shop.' However, if we stay here longer than a trifle, we will discover Ghent to be a fascinating and stimulating city, with many delightful spots, such as the waterfront along Graslei, the ruins of an abbey and a castle right in the heart of the old city.

Visiting Ghent in 1641, John Evelyn wrote: 'The Leys and the Scheldt melting in this vast city divide it into 26 islands, which are united by many bridges, somewhat resembling Venice.' A prospect painted in 1534 and reproduced opposite clearly shows these many islands. One of the delights of Ghent, as indeed in Venice, is to chance upon an unexpected stretch of water as, for example, at the end of St Widostraat (where there is a striking view of the castle), or down the lane called Zwaardsteeg off Brabantdam.

From its earliest days, Ghent has been a tumultuous city, always ready to fight for its independence. Its fiery spirit makes Ghent quite different from the sleepy Burgundian backwater of Bruges, a mere 26 miles away. In the 19th century, while Bruges crumbled and languished, producing little else but lace, Ghent was industrialising at full tilt, and it is now one of the most prosperous cities of Flanders. However, we may not always applaud the consequences of Ghent's restless energy, for it sometimes leads to a neglect of historical buildings, such as the unfortunate baroque fish market on St Veerleplein that is now occupied by a garage. Yet the city still has many beautiful buildings, and some travellers even prefer Ghent to Bruges as it is never overcrowded with tourists.

Ghent grew up around two abbeys founded here in the 7th century. The St Pietersabdij, built on a hill of alluvial sand above the Scheldt, stands in what are now the southern quarters of the town. Its church, designed in 1629 by the baroque architect Pieter Huyssens, was inspired to some extent by its namesake in Rome. The St Baafsabdij (shown opposite), built on another branch of the Scheldt about a mile to the north, is now a romantic ruin.

A castle, 's-Gravensteen, was erected in about 867 to the west of the St Baafsabdij on an artificial hill above the River Leie. Like the Burg in Bruges, 's-Gravensteen was built by Baldwin of the Iron Arm, the first Count of Flanders, to protect his lands from the Vikings.

A sprawling city gradually grew up around the abbeys and castle. In the 13th century a considerable area of flooded land was reclaimed, and in 1251-69 the Lieve canal was cut between 's-Gravensteen and the Minnewater harbour in Bruges. The Lieve was one of the main routes through Flanders up until the construction of the railways; John Evelyn travelled along it in 1641, as did the Duke of Wellington's troops bound for Waterloo in 1815.

The cloth industry developed in Ghent, as in other Flemish cities, in the 13th century. By the mid-14th century some 4,000 weavers and 1,200 fullers worked here, out of a total population of about 50,000. The harsh working conditions led to many revolts and disturbances, including one remarkable incident in 1274 when all the weavers and fullers left the city in a mass protest.

Class conflict is a constant motif in the history of Ghent. In the early middle ages, its patrician families were loyal to the counts of Flanders, who in turn were bound feudally to the kings of France. The cloth-workers, however, relied on steady supplies of high-quality English wool, and so tended to support the English. In the tense atmosphere that developed, the patrician families prudently shut themselves away in rugged stone town houses with crenellated battlements. A few of these austere *stenen* (fortified houses) are still standing, such as the Grote Sikkel on Hoogpoort, the Borluutsteen on Korenmarkt and the Geraard de Duivelsteen on Limburgstraat.

At the Battle of the Golden Spurs in 1302, the Ghent workers' militia, led by Jan Borluut, played a decisive role in defeating the knights sent by Philip the Fair of France. The armed workers of Ghent also fought the French in the Hundred Years War, persuaded by Jacob van Artevelde of the advantages of supporting Edward III of England. Van Artevelde, although born into an aristocratic family, became a champion of the Ghent guilds and in 1337 was appointed Captain of Ghent. However, he later outraged the towns-people by suggesting that a son of Edward III be appointed Count of Flanders, and in 1345 he was murdered when a mob stormed his home. His son, Philip van Artevelde, later led the Ghent militia against Louis de Male, Count of Flanders. He defeated the Count's army in 1381, but

the following year Charles VI of France marched into Flanders and crushed his rebellious vassals at the Battle of Westrozebeke.

Always spoiling for a fight, the folk of Ghent defied the dukes of Burgundy, as they had defied the counts of Flanders. In 1448 they refused to pay a hefty tax imposed by Philip the Good on salt and grain. Somewhat remarkably, Ghent was resilient enough to repel the Duke's forces for five years, but in 1453 its army was finally defeated at Gavre, where some 16,000 towns-people perished. After imposing a crippling fine on the city and cancelling its ancient privileges, Philip the Good indulged a theatrical whim by compelling the leading burghers of Ghent to walk out of a city gate wearing hangman's nooses around their necks, then to kiss the dust at his feet.

Ghent's pugnacious spirit was far from being quashed, however, as Charles V was to discover. Charles had been born in Ghent in 1500 in the Prinsenhof, the magnificent palace seen in Sanderus' print opposite, of which all that remains is the 15th-century gate on Bachtenwalle called the Donkere Poort (Black Gate). The birth of Charles V to Joanna the Mad is romantically portrayed in Browning's famous poem *How they brought the Good News from Ghent to Aix*. However, when Ghent defied him in the 1530's by refusing to pay a tax, Charles had no qualms about punishing his native city. In 1540 he ordered the St Baafsabdij to be demolished to make way for a massive renaissance citadel. A contingent of loyal Spanish troops was garrisoned there, ready to crush any further signs of rebellion.

I probably do not need to tell you that Ghent fought on the rebel side during the Dutch revolt against Charles' successor Philip II of Spain. In 1576 the Spanish troops were expelled from the city, and the massive citadel which had been standing a mere 36 years was razed to the ground. In the same year, representatives from the provinces of the Netherlands met here to sign the Pacification of Ghent. Had this document achieved its aims, the Spanish would have withdrawn from the Netherlands. But Philip II was determined to crush the Protestant revolt in his northern lands and sent Alexander Farnese, Prince and later Duke of Parma, to recapture

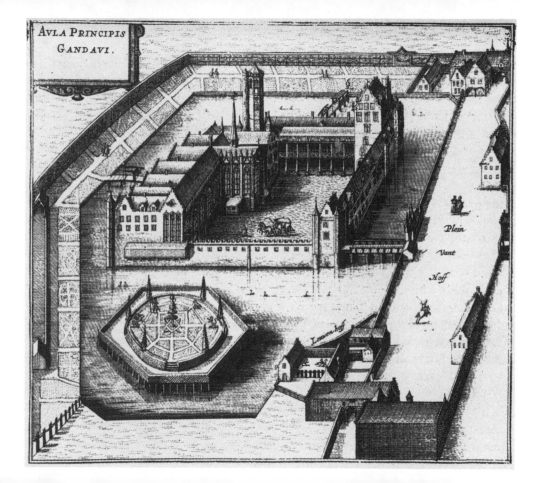

AVLA PRINCIPIS GANDAVI.

Lowenhoff

Plein

Vant

Hoff

the cities from the rebels. Ghent fell to the Spanish in 1584, and with this defeat its spirit of independence finally seems to have been crushed.

French armies marched into Ghent in 1678, 1708, 1745 and again in 1794. The French occupations led to a revival of the ancient class division in Ghent between the French-speaking aristocracy and the Dutch-speaking townspeople. The rich settled in the southern quarters of the city, building the beautiful baroque and rococo palaces on Veldstraat and Kouter (an elegant square where a flower market is held on Sundays), while the workers inhabited the decaying northern areas such as the Patershol.

Yet something did survive of Ghent's rebellious spirit. In 1800 Lieven Bauwens smuggled a spinning jenny out of Britain and set up a cotton-spinning mill in the former charterhouse of Ghent. This swashbuckling deed formed the basis of a flourishing textile industry. Factories were established in 's-Gravensteen, the Prinsenhof and in the many abandoned monasteries, and proved so successful that the population of Ghent trebled in the 19th century, reaching 160,000 in 1900. To improve transportation, a new canal was cut between Ghent and Terneuzen, and a large port built to the north of the city. But the conditions of the 19th-century textile workers were almost as harsh as those endured by the weavers and fullers in the 14th century, prompting the establishment of strong trade unions, which served much the same purpose as the 48 medieval guilds. As if to prove the point, several socialist buildings were erected on Vrijdagmarkt, the square where the guilds had traditionally gathered.

The World Fair of 1913 was held in Ghent's Citadelpark, prompting the city to embark on an ambitious programme of improvements. Much of the old city was restored, including the marvellous row of gable houses along Graslei. Two great buildings erected for the World Fair are still standing: the Feestpaleis, where a flower show is held every five years, and St Pieters Station, which still has a splendid restaurant of banqueting hall proportions, decorated with gleaming ceramic tiles, polychrome capitals and eccentric lamps. However, the mood of optimism in Ghent was crushed by the First World War, when the people of Ghent again fought hard to protect their freedom, as the many war memorials in the city reveal.

Even today, there is a sharp contrast in Ghent between the old Flemish quarters to the north and the elegant French districts to the south. The dividing line is clearly marked by the row of towers of the St Niklaaskerk, the belfry and St Baafskathedraal. The streets of French Ghent such as Veldstraat and Brabantdam have fashionable boutiques, elegant tea rooms and gleaming shopping arcades, whereas Flemish Ghent is an area of narrow cobbled lanes with old brick houses, dark taverns and dusty curiosity shops. It is this contrast, I think, that makes Ghent so fascinating and diverse a city, with an atmosphere very different from Bruges.

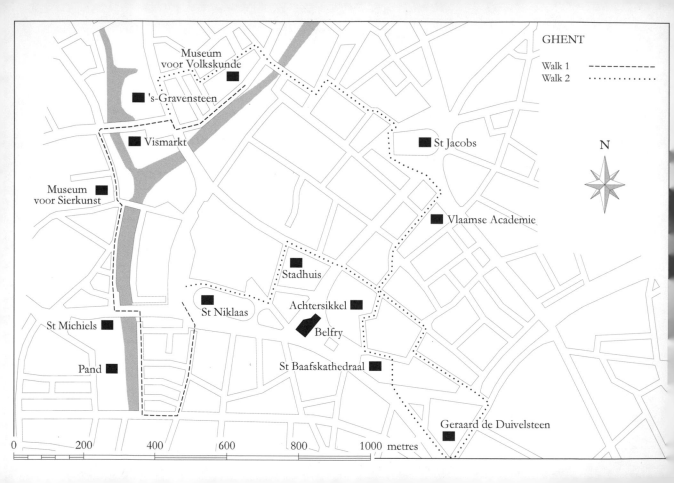

The Waterfront

Our first walk takes us along the old quays of the River Leie, where we enjoy beautiful views of old gables and medieval church towers. After darkness has fallen, a stillness descends upon the old quarters of Ghent like the aftermath of a battle. The quays along the River Leie are particularly delightful at this hour, with floodlit spires and castle walls reflected in the water. 'Now it is merely a city of 26 slumbering islands filled with fantasies,' as the Italian poet Giuseppe Ungaretti wrote in a travel article in 1933.

We may not think of Ghent as a port, but from early times canals have been laboriously dug to provide the city with an outlet to the North Sea. The oldest harbour at Ghent was established on the Leie waterfront in the early middle ages. Grain was shipped here from Artois in northern France and stored in massive romanesque granaries. The fish market and meat market were also erected on this quayside. Nowadays only tour boats use the river, but the magnificent old meat hall is still standing on the waterfront, and there are fishmongers and vegetable stalls on the bustling Groentenmarkt nearby.

Let us begin this walk on **Korenmarkt**, a bustling square where several tramlines converge. Most of the buildings overlooking this former grain market date from the 17th century, but there is one austere stone relic from the early middle ages at Korenmarkt 6-7. Known as the **Borluutsteen**, this 13th-century stone house was built for the Borluut family in a rugged romanesque style. At the Battle of the Golden Spurs in 1302, Jan Borluut, who then lived here, led some 700 Ghent militiamen to victory against the French knights. Isabella Borluut, one of the donors of the *Adoration of the Mystic Lamb* in the cathedral, also came from this family.

We turn down **Veldstraat** to learn a different bit of Ghent history. A brass plaque on the wall of a department store at No. 47 tells us that a delegation of five Americans, led by John Quincy Adams, stayed in this building in 1814, from July until December, to hammer out the fine details of the Treaty of Ghent. This was the treaty that ended the 1812-14 war between Britain and America. The Americans were well received in Ghent, or so it would appear from a plaque put up in 1964 by the National Society of United States Daughters of 1812, 'in appreciation of the hospitality of the people of Ghent'.

Our attention may be diverted by a quaint Alsatian bakery on the opposite corner (at 60 Veldstraat). It is called Bloch and it has been here for at least a century. Long queues gather outside every morning to buy Bloch's famous bread or brioche. There is a tea room at the back which looks like an Alsatian village inn, complete with rustic half-timbered walls and heavy wooden furniture. Let us try to squeeze inside, if only for

a coffee, taking care not to bump into one of the waitresses darting around with trays loaded with silver coffee pots and plates of sticky pastries. The customers tend to be locals who can remember coming here as children fifty years ago. It is a wonderful institution, perfect in every way.

After leaving Bloch, we should take a look at Benito's. Or, rather, we should *smell* Benito's, as this is Ghent's, if not Flanders', best charcuterie shop. We have to retrace our steps down Veldstraat, but only for a short distance, before we turn right into Bennesteeg. Benito's is the shop with the window full of snapshots and magazine articles. Benito is, admittedly, something of a showman, but then he has every right to be, having won the American best bacon award among dozens of other prizes, not to mention producing the world's longest sausage - some 950 metres of best Flemish *worst*.

We had better get back to Veldstraat before we are tempted to buy a kilo of prize-winning sausage. Veldstraat is the most elegant shopping street in Ghent, but it still contains a few 18th-century town houses. One of those, at No. 82, is the Hôtel d'Hane-Steenhuyse, where Louis XVIII of France was offered sanctuary by Count d'Hane during the Hundred Days of Napoleon's return to power. The Duke of Wellington once stayed in the Hôtel van der Haeghen opposite, a decaying palace now used for exhibitions of local urban planning.

We now go back to Bloch's, where the waitresses are still rushed off their feet, and turn left down Hoornstraat to reach the River Leie, then follow Predikherenlei to the right. The waters of the Leie lap against the crumbling brick walls opposite of a former Dominican friary, the **Pand**, founded about 1420. Adjoining it is the **St Michielskerk**, one of the many late gothic churches in Flanders that for one reason or another were never completed. Work began on this church in about 1440 but was halted in 1566 because of Protestant disturbances. The choir was finally completed in 1623-50 in an anachronistic late gothic style. A baroque sacristy, added in 1650 in the corner between the north transept and the radiating chapels of the choir, was partly demolished when the high bridge to the right was constructed, and then rebuilt in neo-baroque style. The west tower is a sad-looking stump; a 17th-century plan to add a soaring gothic spire was abandoned owing to financial difficulties.

We ascend a flight of steps onto the **St Michielsbrug**, a bridge built across the Leie in 1905. From here we have a magnificent view eastwards to the medieval, or mainly medieval, towers of Ghent. We see, from left to right, the sober grey sandstone tower of the St Niklaaskerk, the belfry encrusted with gilded details, and the honey-coloured sandstone tower of St Baafskathedraal. The neo-gothic post office clock tower on the far left, built in 1904, is very much in keeping with the gothic spirit of old Ghent with its gargoyles, statues and coats of arms.

Once across the bridge, we descend the steps in front of the Graaf van Egmont (a restaurant described below, on page 112) to reach the quiet quay of Korenlei. From here we can look across the river to the splendid row of buildings on **Graslei**, which were fastidiously restored for the World Fair of 1913. The **Gildehuis van de Vrije Schippers** (guild house of the free boatmen) at

No. 14 reminds us that this quiet stretch of water was once a bustling harbour. This powerful guild monopolised inland shipping in much of Flanders. The guild house, a confident late gothic building of 1531 designed by Christoffel van den Berghe, is faced with a golden-toned sandstone that is particularly beautiful in the light of the setting sun. The tympanum above the entrance incorporates a relief depicting a three-masted caravel, while two bas reliefs at the top of the gable show boatmen weighing anchor.

A narrow alley that once served as a firebreak separates this guild house from three buildings that emphasize the importance of the grain trade to Ghent. **Korenmetershuis** at No. 11, was the guild house built in 1698 for the grain measurers. To the left, we see a tiny step-gabled house at No. 10 that has been squeezed into another narrow firebreak. Also typical of the Flemish renaissance, this was erected in 1682 as a toll house, where the grain shipments were taxed. A delightful café called **'t Tolhuisje** now occupies the building, an interesting feature of which is the glass-roofed room at the back, built in the former

alley between the toll house and the massive romanesque granary, which was in use until 1734. The rugged stone of its side wall contrasts strikingly with tasteful pale yellow walls and fragile modern lighting. 't Tolhuisje is open daily from 11.30 am, serving coffee, cakes and Belgian beers.

Four years before he designed the guild house of the free boatmen, Christoffel van den Berghe built the **Gildehuis van de Metselaars** (guild house of the masons) at No. 8. But he did not build it here; the edifice was originally erected opposite the St Niklaaskerk, and only moved here in 1912 to improve the appearance of the quay for visitors to the World Fair. The building is an attractive example of Brabant gothic style, decorated with pinnacles and blind tracery which gives it an appearance that is both soaring and ethereal.

At the end of Koornlei we come upon a fine baroque building known as **Het Anker** (The Anchor) at No. 7, erected in 1739 for the Onvrije Schippers, another guild of boatmen. After being subject to the jurisdiction of the free boatmen for many centuries, this guild was finally granted various concessions in the 18th century. The boatmen celebrated by building this jaunty guild house festooned with anchors, dolphins and lions.

Standing upon the **Grasbrug** at the end of the quay and looking north, we see the River Leie joined from the left by the Lieve canal. The magnificent old standstone building on the right bank of the Leie is the former **Groot Vleeshuis** (Great Meat Hall). Built in the early 15th century in a sober gothic style, its roofline is punctuated with dormer windows, like a Bruges almshouse.

The building that stands at the confluence of Leie and Lieve is the 19th-century fish-market. Perhaps you can see the three prongs of a trident glinting in the sun. This is wielded by a splendid figure of Neptune who stands above the entrance to the market on St Veerleplein.

We make our way there along Jan Breydelstraat, a street running behind the houses on our left. Several quirky shops and cafés are found in this street, such as The Fallen Angel at 29 Jan Breydelstraat, whose dim interior is crammed with sepia-tinted picture postcards of East Flanders cities, dolls wearing lace bonnets, 1920's

toy cars and old school ink bottles. At No. 21 in the same street, the exotic-scented Uit Steppe & Oase sells richly decorated chests and pewter jewellery from Pakistan and Afghanistan. It's run by two ex-archaeology students, who venture into remote villages on the old silk road in search of rare treasures. In the summer, they serve Turkish coffee and jasmine sorbets in a Persian garden behind the shop.

Further along we pass the **Museum voor Sierkunst**, a museum of decorative arts occupying a large and decaying baroque mansion at No. 7, built in 1754. A certain interest in interior decoration is necessary to enjoy this museum, but, if you are a reader of *Homes and Gardens* it is not a place to miss. The ground floor rooms are decorated in elegant 18th century styles using furniture and fittings rescued from old Flemish houses. My favourite object, not that I would want it in my house, is a wooden chandelier laden with cherubs and held aloft by an eagle. As we walk through these quiet rooms, our shoes creaking on the floorboards, we might hear a horse clopping along the cobbled street. It is, of course, a tourist coach, but it might as easily be an 18th-century Ghent carriage.

The rear wing may come as something of a shock to our sensibilities. Not only has the old building been gutted to make way for a new four-floor interior, but the works on display are often bizarre. The art nouveau furnishings are elegant enough, but what are we to make of the modern Italian furniture? The quirky 'Banana Chair' by the Belgian designer Muriel Adams looks exceedingly comfortable, but we are not, alas, permitted to try it out.

There are, fortunately, numerous good cafés in the neighbourhood where we can sit down. There is one, indeed, opposite the museum, attached to a bakery called Brooderie (8 Jan Breydelstraat). The sandwiches are wholesome, though the cheesecake is wickedly rich.

We continue now to Burgstraat, where we come upon a splendidly extrovert renaissance house called **Graven van Vlaanderen** (Counts of Flanders), decorated with fourteen medallions bearing portraits of the counts of Flanders and dukes of Burgundy. This façade was put up in

preparation for a visit to Ghent by Philip II, its proud owner aware that the stately procession would pass this way to reach the Prinsenhof.

Turning right across a bridge, the **Hoofdbrug**, we see the massive buttressed walls of 's-Graven-steen rising from the waters of the Lieve canal like a grey cliff. Continuing down Rekelingestraat takes us past the neo-gothic fish market, built in 1872 and decorated with twelve stone reliefs illustrating different types of fish. Then we reach **St Veerleplein**, where the Neptune we glimpsed earlier stands sentinel over a bombastic baroque portal that once led into the old fish market. Built in 1689 and restored after a fire in 1872, this portal now leads to a garage. Nevertheless it is still a splendid sight to behold, decorated by half columns with seaweed-like encrustations. The maritime theme is echoed in the pediment, where Neptune is surrounded by seahorses and dolphins. The window below is flanked by two female figures representing the rivers that meet in Ghent. The Leie is symbolised by a reclining man holding a billowing sail, while the Scheldt is a voluptuous Rubensian woman with a catch of fish at her side.

After crossing St Veerleplein, we continue along Kraanlei, our destination now being the **Museum voor Volkskunde** at No. 65. This captivating museum of local history occupies a beautiful quayside almshouse called the Kinderen Alynshospitaal. The story behind the foundation of this almshouse starkly illustrates the atmosphere of violence and vengeance in 14th-century Ghent. The building stands on the site of a town house owned by Hendrik Alyn, the leader of the guild of fullers. Hendrik Alyn wanted to marry a girl called Godelieve, the daughter of a weaver, but for a fuller to marry a weaver's daughter in Ghent was as unacceptable as for Romeo to marry Juliet. The two guilds were constantly feuding, and in one clash that took place on the Vrijdagmarkt in 1345 some 500 people were slain. To make matters worse, Godelieve was already pledged to a weaver named Simon Rym. However, she broke with him and married Hendrik Alyn in 1354. This so enraged Simon Rym that he murdered both Hendrik and his brother Zeger. In expiation, the Rym family was ordered to build an almshouse and chapel on the site of the Alyns' home.

The almshouse was rebuilt in 1519 in a sober renaissance style, and adorned merely with a statue of St Catherine above the entrance. In 1940 a folk museum was established here, aiming to evoke everyday life in Ghent at the turn of the century. What is appealing about the museum is the diversity of material contained in its 77 tiny rooms, through which we are led through an intriguing route of narrow corridors and winding stairs. The exhibits include numerous photographs, postcards, paintings, toys and utensils. Many of the rooms contain reconstructions of old interiors, such as a grocer's shop, a cobbler's, a weaver's workshop, a tavern with a wall-rack of clay pipes, a candlemaker's shop, a barber's, and a clog-maker's workshop decorated with the mementos of a dedicated pigeon fancier. There is also a small puppet theatre which puts on shows in Dutch on Saturday afternoons.

Entering the chapel, which was rebuilt in the 1540's, we are surprised by two giant figures standing beside the polychrome wooden altar.

These unflattering effigies purport to represent the Archduke Albert and Archduchess Isabella, and were once paraded through the streets during *Reuzen Ommegang* (Giants' Parade). Mock identity papers issued in 1947 for the giant couple are displayed in a glass case, the Archduke's height being given as three metres.

There are also several bourgeois rooms, including a bathroom with an uninviting zinc bathtub and a salon with a brass statuette of Napoleon I on the mantelpiece, suggesting that the upper classes in Ghent still harboured French sympathies in the 19th century. In one of the last rooms, we come upon some souvenirs of the First World War, including a fragment from a Zeppelin shot down by a British pilot near Ghent, and some makeshift chessmen fashioned from spent bullets by Belgian soldiers in the trenches.

On leaving the museum, we may end the walk in a nearby café. Tempting on summer afternoons, the Waterhuis aan de Bierkant, which stocks some 100 types of beer, has a terrace on the right bank of the Leie at the Groentenmarkt. On chilly days, the fashionable **Caffé Wolff** at

Kraanlei 27 is a pleasant place to pause for a coffee, beer or aperitif. Occupying a renaissance step-gabled house built of a cheerful pinkish brick, this tastefully furnished café recalls the interiors painted by the Flemish Primitives. It is decorated with red floor tiles, bare stone walls and a lofty ceiling of wooden beams resting on stone corbels; on wintry days a few logs smouldering in the stone fireplace add to the atmosphere.

When it comes to dinner, there are several attractive restaurants occupying old houses on the quays of the Leie and Scheldt. The Graaf van Egmont at St Michielsbrug 21 is a convivial restaurant situated in a baroque gable house with a good view of the towers of Ghent. It offers traditional Flemish specialities such as stews of one sort or another, and *paling in 't groen* (eel in a green sauce made with chervil).

One of the oddest eating places in Flanders is Tap en Tepel at 7 Gewad, (open Tuesday to Sunday from 7pm to midnight). The Old House of the Dun Dog, says a brass plaque on the door, a foretaste of the obscure spirit that reigns over the place. The interior reeks of the middle ages, with candles dripping hot wax, wrinkled old Flemish paintings of obscure saints, and bizarre folkloric curiosities. We can order a glass of mulled wine, select some cheeses from a wooden sideboard laconically called 'the altar,' and settle down at one of the medieval-size banqueting tables. Maybe someone will eventually lean across and tell us about the dun dog.

The Old City and the van Eyck Altarpiece

On this walk we explore the island known as the **Kuip**, on which the oldest part of the city stands. Originally a neck of land at the confluence of the Leie and Scheldt, the Kuip became an island when the Ketelkanaal was dug. Although the Scheldt now runs underground, leaving only a short stretch of water in which the towers of the Geraard de Duivelsteen are mirrored, we can still clearly see the outline of the island on the map of Ghent. This walk takes us into the cathedral and the castle, and along the quiet, crooked streets of old Ghent which we can compare with the view opposite, painted by the van Eycks. This little glimpse comes from the highlight of the walk: the altarpiece of the *Adoration of the Mystic Lamb* by Jan and Hubert van Eyck, which is the most beautiful medieval Flemish painting in Belgium, if not in the world.

Let us begin (map page 104) in front of the post office on Korenmarkt, where we can admire the west front of the **St Niklaaskerk**, the parish church of Ghent's merchants and guilds. St Niklaas is a marvellous example of Tournai gothic, a sober form of early Netherlandish gothic, modelled on the great cathedrals of northern France. The nave, aisles, transepts, choir and the tower above the crossing were all built in the 13th century in this austere style. In the 14th century, new chapels were added to the aisle by various guilds, and in the 15th century the choir, surrounded by radiating chapels, was completed in a late gothic style. St Niklaas became dilapidated over the years, but it has now been expertly restored to its old splendour.

On leaving St Niklaas, we walk down **Klein Turkije**, a dark street of ancient buildings facing the north side of the church. A quaint row of houses used to stand right up against the north wall of the church, but they have been demolished. Klein Turkije's medieval stone houses are now incongruously occupied by cafés, restaurants and even a throbbing discothèque. In 1521 Albrecht Dürer lodged at an inn within the sombre 13th-century building known as Den Rooden Hoed (The Red Hat) at No. 2. The faded name *Rooden Hoed Hotel* is still to be read above the door, but the blackened building is now a café called Nostalgia.

Upon reaching **Gouden Leeuwplein**, stand in front of the Hotel De Fonteyne (named after a 16th-century salon of rhetoric that met here) for a striking view of the **Belfry**. The sturdy base of Tournai limestone was laid in about 1314, and by 1323 the first four floors had been built. Fifteen years later, the two graceful upper tiers were added using a lighter freestone, and the top was decorated with four corner turrets bearing statues representing the armed officials who guarded the belfry. Only one of the original figures has survived; he is now displayed inside.

The ornate spire with gleaming gilt details was added in 1911-13 as part of the World Fair celebrations. Its design is based on the original 14th-century elevation drawing, now in the Bijlokemuseum. The spire is surmounted by a copper dragon, modelled closely on the belfry's 14th-century weather vane. The privileges granted to Ghent by the counts of Flanders were once kept in a strong box, fitted with three locks, which sat in a ground-floor room of the belfry. This room was in turn protected by two doors each secured by three more locks.

The belfry contains a set of bells which used to be rung on important occasions, including one cast in 1325 that bears the inscription, 'My name is Roeland, if I toll, then there is a fire at hand, if I peal, then there is victory in Flanders land.' Roeland ceased to herald good news or bad in 1540 when Charles V ordered its removal. The great bell was eventually melted down in 1659 and recast by the Dutch bell-maker Pieter Hemony into a 37-bell carillon, which now hangs on the fifth floor. Hemony also cast three large bells known as the Triomphanten, one of which later cracked after an ill-advised attempt to strike it using a charge of electricity. The damaged bell was lowered from the tower and now sits in the square below.

The long gothic building adjoining the belfry was once the **Lakenhalle** (Cloth Hall). Begun in 1425, it was left unfinished in 1445 and only finally completed in 1903. Its vaulted crypt, used as a prison from 1742 until 1902, now contains a cavernous restaurant like the *Ratskellern* restaurants in the cellars of many German town halls. The baroque building attached to the north side of the cloth hall was, surprisingly, also a prison. Built by David 't Kind in the 18th century, it was nicknamed *Mammelokker* (The Suckling) after the relief in the pediment illustrating the story of Cimon and Pero. In this Roman legend, Cimon, an old man, was languishing in prison awaiting execution when his daughter Pero visited him and quenched his thirst from her breast.

Let us now look at Ghent's magnificent **Stadhuis** (Town Hall), illustrated opposite. We reach it by going up Stadhuissteeg, a narrow lane beside the Novotel, then turning right along Hoogpoort.

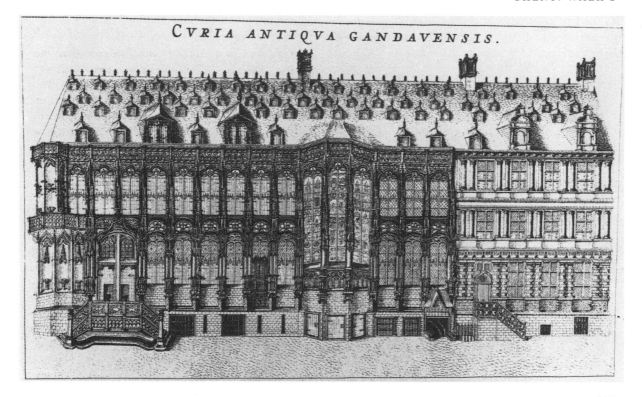

CVRIA ANTIQVA GANDAVENSIS.

We need to cross the street to appreciate the town hall's late gothic façade, which was designed by Rombout Keldermans and Domien de Waghemakere in 1516. Our engraving was proudly made by a fellow-townsman in 1585. We will come upon other late gothic buildings on our wanderings in Antwerp, Brussels and Mechelen, but none quite so delicate and delightful as the frontage of the town hall of Ghent. The main features are the ornate balcony where proclamations were read, the projecting choir of the magistrates' chapel, and the striking polygonal tower on the corner of Hoogpoort and Botermarkt. On studying the tracery at close quarters we will discover delightful details amidst the abstract designs, such as oak leaves and acorns, and vines laden with tiny bunches of grapes.

The problem with buildings in this florid Flemish style was that they were extremely laborious and costly to build. Many of them were therefore abandoned long before they reached completion. Such was the case with Ghent's town hall, of which only one quarter had been built by 1535, when work was halted due to the worsening relations between the city and Charles V. In Ghent's Bijlokemuseum are two detailed elevation drawings made by Keldermans and de Waghemakere in 1517, showing how the town hall should have looked. One drawing depicts the façade on Hoogpoort, which was originally planned to be 21 bays wide, though only 15 bays were ever built. The other shows the façade on Botermarkt, where only four out of 17 planned bays were built. The elaborate niches on the façade were earmarked for statues of the counts of Flanders and dukes of Burgundy, like those on the town hall in Bruges, but these were never produced. Some niches are now occupied by 19th-century neo-gothic inventions, including the figure of Rombout Keldermans stroking his chin contemplatively as he examines a drawing of the town hall, and a glum Domien de Waghemakere holding a model of an elaborate double niche. The 19th-century Ghent gothic enthusiasts once went so far as to propose tearing down several buildings so that the town hall envisaged by Keldermans and de Waghemakere could finally be built. This would have entailed the demolition of the renaissance extensions built in 1572 on Hoogpoort (clearly seen on our print), and in 1620 on Botermarkt, but the plan was quashed by the Belgian Commission for the Protection of Historic Monuments.

Many historic events have taken place in Ghent's town hall. In 1576 representatives of the provinces of the Netherlands assembled in the hall which runs most of the length of Hoogpoort to sign the Pacification of Ghent, a document which unfortunately proved of little consequence in securing peace and religious freedom in the Low Countries. A curious feature of this hall, now known as the Pacificatiezaal, is the intricate maze picked out in the floor in tiles of two different colours. Apparently, offenders in the middle ages who had been sentenced by the court to embark on a pilgrimage might instead follow this labyrinth.

Standing on the corner of Hoogpoort and Botermarkt, we will see the **St Jorishof** opposite at Botermarkt 2. This hotel claims to be the oldest in Europe, dating back to 1228. The ancient step-gabled building of blackened stone

that we see on Botermarkt was erected in 1469-77 as the crossbowmen's guild house. St George, the patron saint of this guild, can be spotted slaying a dragon on the gable top. It was in the St Jorishof in 1477 that Mary of Burgundy, succeeding her father Charles the Bold, was forced to sign the Great Privilege, in which she promised to uphold the privileges of the Flemish cities. Later that year she gave a sumptuous banquet here in honour of the ambassadors sent by the Emperor Frederick III to woo her on behalf of his son, the Archduke Maximilian. The proposal was accepted and Mary married Maximilian that year. Charles V, whose statue stands on the corner of the town hall opposite, also stayed several times in the St Jorishof, and in 1805 Napoleon spent two nights here.

The coats of arms on the front of the hotel recall episodes in its rich history. They are the arms of Ghent, Flanders, Austria, Burgundy, Spain and the guild of St George. At the top of the gable is a window with good tracery, where the crossbowmen had their chapel. Notice, too, the Madonna on the corner of the hotel, a rarer

119

sight in Ghent than in Bruges.

We now cross Botermarkt, of which Dorothy Wordsworth wrote, 'I can hardly endure to call a place so dignified by such a name.' The butter market which gives this square its humble name was once held in the cellars of the town hall, where Ghent's tourist office is now situated.

Continuing along Hoogpoort, we come upon a row of ancient stone houses. Just beyond the St Jorishof are two 15th-century houses known as the **Grote Moor** (Great Moor) and the **Zwarte Moor** (Black Moor). Then come two magnificent houses flanking Biezekapelstraat, built by the van der Sickelen family. To the left of the lane, at Nederpolder 2, is the **Kleine Sikkel**, a rugged romanesque town house built in the 13th century of unhewn stone, with a crenellated curtain wall at the top. The family's coat of arms, much weathered, can still be seen above the door. In 1418 the family quit this fortified town house and moved into the **Grote Sikkel**, a less sombre step-gabled house on the opposite side of the lane.

Venturing down the alluring Biezekapelstraat, we discover a third house once owned by the van der Sickelen family - the **Achtersikkel** - situated, as its name suggests, behind the Grote Sikkel. This secret house overlooking a small courtyard is the most attractive of the three Sikkels, particularly at night when it is floodlit. Various gothic and renaissance buildings and arcades are picturesquely grouped around a lofty round tower of white stone dating from the 15th century. The little turret behind is a 14th-century relic.

The Grote Sikkel, Kleine Sikkel and Zwarte Moor now house the Ghent Conservatory of Music, which generates the cacophony we hear as we wander down Biezekapelstraat. A stone tablet attached to a rear wall of the Achtersikkel depicts, appropriately, Orpheus soothing the wild animals with his lyre. My guess is that this stone was placed here when the building was converted to a conservatory in 1900.

Biezekapelstraat takes us by a delightfully crooked route to the cathedral, past an eerie neo-renaissance house dated 1901 and covered with floral decorations in stone and rusting wrought iron. We then turn left along Kapittelstraat to enter the **St Baafskathedraal** (Cathedral of St Bavo) by the north portal. Let us now sit down in the nave to read the history of this great church.

The St Janskerk, as the cathedral at Ghent was originally named, was constructed in three phases. Following medieval custom, the choir was built first. Grey Tournai sandstone was used in the construction, which proceeded at a snail's pace from the late 13th to the mid-15th century. The choir rests on an immense and impressive crypt, where there are some traces of a 12th-century romanesque church. Another interesting feature of the crypt is its 15 radiating chapels, some still containing family tombs and religious paintings.

In the second phase of construction, lasting from 1462-1534, the tower was built in Brabant gothic style, a more ornate gothic than that of Tournai, and more appealing here because it used a warm, crumbly sandstone from the quarries of Lede was used. In the third period of construction, from 1533-59, the nave and transepts were erected, these too in Brabant gothic style.

This church was the setting for two meetings of the Order of the Golden Fleece. The seventh meeting, or chapter, of the Order was convened here by Philip the Good in 1445, and in 1559 the twenty-third was called by Philip II of Spain, just before he left the Netherlands for the last time. The 51 coats of arms of the knights who attended in 1559 now hang in the south transept, including one above the portal bearing the Medici coat of arms, decorated with the Florentine family's device of five balls. Two years later Philip II elevated Ghent to a bishopric and this church, which already in 1540 had been renamed the St Baafskerk after the old abbey in Ghent of that name, then became St Baafskathedraal.

The rococo pulpit in the cathedral is a flamboyant masterpiece of propaganda. Carved by Laurent Delvaux in 1745, with lavish use of marble, oak, gilt and stucco, it represents Time, an old man, being awakened from his slumbers by Truth, a young maiden holding a book with an admonition of St Paul's to the spiritually asleep. A magnificent double staircase leads up to the pulpit, to which two carved figures are pointing, as if to direct the attention of the congregation towards the priest's words. Yet it would be difficult to concentrate on the priest, given the rollicking drama that is unfolding above, as two angels wrestle with a large cross, while a third places an apple in the mouth of a golden snake entwined around a gnarled tree trunk.

Behind the pulpit is a portrait of the donor, Bishop Triest, who also paid for many other sumptuous baroque embellishments to replace the art treasures destroyed in the religious troubles of the 16th century. He made a gift of the marble choir screen, and the set of four copper candlesticks placed on the high altar. The candlesticks are decorated with the coat of arms of Henry VIII of England, and were designed by Benedetto da Rovezzano to support a canopy above the royal tomb at Windsor. Bishop Triest's mausoleum, which stands in the ambulatory, was carved in 1654 by Hieronymus Duquesnoy the Younger, and shows the sad and aged bishop reclining wearily on his tomb.

The ambulatory and radiating chapels of this church had scarcely been finished, and the tower and nave not yet begun, when Jan and Hubert van Eyck painted the famous altarpiece of the *Adoration of the Mystic Lamb* to stand in a chapel of the church. This work, which took some twelve years to complete, is one of the most remarkable achievements of medieval European art. Returning to the Rooden Hoed Inn after seeing it in 1521, Albrecht Dürer wrote in his diary, 'I saw the St John panel, a stupendous painting of great intelligence.'

In about 1420 Burgomaster Joos Vydt and his wife Isabella Borluut commissioned Hubert van Eyck to paint a polyptych to hang within their family chapel in the St Janskerk, as the church was then called. However, Hubert van Eyck apparently died in about 1426, when the altarpiece was still very far from completion. His brother Jan was called to Ghent from Bruges to take over the work, and it was finally completed in 1432. The interesting question of who painted what is far from being resolved, and some scholars have even cast doubt on the existence of Hubert.

As long ago as 1510, the Flemish renaissance poet Jean Lemaire de Belges described Jan van

Eyck as 'the king of painters, whose perfect and minute works will never fall into vain oblivion'. He was absolutely right, as we discover on entering the chapel in which the painting hangs, joining, probably, a crowd of art-enthusiasts talking excitedly in a dozen or so different languages. The painting, which has drawn travellers to Ghent for more than 500 years, is a large winged altarpiece comprising 26 separate scenes painted on 12 oak panels. It is a truly encyclopaedic work illustrating 14 separate episodes from the Old and New Testaments. The 17th-century art critic Karel van Mander counted 330 complete faces in the painting.

The altarpiece is teeming with delightful details, such as the glint of light on precious jewels, and the almost legible words of an illuminated manuscript. There are numerous tiny gothic inscriptions in the work, sometimes incorporated into a length of fabric, or hidden in a floor tile. Van Eyck has also skilfully depicted the natural world; a botanist once studied the altarpiece and identified some 40 different types of flower.

The figure of God (or Christ, say some critics) fills the middle panel of the upper register. He is portrayed in a cloak of vivid scarlet cloth, the most costly material woven by the Flemish weavers. The Virgins in Jan van Eyck's *Madonna with Canon Van der Paele* in Bruges and *Madonna with Chancellor Rolin* in Paris also wear cloaks made from this sumptuous cloth.

Mary, who is seated to the left of God, has a face of astonishing beauty. Her lips, Karel van Mander observed, 'seem to utter the words that she is reading in a book'. To the right of God is the figure of John the Baptist, who is wearing a hair shirt beneath his rich green cloak, a quaint reminder of the preaching in the wilderness. The inner panels of the wings are decorated with angels singing and making music. The faces of the singers, though not particularly beautiful, are meticulously realistic, capturing the angels in an unguarded moment as they strain to pitch their voices precisely. Notice, too, the bellows operator who is just visible behind the portable organ in the right panel.

We then come to the extraordinary naked figures of Adam and Eve on the outer panels of the wings. Never before in the history of painting were naked figures depicted with such realism. Look at Eve's foot, which seems to be balanced on the very edge of the picture frame. Then compare Adam's right foot, which seems to be stepping out of the frame! This uncanny realism was perhaps intended to remind the medieval viewer that Adam and Eve are part of our world, the world of flesh, whereas God, Mary and the choirs of angels are not.

The panels in the lower register are linked together into a unified composition. The middle panel shows the Adoration of the Mystic Lamb, a theme taken from the Gospel of St John. 'Behold the Lamb of God, which taketh away the sins of the world,' is inscribed in Latin on the rim of the altar upon which the lamb stands, but the letters are too minuscule to read from afar. To the fore stands the Fountain of Life, a symbol of redemption. The prophets are kneeling to the left of the altar, and the apostles to the right. Four other groups of figures converge on the altar. At the bottom left are the patriarchs, who were, according to medieval scholars, the founders of the human race. The figure wearing a white gown and carrying a twig of laurel is sometimes identified as Virgil. Emerging from a copse of exotic bushes behind are bishops and confessors dressed in blue vestments and bearing palm branches. This group is balanced by the virgin saints emerging from the copse to the right, including Agnes, with a lamb, and Barbara, carrying a miniature tower. The final group, occupying the bottom right corner, are saints and martyrs. St Stephen is identified by the stones, symbolising his martyrdom, which he carries in his vestment.

The landscape is painted with supreme clarity, recalling those sunny spring days in the Low Countries when the light inundates the flat landscape. The rolling hills in the distance are more southern European, and the horizon is bristling with exotic Mediterranean trees, probably added by Jan van Eyck after his journey to Portugal, where he had been sent by Philip the Good to paint a portrait of his intended bride. Some of the medieval spires may also be based on buildings that van Eyck saw on his travels. In the middle stands the spire of Utrecht Cathedral, which also appears also in van Eyck's Rolin altarpiece in Paris. We may also recognise Cologne Cathedral and the romanesque church of Gross St Martin on the summit to the right; Memling's *St Ursula Shrine* in Bruges also includes views of these buildings. There is one discrepancy in van Eyck's version, however, for Cologne Cathedral is shown with twin spires; although begun in the middle ages, they were not in fact completed until the 19th century.

Now let us look at the side panels, in which groups of figures advance towards the altar over symbolically rough and stony ground. On the far left are the just judges, whose expressive faces and contemporary costumes suggest that they may be portraits of eminent Burgundians (but there is more to this panel than meets the eye, as we shall discover later). According to an old legend, the horseman in the foreground is Hubert van Eyck, while the figure fourth from the left is said to be his brother Jan. In the adjoining panel are the warriors of Christ, including St George bearing a shield with a red cross, on which there is an inscription, but again illegible from our vantage

point. The two panels to the right show the holy pilgrims led by the giant St Christopher, and the holy hermits led by St Antony Abbot, the founder of monasticism.

Lastly, we should look at the twelve panels on the back of the wings. The donors appear on the outer panels of the lower register. Above we see the Annunciation, set in a lovely Flemish interior with views through windows to the streets of Ghent. These panels, which are in the style of the Master of Flémalle, were probably painted by Jan van Eyck after a visit to the Master's shop in Tournai in 1427. The four panels are linked together by common features such as the roof beams and floor tiles. A gilt inscription in ornate calligraphy fills the gap between the two figures of the Annunciation. *Ave Maria!* the angel declares. The Virgin replies, *Ecce ancilla Domini* ('Behold the handmaid of the Lord'). Notice that the Virgin's reply is upside-down, apparently an odd medieval convention to allow God to read the message.

The tumultuous story of the Ghent altarpiece began in the 1550's when Philip II attempted to ship the work to Madrid. The church authorities refused to permit this, and Philip II had to make do with a copy painted by the Mechelen artist Michiel Coxie, who laboured for two years on this task. At about this time, the predella of the altarpiece, apparently showing a scene of Hell, was mysteriously lost.

The Ghent altarpiece would almost certainly have been destroyed during the Protestant disturbances in 1566 had the church authorities not hidden it in the church tower. During the period of Protestant rule, the altarpiece was moved to the town hall, and the aldermen on one occasion came close to presenting the work to Queen Elizabeth I of England to repay a loan. After Ghent was recaptured by the Spanish in 1584 it was moved back into the church, where it remained undisturbed for the next two centuries, until in 1781 Emperor Joseph II of Austria expressed his distress at the naked figures of Adam and Eve. The church authorities dutifully removed the offending panels and replaced them with copies in which Adam and Eve are clothed in shaggy cloaks. These ridiculous panels now hang at the west end of the nave.

After Napoleon invaded the Low Countries, the four middle panels were carried off to Paris, but the side panels were concealed from the pillaging army. Following Napoleon's defeat, his booty was returned, but a few months later the church authorities sold the six remaining side panels to an antique dealer for 3,000 florins. This dealer promptly resold all six to a collector in Britain for the princely sum of 100,000 florins, and in 1821 the shrewd British dealer earned an even more handsome profit by selling them to the Kaiser Friedrich Museum in Berlin for 400,000 florins. To add to Ghent's sorrow, the four panels left hanging in the cathedral were badly damaged by a fire. During the three years spent restoring these panels, there was nothing at all to be seen of van Eyck's altarpiece in Ghent.

A series of fortuitous events then brought the scattered pieces of the altarpiece together again. In 1861 the original Adam and Eve panels resurfaced, having been lost since their replacement in 1781, and were purchased by the Musée des Beaux-Arts in Brussels. At the end of the First World War, under the reparation terms of the Treaty of Versailles, Germany was required to give Belgium a number of works of art, including the panels sold to the Berlin gallery in 1821. The original Adam and Eve panels were then returned to Ghent in 1920, and the altarpiece was again complete, for the first time in 141 years. But this happy reunion was of short duration, for in 1934 a thief broke into the church and removed the panel at the bottom left-hand corner, with the just judges on one side and the grisaille St John the Baptist on the other. This was one of the panels that had been sold to the Berlin gallery, and the wooden frame had been carefully sawn down the middle so that the two paintings could be hung separately. The thief prised apart the two pieces, keeping the painting of the just judges and depositing St John the Baptist in a left luggage locker. He then demanded an enormous sum of money for the return of the former. The authorities refused to pay the ransom, however, and the painting has never been recovered. In its place is a copy painted during the German occupation in the Second World War. Various theories have been proposed as to the whereabouts of the 'Just Judges'. In Albert Camus' novel *The Fall* the panel turns up hidden in a cupboard in an Amsterdam house, an emblem of sin. There is a further twist to this bizarre story, for the artist who made the copy apparently expressed his patriotism by secretly altering the face of one of the just judges to resemble King Léopold III, who was then being held prisoner in the palace at Laeken.

Later in the war the altarpiece was removed from Belgium for safety, first to Pau, then to 'Mad' King Ludwig's castle of Neuschwanstein, and finally to Munich. It was returned to Ghent after the war, and has only moved once since then, when it was transferred from the Vydt chapel to its present secure location in a windowless chapel in the nave.

Once we have explored the cathedral, we head down Limburgstraat, past a bronze sculptural group of Jan and Hubert van Eyck surrounded by admirers. This work was unveiled, like so much else in Ghent, for the World Fair in 1913. Further on we come to a bridge where the River Scheldt makes a brief appearance before vanishing below the streets. Under the terms of the Treaty of Verdun in 843, the Scheldt formed a frontier between the lands of the French kings to the west and those of the German emperors to the east. Rising like a cliff from the water is the **Geraard de Duivelsteen**, a massive fortified town house of blackened Tournai sandstone. This *steen*, once much larger than it is today, was erected in the 13th century for Geraard de Duivel (Gerald the Devil), whose sinister epithet was apparently due to his extremely dark skin.

We now turn left along Reep, left again up Hoofdkerkstraat and right into Kapittelstraat. On reaching Nederpolder we turn left, then right into **Zandberg**, an attractive little square with a curious pump surmounted by an obelisk, put here in 1810 by the Napoleonic administrators. In Koningstraat, straight ahead, we come upon the **Vlaamse Academie** (Flemish Academy) at No. 18, which occupies a beautiful rococo town house designed by David 't Kindt in 1746. A pleasing effect is achieved by the mock drapery, which seems to flutter from the window ledges and balustrades. In the setting sun the golden-hued sandstone of the building is particularly striking. This street leads to the **St Jacobskerk**, a sober church with twin romanesque towers, and a 13th-century gothic choir and nave.

Wijzemanstraat leads thence into **Vrijdagmarkt**, a cheerful square surrounded by cafés and restaurants. Vrijdagmarkt is especially lively on Fridays, market day, when the heavy smell of waffles and *frites* wafts around stalls selling clothes, smoked sausage and boiled sweets. Many important events in Ghent's history have taken place on this square. The imposing neo-gothic statue of Jacob van Artevelde in the middle commemorates the rousing speech he made here urging the citizens of Ghent to support Edward III of England against the king of France. The three bas reliefs on the base are decorated with allegorical female figures representing the treaties concluded by van Artevelde. The polychrome coats of arms of the guilds of Ghent also appear on the base, recalling that van Artevelde was at one time captain of each of the 48 guilds. It was also here, on a day in 1345 that became known as Evil Monday, that the weavers and fullers clashed

following a dispute about wages, leaving some 500 people dead.

Of the many guild houses that once stood on Vrijdagmarkt, only one remains. Built in about 1450 for the guild of tanners, **Het Toreken**, as it is called, stands on the corner of Kammerstraat, its elegant round watchtower attractively restored and emblazoned with the guild colours. On the opposite side of the square is a warehouse designed in 1899 by Ferdinand Dierkens for the Ghent socialist society *Vooruit*, bearing the Dutch equivalent of 'Workers of the World Unite'.

Meerseniersstraat leads down to the River Leie, a short distance downstream of a 15th-century cannon known as Dulle Griet. Facing us on the other side of the bridge are two interesting baroque houses. **De Fluitspeler** (The Flautist) at Kraanlei 79 is decorated with six terracotta reliefs representing the five senses, and a flying deer. The house takes its name from the figure of a flautist in a medallion at the top. Allegorical figures on the cornice representing Faith, Hope and Charity finish off this crowded composition. **De Zeven Werken van Barmhartigheid** (The Seven

Works of Charity) at Kraanlei 77 is decorated with six panels. The top three represent the charitable works of burial of the dead, comforting prisoners and visiting the sick; the lower ones depict feeding the hungry, refreshing the thirsty and clothing the naked. The seventh work of charity - lodging travellers - was represented by the building itself, which was once an inn.

Rodekoningstraat leads straight ahead into the **Patershol**, a picturesque medieval quarter first settled in the 10th century by leather workers. After years of neglect, the lanes and houses in this corner of Ghent are being carefully restored, and cafés, restaurants and art galleries are transforming an area that was once a notorious slum. The street to the left named Corduwaniersstraat (Cordwainers Street) is a reminder of Ghent's old leather trade. The word cordwainer derives from Cordoba in Spain, which produced luxurious leather products. Spanish leather workers were particularly renowned for *guadamacil*, a gilded leather introduced to Spain by the Moors, and used in Flanders for wall hangings. There is a beautiful room in the Plantin-Moretus Museum in Antwerp that is hung with this sumptuous Spanish leather.

If we turn right from Corduwaniersstraat along Hertogstraat, we come upon a lane to the left named Haringstraat. Here we glimpse the grey stone walls of 's-Gravensteen, a louring castle which we reach by walking down the lane and turning left along Geldmunt.

Dark and dank, bristling with turrets and battlements, **'s-Gravensteen** (The Count's Castle) is a stark symbol of medieval power, as is still clearly visible behind all the accretions of more mercantile periods in the 17th-century engraving opposite. On a chilly winter's day, the castle is gloomy, but when the sun shines, it is delightful to climb up to its breezy battlements and look down upon the old city.

This is a motte-and-bailey castle, consisting, that is, of a raised mound (the motte) surmounted by a tower, and surrounded by a courtyard (the bailey) enclosed by an elliptical outer wall with 24 turrets. It stands on the site of a castle erected in the 9th century by Count Baldwin of the Iron Arm, which was rebuilt in 1180 by Count Philip

ECCLESIA COLLEGIATA
Divi Pharahildis ·

Domus Prætoria
Castellaniæ Auderburgensis

PETRA COMITIS
vulgo
HET GRAVEN CASTEEL

of Alsace, Duke of Flanders, to curb the rebellious spirit of the townspeople of Ghent.

Entering 's-Gravensteen, we see a sinister cruciform window with dripping stalactites, flanked by twin octagonal towers of blackened stone. This unusual window may have been intended by Philip to remind his vassals of his crusading zeal. Eleven years after erecting this castle, he died in the Holy Land at the siege of Acre.

In the 13th century a building known as the Count's Residence was added alongside the keep. It was in a less severe style of architecture, with stepped gables and romanesque windows. Despite this improvement, the castle was not a comfortable place to live. By the 14th century, the counts of Flanders had moved to a new residence built on the island to the west, which eventually became the magnificent Prinsenhof, where Charles V was born in 1500.

In 1779 the abandoned 's-Gravensteen was sold to a local architect who conceived an ambitious plan to convert the buildings into houses and artists' ateliers, but this was never realised. During the industrial revolution, 's-Gravensteen was one of many old buildings in Ghent used as a textile mill, and looms clattered in the vacated rooms of the Count's Residence. In 1888 a zealous restoration was begun; families living within the castle were evicted and the houses that had been built against its walls were torn down. The old castle buildings were then purged of looms and litter, and rebuilt in a style that owed as much to Victorian values as to the architecture of the early middle ages. A century on, weeds have sprung up on the battlements and pigeons have returned to their old haunts in the stone walls, restoring a patina of desirable decay to this ancient hulk.

Many of the rooms of 's-Gravensteen seem to have been used at one time or another as prisons, including the room in the gatehouse with the cruciform window. The most dreadful sight in the castle is the oubliette sunk deep below the floor in one of the rooms in the Count's Residence. Another unlovely feature is a small room with an exhibition of torture instruments. The grim impression that these rooms inevitably leave is quickly dispelled, however, as soon as we ascend the dark spiral stairs to emerge on the windy battlements, where we are greeted by a magnificent panoramic view of Ghent's old stone and brick houses, the glorious row of towers, and the cluster of cranes around the port.

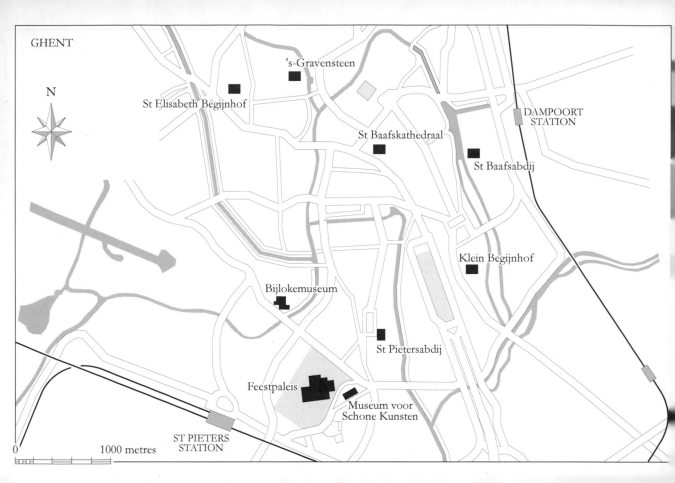

Ghent Explored Further

If time permits it is worth venturing further afield in Ghent, for there are numerous interesting sights outside the centre. Many can be reached by tram from Korenmarkt, although it is also pleasant to wander along the quays of the Leie, Schelde and Lieve to reach the outlying quarters.

I. Southern Ghent. Southern Ghent has an elegant 19th-century character, with broad, leafy avenues and imposing mansions. The main attractions of this quarter are the antiquities collection of the Bijlokemuseum and the paintings in the Museum voor Schone Kunsten. We might also stroll into the **Citadelpark**, an attractive park laid out in the 1870's. It stands on the site of a citadel erected in 1819-31 by the Duke of Wellington at the time of the short-lived Kingdom of the Nether-lands. A solitary gate is all that survives of the citadel, which was once one of the strongest fortresses in Europe. The sonorous Latin inscription above the gate proclaims, *Anno XI Post Proelium ad Waterloo Exstructa* ('Erected nine years after the Battle of Waterloo'). Another device in French declares, *L'union fait la force* ('Strength through unity'). This slogan did not convince the Belgians, who in 1830 severed their links with the Dutch.

Behind the park is the attractive, if small, **Kruidtuin**, a botanical garden tended by the university. Here some 7,000 species of plants from all over the world thrive in Alpine gardens or shady glades. A lake bordered with magnolias and pines adds a certain romance to this scientific garden.

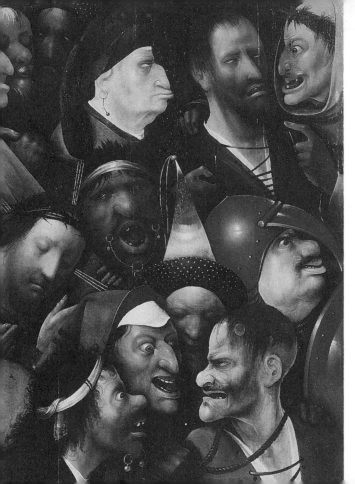

Opened in 1904 beside the Citadelpark, the **Museum voor Schone Kunsten** (Museum of Fine Arts) houses a diverse collection of paintings by Flemish, Dutch, British and French artists. Ghent has always been more interested in industry than art, one feels, and its collection of old paintings does not compare with the galleries at Brussels, Antwerp and Bruges, although its contemporary art collection is one of the best in Europe. Before visiting the gallery, we might pause for a coffee in the airy neoclassical apse at the centre of the building.

Room 1 contains a long and narrow painting, once part of a retable, which depicts the Capture of Jerusalem by Titus in a most detailed manner. Also in this room is a 16th-century set of three double portraits representing Philip the Good and his third wife Isabella of Portugal, John the Fearless and Maria of Bavaria, and Charles the Bold and his second wife Isabella of Bourbon.

The most remarkable paintings in the collection are two works by Hieronymus Bosch in room 2. The *Bearing of the Cross* is a nightmarish painting filled with 17 of the ugliest physiognomies in the history of art. Besides Christ's, the only remotely attractive face is that of a woman who is turning her head away from the scene. This is St Veronica (carrying her holy handkerchief stained with the image of Christ) but even she is not an entirely appealing character, however, and looks mildly amused by the mockery that Christ is suffering. The other work by Bosch is a *St Jerome*, set in a bizarre landscape with curious plants and animals.

The rooms of 19th-century art contain many attractive works, in particular views of the River Leie by Emile Claus. The Leie was known to the English in the middle ages as 'The Golden River' because it flowed through extensive fields of flax. This peaceful landscape attracted Flemish Impressionists in the 19th century, rather as the Seine attracted their French counterparts.

Not far from the Citadelpark, the **Bijloke-museum** at Godshuizenlaan 2 occupies an attractive Cistercian abbey founded in 1228 by Ferrand of Portugal. The oldest buildings still standing are the 14th-century infirmary and refectory. The rest of the abbey was destroyed when the Dutch rebels built new ramparts here. After the Spanish recaptured the city, a relatively stable period followed when the Cistercian nuns slowly rebuilt their abbey, sometimes (as we will discover) in an unexpectedly ostentatious style. The abbey was used as a hospital up until the 1920's, then converted to house a museum of antiquities established in 1884.

The museum has amassed a diverse collection of local curiosities, including furniture, guild relics, armour, decorated tiles, ship models, paintings, maps, plans, sculpture, old doors, coins and ironwork. The collection is not as carefully tended as the Gruuthusemuseum in Bruges, I suspect because Ghent looks towards the future rather than the past. It is fascinating nevertheless, in much the same way as the overcrowded attic of an old stately home might be.

We first explore the four walks of the lower cloister, where we come upon a surprising room decorated with lavish stucco. Dated 1715, it looks as if it might have once been a ballroom in one of the palaces on Veldstraat. Not so; this room was built by the Cistercian nuns *inside* the ancient abbey refectory. During a recent restoration of the abbey, this baroque oddity was removed, thankfully, and rebuilt here. An interesting painting in this room shows the *Inauguration of Charles II of Spain as Count of Flanders*, a splendid ceremony that took place on the Vrijdagmarkt in 1666. A grandiose baroque stage was erected on the east side of the square for the occasion, behind which the watchtower of the guild house of the tanners is just visible.

The lower cloister contains several rooms furnished in period style, including an Empire drawing room filled with mementos of the Napoleonic era. The most attractive of these rooms is the former Treasury of the Stadhuis at Ghent, a rich and dark baroque interior, made mysterious by the greenish light that filters in from the overgrown courtyard. The walls are hung with sumptuous gilt leather from Mechelen, and a magnificent polychrome mantelpiece dated 1682 is decorated with a painting of the *Four Seasons* by Joos van Cleef.

Mid-way up the staircase, we come upon the abbey's 14th-century refectory, a majestic gothic structure with a painted oak roof resting on columns of grey Tournai sandstone. On the west wall is a 14th-century fresco with John the Baptist and St Christopher. Pilgrims often lodged at the abbey, which explains the figure of St Christopher, patron saint of travellers. The fresco at the east end is a Last Supper, a subject often found in abbey refectories. The long side walls are decorated with neo-gothic frescos. Placed in the middle of this vast room is the tomb of Hugo II, chatelain of Ghent, who died in 1232. The recumbent figure is dressed in chain mail, and rests on a stone slab supported by four fanciful animals. A castle at his head recalls his function as chatelain (keeper of the castle), and a dog at his feet symbolises his duty of fidelity.

At the top of the stairs we enter the former dormitory where an interesting collection of guild relics is displayed. Notice the eighteen wooden guild emblems once carried in processions, including those of the carpenters, boatmen, millers (a windmill), weavers (a loom) and porters (a figure in 18th-century dress carrying an enormous sack on his head). The upper cloister contains further curiosities, including a strange little room decorated entirely with Delft tiles.

On leaving the cloister, we enter a garden with a clipped hedge for a good view of the west gable of the refectory. This grandiose brick gothic design dates from the 1320's, with a large trefoil cornice surrounded by niches, rose windows and blind arches.

The former house of the abbess, which we enter from the garden, contains various furnished rooms including an attractive Flemish kitchen. On leaving this house, we still have one room to visit, which we might easily overlook. Situated at the end of the corridor opposite the porter's lodge, it is the Room of the Governors of the Poor Board, a splendid baroque interior designed in 1689, with panelling by Norbert Sauvage. A chimneypiece painting by Joos van Cleef depicts the foundation of the Poor Board at Ghent by Charles V in 1531, the spires of Ghent looming in the background. The other paintings in the room depict the Seven Works of Charity.

II. Begijnhofs in Ghent Ghent has three large Begijnhofs, all of them interesting to explore if we have time to spare. The oldest in the city, and probably in Flanders, is the **St Elisabeth Begijnhof**, to the north of Begijnengracht. In 1234 Countess Joanna of Constantinople granted the Beguines this site, which was then an area of marshy ground to the west of the city boundary. Although the walls of the St Elisabeth Begijnhof are no longer standing as they do so stoutly in the print overleaf, it has not entirely lost its enclosed and protective atmosphere. Proveniersstersstraat is particularly attractive, with houses dating from the 16th and 17th centuries, their doorways delightfully adorned with iron grilles, elaborate bell-pulls and saints in niches.

The **Klein Begijnhof** on Lange Violettenstraat is the most appealing of Ghent's Begijnhofs. Also founded in 1234 by Countess Joanna, it has the advantage of retaining its walls and portal, so that the outside world is kept at bay. The houses, dating mainly from the 17th and 18th centuries, surround a spacious grassy square like an English village green; there are birds singing in the lime trees. Each house has its own small portal with a statue of a saint to identify it. The doors, as

139

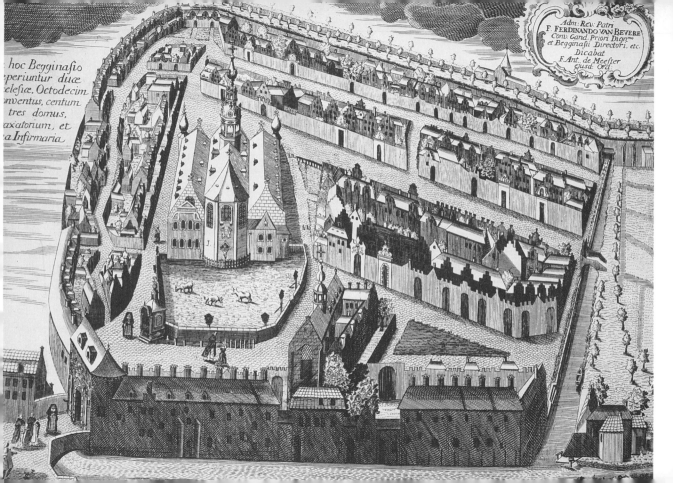

hoc Begginasio
periuntur duæ
clesiæ. Octodecim
onventus, centum
tres domus,
axatorium, et
a Infirmaria

J.

always, have elaborate if rusty bell-pulls and tiny grilles through which to scrutinise visitors.

There is another Begijnhof, the **Groot Begijnhof**, in the eastern suburbs of the city, beyond Dampoort station. Built in 1874 to rehouse the women of the St Elisabeth Begijnhof, this large neo-gothic complex is less appealing than the older Flemish Begijnhofs, though it has a certain dusty and dilapidated charm.

III. St Baafsabdij With its crumbling slate walls and overgrown romanesque windows, the ruined **St Baafsabdij** is perhaps the most romantic spot in Ghent. After the roar of traffic along the quays of the Scheldt, it is a pleasure to enter this unexpected ruin and hear only the cheerful twitter of the caretaker's budgerigars.

A Benedictine abbey was founded here in about 630 by St Amandus, a missionary from Aquitaine. It is named after Bavo, a Brabant landowner who lived a debauched life until his wife died, whereupon he mended his ways, gave away his possessions and lived as a hermit in a hollow tree near Ghent. The abbey was later granted to Eginhard, Charlemagne's biographer. When Charlemagne visited Ghent in 811 to inspect the fleet he had assembled to fight the Vikings, he probably stayed here as a guest. Despite Charlemagne's efforts, the Vikings reached Ghent in 851, and this abbey was one of the buildings they sacked.

The monks returned in the 10th century, and in 940-50 rebuilt the abbey in splendid romanesque style. It was here that Edward III of England and Queen Philippa stayed when they visited Ghent in 1341 and it was here that their third son, John of Gaunt, was born; his epithet is an anglicisation of Gand, the French name for Ghent. Twenty-eight years later the marriage of Philip the Bold and Margaret of Flanders took place in the abbey church.

Little now remains of the abbey church, which we can see in the foreground of the prospect of Ghent on page 96, or of the guest quarters where John of Gaunt was born. In 1540, enraged by Ghent's refusal to pay a new tax, Charles V ordered the abbey's destruction. In its place a huge fortress was erected, on the model of the citadel in Verona, and designed by an Italian military architect. The Spanish citadel, as it was nevertheless called, was square in plan, with pointed bastions at the corners, and was surrounded by a moat. It was the first renaissance fortress built in the Low Countries, but was soon followed by similar oppressive strongholds at Antwerp and Utrecht. Only the abbey choir was spared, to serve as a chapel for the Spanish troops. The parish church on this island and numerous houses in the neighbourhood were also razed to the ground by the military.

After a long siege in 1576, the Spanish garrison here surrendered to the Dutch rebels, and much of the citadel was then demolished. The last vestiges were finally removed in 1831, leaving only street names such as Spanjaardstraat, and two tombstones inscribed in Spanish, to recall its existence.

The abbey buildings have been left as romantic ruins, quite unlike the mint condition of 's-Gravensteen, which was the victim of restoration for the 1913 World Fair. The decay of these ancient buildings provides a fitting setting for the **Museum van Stenen Voorwerpen** (Lapidary Museum) established here in 1887. In the mysterious and melancholy cloisters, we discover a miscellany of tombstones, columns, boundary stones, capitals, urns, balustrades, doorways and tympana.

The chapter house, dormitory and refectory are still standing, the Spanish garrison having used these as barracks and store rooms. The oldest part to survive is an unusual octagonal building off the east walk of the cloister, erected in 1171 in a sober romanesque style. The ground floor originally served as a lavatory, and a sanctuary above held the relics of St Macharius, an 11th-century saint who allegedly saved Ghent from an outbreak of plague. The cult of St Macharius revived during an outbreak of plague in the 17th century, and the lavatory was then converted into a small chapel.

An early gothic Chapter House was added to the east of the cloisters in the 13th century. In this now sadly dilapidated building, we see fragments of the stone benches on which the monks sat, and a few broken columns from which the vaulting sprang. There are also a number of unusual stone tombs set into the floor.

The north cloister contains two tombstones (Nos. 25 and 26) bearing Spanish inscriptions and both dated 1625. Rescued from the chapel of the Spanish citadel, these marked the graves of the garrison commander, Luis Espinola, and its chaplain, Franco Henriquez. Above, we see three tympana reliefs (No. 31) salvaged from a house dating from 1660. The original owner was a local surgeon who commissioned the reliefs to advertise his trade. They depict an unfortunate woman being bled, the Good Samaritan helping the injured traveller, and the dissection of a corpse.

Three rooms off this cloister contain an interesting collection of sculptural fragments which have been imaginatively exhibited on scaffolding, as if in a mason's yard. The most striking work is a romanesque baptismal font (No. 119) with reliefs on its four sides depicting Adam and Eve in Paradise, the Expulsion, the Magi before Herod, and (now damaged) the Adoration of the Magi. This 12th-century font presumably came from the parish church demolished during the construction of the Spanish citadel.

We also see the tombstone of a Ghent boatman named Jan van den Poele (No. 154), decorated with a three-masted caravel of the type used to ship goods to Ghent during the 16th century. Notice, too, the enigmatic fragments of a head and hands (No. 171) which were saved from the baroque fish market after the fire in 1872.

The third room we enter was designed in a graceful late gothic style in 1495. Known as the **Mercatelzaal**, it was built for Abbot Raphael de Mercatel, a bastard son of Philip the Good born in Bruges and given the name of the Venetian merchant his mother married. From the paintings and engravings reproduced in this room, we can form an impression of the vanished abbey buildings, and also of the citadel erected by Charles V. A 17th-century engraving by Sanderus (No. 194) shows us the plan of the latter with the abbey cloister clearly visible in the top left corner.

Directly above the Mercatelzaal is the extraordinary romanesque refectory, to which we climb by a flight of steps off the cloister. Extending along the entire north walk of the cloister, this huge and gloomy hall dates from the end of the 12th century. The solemn rhythm of the arched windows along the south wall is broken only by a single niche, where a monk would read from the Benedictine orders during meals. After being used by the Spanish garrison as an arsenal, the refectory served as a parish church in the 19th century. It now houses a collection of medieval tombstones, which came here in a peculiar way. Up until the 18th century, churches and monasteries in Ghent were accustomed to raise funds by selling off ancient tombstones to the city authorities. These were then used in the foundations of bridges, sluices and other public works. In the 19th century, when many of these buildings were renovated or demolished, several old tombstones were uncovered. These were presented to the newly established lapidary museum, and are now displayed here. The most interesting find was the probable tombstone of Hubert van Eyck (No. 79), discovered in 1892.

Further curiosities salvaged from Ghent's past are displayed in the overgrown garden to the west of the cloisters, where the guest house and kitchens once stood. The gigantic head of a river god (No. 199) is all that remains of a 19th-century bridge blown up in the Second World War. Equally impressive is a large 18th-century figure of Diana the huntress, which adorns a tympanum (No. 203). Notice, too, the chimney stack planted in the grass, and the superstructure of the Miraculous Well of St Macharius, moved here in the 19th century when the neo-gothic church that looms above us was built over the well itself.

Before leaving the abbey, we should briefly explore the overgrown corner to the south of the cloisters, where the nave of the church once stood. The forest of columns nonchalantly planted in the grass came from the cellars of various medieval Ghent houses. The museum guide book has nothing to say about other odd fragments, such as an upturned leg and a pile of three capitals. This enigmatic corner is an appropriate place to end a tour of Ghent, the most curious and baffling of Flemish cities.

Antwerp

Antwerp

There is a shop in Antwerp called Extra Large, that sells large-scale replicas of everyday objects. The selection of items includes a pencil as tall as a child, a bottle filled with 18 litres of best claret and a tennis ball the size of a football.

After a few hours in Antwerp, we may well decide that the Extra Large shop has supplied the city with much of its architecture and art. The grand neo-baroque railway station at the end of De Keyserlei; the buildings on Meir and Suikerrui adorned with muscular sea gods and fleshy maidens; the paintings of Rubens hanging in the churches; everything - even the figures of the Virgin and Child attached to the corners of old houses - seems to be several sizes too large. Visitor to Antwerp may soon feel that they have wandered, like Gulliver, into a land of giants.

In its heyday, Antwerp was sometimes simply called the Metropolis. It was a city of superlatives, the Manhattan of the 16th century, attracting artists and scholars from the whole continent. Thomas More came here in 1515 with Erasmus, and set the opening scene of *Utopia* in an Antwerp inn; Albrecht Dürer arrived five years later and stayed for nine months in a house on Wolstraat; and the English merchant banker Thomas Gresham, who formulated Gresham's Law, settled here in 1555, borrowing large sums of money for Elizabeth I on the Antwerp exchange as he mulled over the principle of bad money driving out good.

Visitors to Antwerp could hardly find words to express their admiration. Lodovico Guicciardini, a 16th-century Florentine writer, described

Antwerp as: 'the most beautiful city in the world'. On a visit there in 1641 John Evelyn wrote in his diary: 'Nor did I ever observe a more quiet, cleane, elegantly built, and civil place, than this magnificent and famous Citty of Antwerp.' Anna Roemers Visscher, a 17th-century Dutch poet, was equally impressed, proclaiming it to be: 'The fairest town the Netherlands have ever seen.' Antwerp is still one of the most beautiful and artistic of Europe's northern cities, with many hidden joys, including exquisite gothic chapels, secret baroque gardens, and beautiful renaissance interiors hung with gilt leather. At the end of our explorations, we may agree with Victor Hugo, who said of Antwerp in 1837, 'The city is delightful: paintings in the churches, sculpture adorning the houses, Rubens in the chapels, Verbruggen on the gables; the city is literally overflowing with art.'

A marvellous woodcut made by an unknown master in 1515 shows all the bustle of the harbour; I have not been able to resist including three details from this view (pages 146, 149 and 151), on which we will still be able to identify many of the buildings that stand today. When this work was being cut, Bruges was already in decline , and Antwerp was fast becoming the main seaport of northern Europe. Up until then, the city's main role had been as a fortress at the western frontier of the loose confederation of German states known as the Holy Roman Empire, a frontier which, under the terms of the Treaty of Verdun, had followed the River Scheldt. However, Antwerp's fortunes improved dramatically after 1505, when the Fuggers of Augsburg moved their trading house here from Bruges. These powerful German bankers erected a splendid late gothic building, no longer extant, in the southern quarter of the city. Other trading nations followed the Fuggers to Antwerp, and the old Bruges trading houses on Oosterlingenplein and Vlamingstraat were left to decay. Buildings in the flamboyant late gothic style multiplied through Antwerp, each with an ostentatious watchtower to espy ships as they sailed up the Scheldt.

Antwerp enjoyed a period of extraordinary prosperity during the reign of the Emperor Charles V. Born in Ghent and raised by his aunt, Margaret of Austria, in Mechelen, Charles V

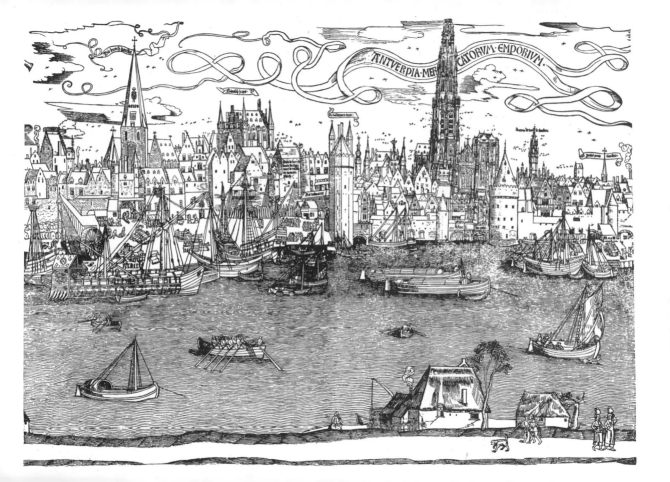

chose Antwerp as the principal port of his domains. The nineteen states he governed formed one of the greatest empires ever to exist. It encompassed the Burgundian Netherlands, which he inherited in 1515, the Spanish Empire, including lands in South America, acquired through his mother in 1516, and the Holy Roman Empire, which fell into his hands in 1519.

Antwerp eventually became the most important commercial centre of the 16th-century world, eclipsing Bruges, Genoa and even Venice. The commodities which passed through its warehouses must have seemed unbelievably rich compared to the wool and cloth which until then had formed the basis of Flemish trade. Sugar and exotic spices, including pepper and cinnamon, were trans-shipped from Portugal; velvet, silk and cloths of silver and gold filigree were brought from Italy; wines came from the Rhineland and fruits were imported from Spain. The paintings of the Antwerp mannerists provide us with a vivid impression of the jewel-encrusted objects of the age of Charles V, just as the paintings of Jan van Eyck depict the fabrics and furnishings of the Burgundian world. A favourite Biblical theme of this 16th-century school was the Adoration of the Magi, for this afforded an ideal opportunity to depict the opulent clothes and ornate objects that were flooding into Antwerp from all parts of the world.

The old warehouses in the northern quarter of Antwerp now lie empty, although a few have been put to new uses as jazz clubs or bars. However, the confidence of the 16th century is still reflected in the renaissance architecture of the town hall, and the splendid merchants' palaces that we sometimes glimpse behind sturdy portals. Even in the somewhat shabby streets of the northern quarter, there are still some imposing edifices, such as the **Hessenhuis** at Falconrui 53, a vast renaissance building erected in the 1560's to provide stabling and lodgings for the waggoners who shipped goods between Antwerp and the German cities.

The abdication of Charles V in 1555 brought an end to Antwerp's golden age. His son, Philip II, inherited the Spanish Empire and the Netherlands from his father, while the Holy Roman

ACTVM·1515· Vlaenderen·

Empire passed to the Austrian Hapsburgs. Philip II's passionate Catholicism quickly brought him into conflict with the traditionally free-thinking and tolerant people of the Low Countries. Antwerp's troubles began in 1566 when a group of zealous Protestants broke into Catholic churches and monasteries, destroying religious paintings and sculpture. Philip responded in 1567 by sending an army under the Duke of Alva to erect a huge renaissance citadel to the south of the city, similar to the one built by his father at Ghent in 1540. In 1576 the Spanish troops quartered in Antwerp plundered the city during a horrifying episode known as the Spanish Fury, which left some 7,000 townspeople dead. The Spanish troops were briefly expelled in 1577 by the Protestant leader William the Silent, but they were soon back, led by Alexander Farnese, then Prince of Parma, and after a gruelling siege lasting 14 months the city was recaptured in 1585.

We can obtain an impression of the disastrous turn of events if we look at the population figures. In 1526, some 55,000 people lived in Antwerp, and by 1567 the population had almost doubled, to 100,000, according to the *Description of All the Low Countries* published in Antwerp by Ludovico Guicciardini, son of the famous Florentine historian and at one time Tuscan ambassador to the Netherlands. At the outbreak of the Dutch Revolt in 1568, the population had climbed yet further to 125,000, but then it dropped rapidly, as citizens were brutally slain or forced to flee to Holland or England. By 1589 the population had fallen back to 55,000, while in the 18th century a mere 40,000 people lived here. James Howell, who saw Antwerp in 1619, described the city as: 'a disconsolate widow, or rather some super-annuated Virgin, that hath lost her Lover, being almost quite bereft of that flourishing commerce wherewith before the falling off of the rest of the Provinces from Spain she abounded to the envy of all other Cities and Marts of Europe.'

We may find it surprising that this observation was made at the time when the painter Pieter Paul Rubens was active in Antwerp, for his paintings suggest a boundless energy and creativity. Rubens, however, was painfully aware of Antwerp's decline, and he once described the city as 'languishing like a consumptive body, declining little by little'. His baroque painting and architecture were an heroic attempt to rescue the dying northern city by importing the vivacious style he had encountered on his travels in Italy. Numerous works by Rubens have remained in Antwerp: ten in the Museum voor Schone Kunsten, eighteen portraits in the Museum Plantin-Moretus, two works in the Rubenshuis, four altarpieces in the cathedral, a religious painting in the St Pauluskerk, and two works in the Rockoxhuis. Rubens' palatial home is also still to be seen, as is a magnificent Jesuit church built partly to his designs. The indefatigable painter also undertook various diplomatic missions on behalf of the Archduchess Isabella, in the hope that peace in Europe might rescue Antwerp from economic ruin. In 1630 he successfully negotiated a treaty between England and Spain, which led to a temporary hiatus in hostilities.

The Treaty of Münster of 1648, signed eight years after Rubens' death, secured a more lasting peace in the Low Countries. But its terms were disastrous for Antwerp: the Scheldt was closed to shipping, and Antwerp's hopes of economic recovery were dashed. Amsterdam and Rotterdam became the main ports of northern Europe, and Antwerp followed Bruges into decline and decay.

And so it remained until well into the 19th century. There was some recovery under Napoleon, when a new naval dock, the Bonapartedok, was built to the north of the city. But Napoleon, like Philip II, was interested only in Antwerp's strategic position, which he pugnaciously described as 'a pistol pointed at the heart of Britain'.

After three centuries of stagnation, Antwerp finally revived as a commercial city in the 1860's with the abolition of the Dutch right to levy tolls on ships navigating the Scheldt. Its economy suddenly boomed, and a second golden age dawned. The elegant boulevards, railway station, museum of fine arts and Stadspark are mementos of this confident period in Antwerp's history.

But perhaps the most remarkable 19th-century creation is the boulevard in the southern suburbs known as **Cogels Osylei**. Two entrepreneurs,

Baron Edouard Osy and his sister Joséphine Cogels Osy, shrewdly realised that this corner of Antwerp was an ideal residential area for commuters, thanks to two suburban railway stations nearby. They bought an old castle called Zurenborg that stood on the site, promptly demolished it, and by the 1880's architects were beginning to erect opulent Victorian mansions on Cogels Osylei and neighbouring streets in every imaginable architectural style. There is a Greek Classical building at Transvaalstraat 23, a reconstructed renaissance house at No. 59, a magnificent Venetian palace at Cogels Osylei 65, and several beautiful art nouveau houses at the southern ends of Cogels Osylei and Waterloostraat (the photograph is of one of these).

Antwerp again became an important military stronghold in the 19th century. Although the 16th-century walls had been demolished in 1859, new forts were built around the city in the 19th century, making it again one of the most heavily fortified cities in Europe. But the elaborate defences, parts of which survive in the modern suburbs, failed to halt the German advance in

1914. British troops led by Winston Churchill rushed to the defence of the city, but succeeded only in delaying the German army for a few days. The British were pushed back to the Channel ports, and the Belgian army dug in beyond the River Yser.

Antwerp was also badly bombed in the Second World War, and the damaged areas have still not been completely rebuilt. Although a huge modern port was constructed after the war to the north of the old Napoleonic dock, the city still sometimes has the look of a 'disconsolate Widow', particularly in the neighbourhood of the Stadswaag and the St Pauluskerk. Yet Antwerp is, I think, one of the most captivating of northern European cities, its architecture and art a blend of Amsterdam, Rome, Paris, London and New York.

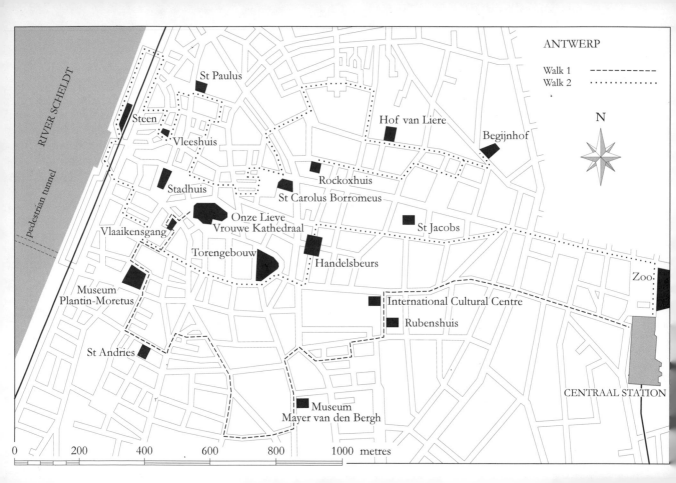

ANTWERP

Walk 1 ----------
Walk 2 ···········

N

RIVER SCHELDT

pedestrian tunnel

St Paulus

Steen

Vleeshuis

Hof van Liere

Begijnhof

Rockoxhuis

Stadhuis

St Carolus Borromeus

Onze Lieve
Vrouwe Kathedraal

St Jacobs

Vlaaikensgang

Torengebouw

Handelsbeurs

Museum
Plantin-Moretus

International Cultural Centre

Rubenshuis

Zoo

St Andries

CENTRAAL STATION

Museum
Mayer van den Bergh

0   200   400   600   800   1000 metres

Rubens, Bruegel and Plantin

On our first walk in Antwerp we will explore the baroque home of Rubens and the former printing works of his fello-citizens Christopher Plantin and Balthasar Moretus. 'Our City of Antwerp is proud to possess two such great citizens as Rubens and Moretus,' wrote Jan Woverius, a counsellor to the Archduke Albert and Archduchess Isabella in the 17th century. 'Foreigners will stare at the houses of both, and travellers will admire them.' And so we will.

This walk also takes in the Museum Mayer van den Bergh, a remarkable and virtually unknown art collection, which includes the only two paintings by Pieter Bruegel the Elder to remain in Antwerp, where he lived from 1555 to 1563. As this walk is mainly concerned with museums, each deserving at least an hour of our time, it is an ideal way to pass a rainy day.

We begin at **Centraal Station**, the main railway station, which was designed in 1895-1905 in the extravagant neo-baroque style favoured by Léopold II. We may notice that Léopold's monogram, a florid L, appears on numerous cartouches, as if he sought to model his little kingdom on the absolute monarchies of baroque Europe. The architect of this palatial railway station, we may be surprised to discover, was Louis Delacenserie, who hitherto had made his mark as the fastidious restorer of Burgundian gothic buildings in Bruges, such as the Gruuthuse mansion. After admiring the houses of Rubens and Moretus, foreigners will perhaps now stare at the station café next to Platform 1, with its ball-room mirrors, moulded ceilings and enormous clock. The café used to be in a dilapidated state, but it was carefully restored in 1993 to its original grandeur as part of the cele-

brations marking Antwerp's year as European City of Culture.

Antwerp's **Zoo**, situated next to the station, is one of the oldest in Europe, dating back to 1843. It was once, according to Baedeker's 1905 guide book, 'a favourite resort of the fashionable world', and it still boasts some splendid architecture, although many of the buildings were destroyed in the last war. There is a delightful Greek temple set on an artificial hill, a Moorish villa which is home to the rhinoceroses and an Indian temple where Central African okapis ruminate. But the most astonishing building is a large Egyptian temple, photographed here, which serves as an elephant house. This spectacular souvenir of the Victorian cult of Egyptology was designed by Charles Servais, who modelled it upon the Egyptian Court at the Crystal Palace in London. It is decorated with intriguing hieroglyphics composed by an Antwerp Egyptologist, including one sonorous inscription which declares, 'In the Year of Our Lord 1856, in the reign of His Majesty the King, Sun and Life of Belgium, Léopold the First, this building was erected as a book for the glorification of Antwerp and the edification of its inhabitants.'

Perhaps we should leave the delights of the zoo for another day, however, and proceed at once down De Keyserlei, then cross Frankrijklei, one of the boulevards laid out in 1859 on the site of the renaissance city walls. Continuing down Leysstraat, we should pause to admire the 19th-century house at **Leysstraat 15**. The balcony is in the shape of a ship's prow and there are reliefs decorated with whales and other maritime details. We are clearly looking at the house of someone with the sea in his blood.

We come next to the beautiful street **Meir**, where we soon turn left down Kolveniersstraat, there discovering an unexpected pleasure at No. 16. Through an open door we see the renaissance courtyard of the **Kolvenicrshof**, built in the 1630's as the guild house of the arquebusiers.

The drill yard of the arquebusiers happened to back onto Pieter Paul Rubens' garden. Rubens, inspired by the formal baroque gardens he had seen during his eight-year stay in Italy, returned to Antwerp determined to create his own Ital-ianate garden, and he approached Burgomaster Rockox, captain of the arquebusiers, to buy the land he needed. Conveniently, Rockox was already one of his enthusiastic patrons, and in 1608 had commissioned an *Adoration of the Magi* - now in the Prado - to hang in the town hall. The Burgomaster therefore proposed to Rubens that he pay for the plot of land with a painting. The subject was to be a portrait of St Christopher, the guild's patron saint, for the banqueting hall. Rubens responded with characteristic gusto and, instead of a portrait of St Christopher, the arquebusiers received the magnificent *Triptych of the Descent from the Cross*, which we will see in Antwerp Cathedral. The members of the guild were apparently none too pleased at this breach of contract and ordered Rubens to add a portrait of St Christopher (who had not appeared on the original) to one of the wings.

We return to Meir, to see facing us at No. 85 the elegant **Osterriethhuis**, now a bank, built in Flemish rococo style by Jan Pieter van Baurscheit in 1748. Turning left along Meir, we soon come upon another fine rococo palace at No. 50

completed by the same architect three years earlier. Occupied briefly by Napoleon in 1811, this decayed palace now houses the **International Cultural Centre**, which screens films in the first-floor rooms. We should glance inside, if time permits. The ballroom is now empty and tragic, but the stables at the far end of the courtyard have been maintained in immaculate condition and the polished wood and brass fittings are glinting like new.

Now let us visit the **Rubenshuis** at Wapper 9. We can begin our tour of the house at once, if we wish, though should the sun be shining we may be tempted to pause on a bench in the garden to read about the building.

The baroque garden designed by Rubens in the former drill yard provided a setting for many of his most felicitous paintings, such as *Amidst Honeysuckle* in Munich's Alte Pinakothek, and *The Garden of Love* in Madrid's Prado. These paintings greatly influenced later artists such as Watteau, Fragonard and Gainsborough. Another picture in Munich (reproduced opposite) shows him in this garden with his second wife, Hélène Fourment,

whom he married in 1626, four years after Isabella died. 'I am determined to remarry,' Rubens wrote somewhat defensively, 'considering myself not yet old enough to surrender to the abstinence of celibacy and, as it is sweet after one has been thrown into desolation to enjoy permissible pleasures, I have taken myself a young girl.' Many of the charming scenes painted here feature this voluptuous second wife, who was only 16 when she married. Hélène was also cunning, however, for when Rubens died in 1640 she immediately sold off his huge collection of paintings and antiques to prevent the children of his first marriage from inheriting anything.

We will find the little garden temple seen in the painting still there, framed by the handsome portico that confronts us as we enter the Rubenshuis. Both temple and portico (which links the two wings of the house) were designed by Rubens in an Italianate baroque style, and were to appear in many of his paintings, as also in works by his pupils, such as the portrait of Isabella Brant by van Dyck in Washington's National Gallery, and *Diana in the Bath* by Jacob Jordaens in the Prado.

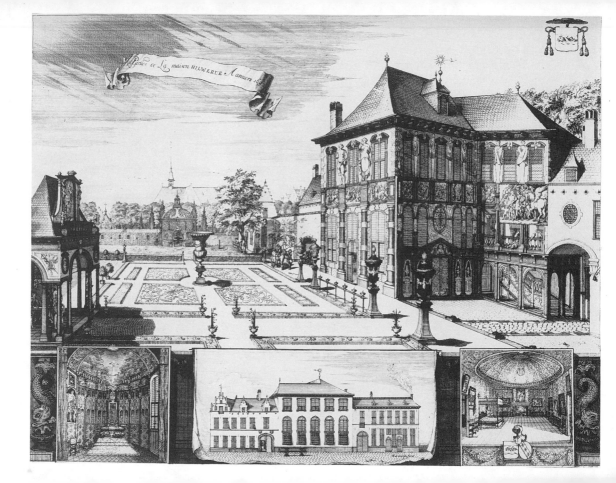

Veües de La maison HILWERUE Aanuers des

When Baedeker's 1905 guide book was written, only the portico and pavilion were in fact still standing. The house was painstakingly reconstructed during the last war, using as guidelines paintings by Rubens and his pupils, or old prints such as the one opposite, made in 1692 (which seems to have a painting - or is it a tapestry - hanging out of a top-floor window). The building to the right of the portico is a reconstruction of the original 16th-century house bought by Rubens, a typical Flemish late gothic building with alternating courses of brick and sandstone. The reconstructed kitchen, dining room, picture gallery and bedrooms are in this wing. Annexed to the picture gallery is an apsidal Pantheon where Rubens displayed his collection of classical busts (in the print this is shown bottom left, converted into a chapel by the next owner, a cardinal).

Rubens also designed the magnificent baroque wing to the south of the portico. This is almost entirely taken up by Rubens' lofty atelier, where he and his many pupils laboured tirelessly to produce the scores of baroque paintings that now hang in art galleries throughout the world. An interesting feature of the atelier is the viewing gallery at the far end, where Rubens took his clients to show them the large canvases in progress.

A youthful study by Rubens of *Adam and Eve*, with a rabbit in the foreground to symbolise fecundity, hangs in the atelier. But the most interesting painting in the house is not by Rubens at all; it is *The Picture Gallery of Cornelis van der Geest* by Willem van Haecht, who was keeper of the picture gallery depicted in the painting. The work (reproduced on page 165) now hangs in Rubens' own gallery. Painted in 1628, it is a fascinating example of a curious type of work called a *kunstkamer* painting. The object of these paintings, which were very popular in 17th-century Antwerp, was to record a private collection, often with the patron's family and friends.

Most of the guests in the painting by van Haecht can be identified, including the Archduke Albert and Archduchess Isabella, who are sitting on the left. Van der Geest is showing them a *Virgin and Child* by the Antwerp artist Quinten

Metsys. Rubens, who is also among the guests, looks to the Archduke, while Anthony van Dyck stands behind van der Geest. Burgomaster Rockox is also in the painting, standing directly behind the Archduchess Isabella, and the figure entering the room from the street may be the artist himself. The house of Cornelis van der Geest overlooked the Scheldt, and some ships can just be glimpsed through the windows of the picture gallery.

The painting shows three walls of the picture gallery, which is crammed from floor to ceiling with works of art. A number of paintings are propped against the furniture, presumably having been taken down from the fourth wall to allow the entire collection to be depicted. Of the 43 works copied here in miniature, 24 have survived and been identified. One of the best known is Rubens' *Battle of the Amazons*, now in the Alte Pinakothek in Munich, which is given pride of place by the window. Above it hangs a small portrait by Metsys of the Swiss physician Paracelsus. The Musée d'Art Ancien in Brussels owns a copy of this painting made by Rubens.

The most intriguing work displayed in van der Geest's collection hangs in the right-hand corner above a statue of Venus and Cupid. It depicts a naked woman taking a bath in the company of another woman. The woman on the right is holding a phial (symbolising cleanliness) and an orange (symbolising fertility), suggesting that the scene represents a prenuptial bath. Some scholars have argued that this is a lost work by Jan van Eyck, painted as a companion to the *Arnolfini Wedding Portrait*, now in the National Gallery in London. The rooms in both paintings are strikingly similar; each has a window on the left with three wooden shutters, and a convex mirror reflecting the people in the room. A dog (symbolising marital fidelity) also appears in both works, and similar wooden shoes lie discarded on the floor. Giovanni Arnolfini, the husband in the wedding portrait in London, was a merchant from Lucca who had settled in Bruges in 1420. Jan van Eyck was a witness to the wedding that took place in 1434 in Arnolfini's home in Bruges, when Arnolfini married Giovanna Cenami, also from Lucca. If the painting in Cornelis van der

Geest's *kunstkamer* is indeed a lost prenuptial portrait, then it would seem to cast some doubt on the popular belief that Giovanna Cenami, who is wearing a voluminous dress in the London painting, was pregnant when she married.

The painting of van der Geest's *kunstkamer* also includes a small drawing lying on the table in the foreground. It is a work by Johan Wierix, dated 1600, of *Alexander in the Studio of Apelles*. The drawing depicts the Greek legend in which Alexander the Great commissioned the renowned Greek artist Apelles to paint a nude portrait of his favourite mistress, Campaspe. While working on the painting, Apelles fell in love with Campaspe. To demonstrate his admiration for the painter, Alexander made him a gift of his mistress. By a nice coincidence, the drawing by Wierix is now in the collection of the next museum we will visit.

On leaving the Rubenshuis we turn left down Wapper, right along Schuttershofstraat, and left into Arme Duivelstraat, where we might be tempted to stop for lunch in De Varkenspoot, an attractive Flemish bistro. Turning right along Kelderstraat, right again on Komedieplaats, and then left on Huidevettersstraat, we reach Lange Gasthuisstraat.

Our destination is the marvellous **Museum Mayer van den Bergh** at Lange Gasthuisstraat 19. This forgotten museum boasts a large collection of paintings, sculpture, stained glass, tapestries and rare manuscripts. The works were amassed in the 19th century by Fritz Mayer van den Bergh, a passionate art connoisseur, whose portrait hangs on the main staircase. When he died, aged only 43, his mother resolved to create a museum next to the family home. A local architect was commissioned in 1904 to design the building in the richly eclectic renaissance style of 16th-century Antwerp, incorporating heavy mannerist furniture, gilt leather walls, and old leaded glass windows. The Mayer van den Bergh is a wonderfully intact example of Belgian nostalgia, still furnished with its original display cabinets. The most intriguing of these is hidden behind a renaissance door to the left of the fireplace in room 10, which opens to reveal some 17th-century drawings. According to the museum's guide book, Johan Wierix's of *Alexander in the Studio of Apelles* should be here, although it was missing when I last looked.

Room 3, a finely vaulted room, contains two beautiful 12th-century carved figures. These are rare relics from the monastery of Notre-Dame-en-Vaux, which once stood in Châlons-sur-Marne. The monastery was demolished in the 18th century, and its stones used locally as building material. Recent excavations have unearthed some extraordinary fragments of sculpture, suggesting that this vanished monastery must have been one of the finest early gothic buildings in France.

Room 4 contains a *Crucifixion Triptych* by Quinten Metsys, an Antwerp painter who lived for the last nine years of his life in a house on Schuttershofstraat, a street we have just walked down. The wings bear portraits of the donors, whose identities are unknown, although we can deduce their Christian names from the patron saints alongside. Mary of Egypt - the woman's patron saint - was a penitent whore who lived naked in the desert, sustained only by three small loaves.

Perhaps the most delightful medieval work in the museum is the double panel from the *Antwerp-Baltimore Polyptych*, displayed in a glass case in room 6. Painted in about 1400 by an artist living in the vicinity of Aachen, it formed part of a travelling altar, the rest of which is now in a museum in Baltimore. One panel is decorated with a scene showing St Christopher, the patron saint of travellers, crossing a stream. Looking closely in the water, we see numerous fish and even a mermaid admiring herself in a looking-glass. Another panel of the polyptych depicts a charming, if fanciful, Biblical episode in which Joseph cuts his stockings to provide swaddling clothes for the infant Christ. Some photographs displayed in the case show what there is to see of this work in far-off Baltimore.

The undoubted highlights of this collection are the two paintings in room 9 by Pieter Bruegel the Elder. There are only seven works by this great artist still in Flanders: five are in Brussels, and the other two are here. The most famous of the two paintings in Mayer van den Bergh's collection is *Dulle Griet*, painted in about 1562-4.

If we tend to think of Bruegel as the painter of hunters in the snow and merry peasant weddings, we may be shocked by this work; it is in the style of Hieronymus Bosch and shows an irate, perhaps insane, woman rampaging through the chaos of war. The meaning of the work is not clear; some scholars have interpreted it as a warning by Bruegel about the dangers of allowing women to rule, while others say that it is an allegory of folly. The other work by Bruegel is an engagingly whimsical study of *The Twelve Proverbs*, with twelve miniature scenes illustrating popular Flemish sayings, such as falling between two stools and belling the cat.

On leaving the museum, turn left and walk down Lange Gasthuisstraat. At No. 33 is the beautiful **Maagdenhuis**, an orphanage for girls founded in 1564 by Jan van der Meeren and Gilbert van Schoonbeke. Van Schoonbeke, a leading light of the Flemish renaissance, was constantly occupied with schemes to improve the city of Antwerp, several of which we come across in our wanderings. Not all, however, were popular with the folk of Antwerp, and eventually he had to flee to Brussels, where he died at the age of only 36.

Above the entrance to the orphanage is an enchanting mannerist relief dating from 1564. It depicts orphaned girls being admitted to the Maagdenhuis, and a classroom scene so finely detailed that it even includes shelves lined with school books. If the gate is open, we can glance into an arcaded courtyard dating from 1636, with a 17th-century wooden figure of an orphan.

A short distance further, we turn right along Boogkeers, continue along Rosier, then right up Bredestraat. This brings us out on a little square where a statue of the Virgin illuminated by a quaint old iron lamp smiles down on us. As in Bruges, there are numerous statues of the Virgin in Antwerp. The difference is that the Virgins of Bruges look frail and pious, whereas those of Antwerp are voluptuous Rubensian women wearing glittering crowns and surrounded by gaudy ornaments.

We continue along Kammenstraat, past a baroque church designed in 1615 by Wenceslas Coeberger, then turn left into Ijzeren Waag. This brings us to a square where, if tempted, we can buy *frites* at a small wooden chalet. After crossing Nationalestraat, we continue down Augustijnenstraat, watched over by another magnificent Virgin and Child illuminated by a dusty iron lamp. Standing opposite the north transept of the **St Andrieskerk**, we obtain a marvellous view of the baroque church tower rising above a picturesque cluster of roofs. St Andries was built in 1514-23, and the tower added in 1756-63. Inside the church, which is unfortunately seldom open, there is an unusual memorial to two ladies-in-waiting to Mary Queen of Scots, who both died in exile in Antwerp.

This corner of Antwerp was badly damaged in the Second World War and it has only recently been redeveloped. There remains one intriguing 16th-century lane, the Maesganck, at Korte Ridderstraat 23. Continuing down Korte Ridderstraat, we then cross Steenhouwersvest and into Vrijdagmarktstraatje. This little lane emerges on the **Vrijdagmarkt**, the scene every Wednesday and Friday morning of a market in second-hand goods. The market was established here in 1549 by Gilbert van Schoonbeke, co-founder of the girls' orphanage.

But we have not come to the Vrijdagmarkt to pick up framed sepia photographs of Antwerp harbour or dusty art deco lamps, but to look around the **Museum Plantin-Moretus**. This extraordinary museum filled with old books and printing presses used to be one of the great publishing houses of renaissance Europe. For more than four centuries, European scholars and book collectors have trekked to the Vrijdagmarkt to buy luxurious editions of religious works, world atlases, multilingual dictionaries, and the latest philosophical writings.

The famous publishing house was founded in 1555 by Christopher Plantin, a Frenchman who moved to Antwerp to work as a book binder. Antwerp already had a booming book publishing industry, but Plantin managed to carve himself a niche by producing superb editions in the world's major languages. His first publication was a modest bilingual volume in French and Italian providing young women with advice on manners (a useful undertaking for a man with five

daughters); but Plantin soon moved on to bigger projects, including a massive eight-volume edition of the Bible with parallel text in five languages.

Plantin's imprint was a golden compass with the words *Labore et Constantia*: 'Through hard work and diligence.' The device appears on the title pages of his many publications, and is even to be spotted in carved form on the living-room woodwork. Phillip II of Spain was so impressed with Plantin's hard work and diligence that he appointed him Head Printer to the Crown.

Plantin dutifully continued to publish lists of prohibited books for the Catholic authorities, although secretly he remained a Calvinist. Godly or not, publishing was a dangerous business in Plantin's day, and he risked his life several times by printing 'heretical' works. He clashed with the authorities more than once, and ultimately saved his skin only by paying a crippling ransom. Plantin's business was almost ruined in the process; he had to lay off most of his workers, and sell 17 of his 22 printing presses.

When Plantin died in 1589, the publishing house passed to his son-in-law, Jan Moretus. The concern was then managed by successive members of the Moretus family until 1865, when the city of Antwerp eventually bought up the ailing business. The rooms were then fastidiously restored by the city fathers to create a unique museum of printing which opened in 1877.

A must for bibliophiles and print-lovers alike, the Plantin-Moretus Museum is crammed with old books, wooden printing presses, and dusty cases of old-fashioned movable type. Built around a handsome renaissance courtyard, the dark red brick edifice is a mixture of domestic rooms and workshops. The kitchen is next to the proofreaders' room, while the type foundry is tucked away in the attic, above the bedrooms. We can visit some 33 different rooms, most of which are furnished in Flemish baroque style with wooden cabinets and glinting chandeliers. Even on a grey morning in the dead of winter, the building is bathed in a mellow golden light.

We soon get to know the family traits of the Plantins and Moretuses from portraits hung in the former drawing-room. No fewer than eighteen paintings bear the signature of Pieter Paul Rubens, who frequently strolled across town from his palatial home on Wapper to visit his friend Balthasar Moretus. The museum still owns an old ledger showing that Rubens obtained the latest architectural books published by Plantin in exchange for painting portraits of the family, or engraving illustrations for the title pages of new publications.

The Italian historian Ludovico Guicciardini praised the Plantin Press in his famous 16th-century description of the Netherlands. 'Such an establishment has never been seen in the whole of Europe, with more presses, with more types of various kinds, with more moulds and other instruments, with more capable and competent printer's assistants, earning higher wages by working, correcting and revising in all languages, strange as well as familiar, which are used throughout the whole of Christendom.'

Maybe some of this was just hype (Plantin happened to be Guicciardini's publisher), but even today the former printing works exude an impressive air of deep scholarship. We can pore over carefully-marked page-proofs from Plantin's day, or study the racks of different typefaces - including musical notation and Hebrew.

The first three rooms originally formed part of the family's dwelling house. Hanging in these rooms are several portraits by Rubens of prominent persons associated with the publishing house, among them a gaunt Christopher Plantin, his wife Jeanne Rivière, Jan Moretus and his wife Martina, the geographer Ortelius and the classicist Lipsius.

The bookshop (room 4) is entered from the arcade. Several well-known people have visited this shop to make purchases, including John Evelyn, who noted in his diary, 'Returning by the shop of Plantine, I bought some bookes for the namesake onely of that famous printer.' The dusty old books on the shelves are not for sale, but we can buy an excellent little guide to the museum written by Leon Voet and printed in a handsome Plantin typeface.

Sales of books were once recorded in a large ledger by the book-keeper, who perched in the little office next door. The old account books are still preserved, including the 17th-century ledger displayed in room 19 in which Rubens' account is entered.

The adjacent wing contains an evocative series of rooms in which the printers, editors and proof readers worked 'in all languages, strange as well as familiar'. In room 9 is the aged wooden desk at which the proof readers toiled by candlelight, marking the texts with symbols still used today (as we see from the old proof copy displayed in a glass case). Room 10 is hung with gilt leather from Mechelen, which bathes the interior in a captivating golden light, like a shaded glade on a summer day. Even more exquisite is the 16th-century gilded leather of Cordoba known as *guadamacil*, which hangs in room 12. This is

believed to be the room in which Justus Lipsius worked when he visited the Plantin Press. We then walk through a room with cases of old type to enter the remarkable printing workshop built by Plantin in 1579, with sturdy wooden beams anchoring the old printing presses to the roof. The smell of printers' ink still pervades this room, and occasionally one of the old presses is put back into service to turn out copies of Plantin's ode, *Le bonheur de ce monde*. The printer's assistants here are still apparently able to work in 'all languages... employed throughout the whole of Christendom', for Plantin's ode to contentment is available in seven European languages. There is even a Russian version, perhaps for the benefit of the sailors who are often to be seen roaming the streets of Antwerp in search of souvenirs.

We then leave the printing works and ascend the creaking stairs to the first floor. Room 19 contains a collection of books and prints recalling Rubens' long association with this publishing house, which began in 1608 when he and his brother Philip published a book on the social customs of Rome.

One of the most amusing books to be published by this house is the *Dictionary in Seven Languages* written by the humanist Ficardus in 1616 and displayed in room 20. This provided 17th-century travellers with essential phrases such as 'You seeke noothing but to begyle me', the Flemish equivalent of which, should we ever find ourselves being unwantedly *begyled*, is *Ghy en soeckt niet dan my te bedrieghen.*

Room 23 is filled with fascinating maps, including the only surviving copy of the 1565 map of Antwerp by the renaissance cartographers Virgilius Boloniensis and Cornelis Grapheus, a detail from which is reproduced here. We then ascend to the second floor, there to visit the stone-floored attic room. The type founders were banished here to minimise the danger of them setting fire to the building with molten metal. The typeface known today as Plantin was based on the designs of Claude Garamond, a French designer, after whom another typeface is named. Standing by the ancient stove which once took the chill off this room, we may glimpse through the small window a nearby watchtower embellished with

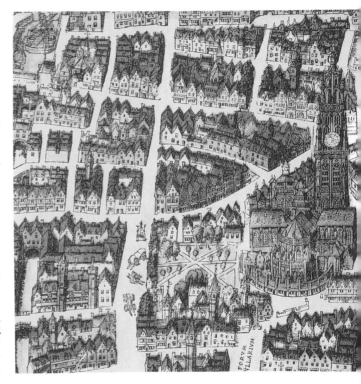

an unusual onion-shaped dome. We shall soon see the house to which it belongs.

Upon leaving the museum, we turn down the lane to our left, Heilige-Geeststraat, and enter the courtyard of the **Huis Draeck** at No. 9. A city official built a house here in the 15th century, of which all that survives is the small chapel on the left. In 1540 the building was bought by Wolf Puschinger, a merchant from Leipzig, who rebuilt it in late gothic style and added the octagonal watchtower that we spied from the attic foundry of the Plantin Press.

We see this watchtower again from another angle upon entering the nearby courtyard of the **Jordaenshuis** at Reyndersstraat 4. To reach it, turn right at the end of Heilige-Geeststraat into Hoogstraat, then again right. The attractive, if somewhat decayed, baroque house was built by Jacob Jordaens, a pupil of Rubens and painter of numerous fleshy and grotesque baroque works, such as *The King Drinks* in the Musée d'Art Ancien in Brussels.

On leaving the courtyard of Jordaens' house, we turn right and soon come upon yet another secret courtyard, at Reyndersstraat 18. The dear old café that was here, De Grote Witte Arend, has sadly just been closed. Pelgrimstraat, directly opposite where it used to be, was once, as its name suggests, the route taken by pilgrims bound for the cathedral. The view of the soaring cathedral spire from the end of the street is breathtakingly beautiful. From here, I suggest that we take a somewhat indirect route to the cathedral, retracing our steps and turning down the passage at Pelgrimstraat 8. This takes us into the **Vlaaikensgang**, an undisturbed 16th-century corner of Antwerp, where narrow crooked lanes run between whitewashed houses with bluestone pumps, all overgrown with rambling creepers.

We emerge from this almost rural warren of lanes on the bustling Oude Koornmarkt, from which no directions are needed to reach the cathedral. Begun in 1352, **Onze-Lieve-Vrouwekathedraal** (Our Lady's Cathedral) is one of the finest gothic churches in the Low Countries. It was built on the site of a 12th-century romanesque church that was slowly demolished as the new church was built. The overall design was the work of the French architect Jean Appelmans, who is commemorated by a charming 19th-century statue at the foot of the unfinished south spire. The choir was built first, then the west front, and finally the nave, probably to the design of Herman de Waghemakere. The north spire of the cathedral, constructed between 1420 and 1518, is its greatest glory. For several centuries this graceful spire was the tallest structure in the Low Countries. The lowest tier (which we see in Jan van Eyck's drawing of St Barbara in Antwerp's Museum voor Schone Kunsten, reproduced on page 197) was designed by Master Everaert, while the two upper tiers were added later by Herman's son Domien in a thrilling Brabant gothic style. In 1519 Domien de Waghemakere and another scion of a building dynasty, Rombout Keldermans, were commissioned by Charles V to rebuild the choir in Brabant gothic style, but following a fire in 1533 the project was abandoned.

The interior of the cathedral was badly damaged by the Protestants in 1566, and the main relic to survive from the middle ages is a bronze recumbent figure of Isabella of Bourbon, attributed to Jacob van Gerines. It was moved here when the St Michael's Abbey on Kloosterstraat was demolished. Isabella, the second wife of Charles the Bold, died there in 1465.

The main glory of the cathedral is its collection of altarpieces by Rubens. The most impressive work is the *Descent from the Cross*, which stands on a baroque altar teeming with saints and cherubs. We have already related the story of this painting, which was commissioned by the guild of arquebusiers (see page 159). The other great work by Rubens in the cathedral is the *Elevation of the Cross*, an ambitious early work painted in 1610. Rubens had then just recently returned from an eight-year sojourn in Italy and his style was still heavily influenced by Michelangelo. The Treasury contains another work by Rubens, the *Resurrection Triptych*, painted in 1612 for the tomb of his friend Jan Moretus.

The *Marriage at Cana* by Martin de Vos is an interesting example of Antwerp mannerism. True to the artistic conventions of the day, the scene is set in a 16th-century Flemish interior complete with a minstrels' gallery. Notice, too, the little chapel on the north side of the cathedral, which contains several paintings in Pre-Raphaelite style, including an altarpiece called *Our Lady of Peace*, a strange and sad First World War memorial. The soldiers are depicted in the guise of medieval knights, and dark scenes at the base show the bombardment of Antwerp.

As so often happens in the crowded cities of the Low Countries, the cathedral is enclosed by a jumble of dwelling houses. Baedeker stiffly condemned these 'mean houses', but I think that they add a certain picturesque charm to the scene. Many of these buildings now contain cafés and tea rooms, and there are others on the nearby Groenplaats. The café terraces hereabouts are particularly pleasant when concerts are given on the cathedral carillon.

A café with a hint of Surrealism in its decor faces the north transept of the cathedral at Torfbrug 10. Wickedly named De Elfde Gebod (The Eleventh Commandment), it has a most curious interior crammed with 19th-century plaster-cast saints and neo-gothic altars salvaged from old churches. One of the oddest features is the door to the kitchen on which, as a 'Homage to Diderot', all the parts have been labelled with a flourish of calligraphy.

There are also many attractive restaurants in the neighbourhood of the cathedral, including the celebrated Sir Anthony van Dyck at Oude Koornmarkt 16, where excellent Flemish cuisine is served in attractive rooms with flagstone floors, renaissance cabinets and old Flemish paintings. More modest restaurants include Pasta at Oude Koornmarkt 32, a striking modern Italian restaurant with a magnificent view of the cathedral from the upper floor, and the Tapas Bar at 21 Pelgrimsgang. Among dozens of good cafés in the neighbourhood, it is worth hunting out the monkish De Cluyse at 26 Oude Koornmarkt, where candles flicker under the stone vaulting of a 13th-century cellar.

The Old City

There are many delightful buildings and engaging curiosities to be discovered in the winding lanes of the old city, yet we should be prepared too for a certain amount of decay and sad neglect. Already in 1789, Samuel Johnson's friend Mrs. Thrale complained that Antwerp was 'a dismal heavy looking town - so melancholy!' Despite the revival of Antwerp's trade in the 19th century, the old city still at times seems somewhat ravaged, but if we can ignore this we will find the old town fascinating to explore.

During the walk (*map on page 156*), which will take a full day, we will pass through the world's first stock exchange building, stand in front of the house where *Utopia* was conceived, and hear about a practical joke played on Albrecht Dürer. We begin once again at **Centraal Station**, but this time we leave by the north entrance to reach Koningin Astridplein. We cross this square, dodging the parties of children bound for the zoo, and turn left along Gemeentestraat, past the opera house and under an unsightly overpass, to enter the narrow streets of the old city. We then take a left fork down Lange Nieuwstraat (Long New Street), not quite so new as in 1315 when it was named. This gently curving street, with an enticing view of the cathedral spire to tempt us onwards, was one of the most desirable streets in Antwerp in the 15th and 16th centuries, though it is now the worse for wear.

We have come down this street to visit the **St Jacobskerk**, which is entered by a small door in the south transept, at No. 73. The church was begun in 1491 by Herman de Waghemakere and continued, after his death, by Domien, his son, and Rombout Keldermans the Younger, who came from Mechelen. In 1526 the work was halted because of lack of funds (a familiar story in 16th-century Flanders) and it was not until 1656 that the church was finally completed. The tower, like so many late gothic towers in the Low Countries, remains unfinished, a symbol of failure. It was simply too costly to complete these ambitious late gothic towers, and in any case the style became totally outmoded in the 16th century.

Unfortunately the delicate late gothic interior of St Jacobs is now buried beneath masses of heavy baroque sculpture added in the 17th century. The effect is overpowering and dizzying, as it was intended to be, for the aim was to win converts to the Catholic faith. A sign directs us to Rubens' mausoleum in the ambulatory, one of the largest baroque monuments in the church. It is far more impressive than the memorials to other northern baroque artists such as Rembrandt and Vermeer. But we must remember that Rubens was a diplomat as well as a painter and architect; should we have forgotten the fact, there is a lengthy 18th-century inscription in Latin recall-ing his many achievements. The painting on the tomb of *The Virgin Surrounded by Saints*, executed by Rubens towards the end of his life, is virtually a family group portrait, for it has Rubens posing as a gallant St George, his two wives as saints, and his father, probably, as St Jerome. The Virgin is portrayed with deep tenderness and, interest-ingly, looks more like a Raphael Madonna than one of the typically plump models that Rubens usually preferred. Perhaps the elderly Rubens imagined Paradise to be like the Italy he had once known so well.

The tomb of Nicolaas Rockox, Rubens' faith-ful patron and close friend, is in the north aisle of the church. Above it hangs a *Triptych of the Last Judgement* by Bernard van Orley of Brussels. The left wing includes a portrait of Rockox and his three sons, while the right wing shows his wife and ten daughters.

Looking at too many tombs can be a gloomy pursuit, so let us leave this church where so many eminent citizens of Antwerp are buried and continue along Lange Nieuwstraat. The renais-sance house at **Lange Nieuwstraat 43** was purchased in 1559 by the English diplomat and merchant banker Sir Thomas Gresham, who gave his name to Gresham's Law, the economic principle that bad money drives good money out of circulation. Gresham belonged to a community of 5,000 or so foreign merchants who carried on business in Antwerp's Handelsbeurs, the world's first purpose-built stock exchange. Gresham worked here intermittently from 1551 to 1574 as financial agent of the crown, often securing large loans on behalf of Queen Elizabeth. So impressed was he with the Antwerp exchange that, on his return to London in 1566, he founded a similar institution, originally called the Bourse and later renamed the Royal Exchange.

Further along this street, the **Bourgondische Kapel** at No. 31 is an elusive gothic chapel which is only open a few hours every week. The chapel, all that survives of the 15th-century palace of Jan van Immerseel, was built in 1496 by Herman de Waghemakere. It is decorated with murals commemorating the marriage in that year of Philip the Fair to Joanna the Mad of Castile.

There is another concealed chapel, the St Niklaaskapel, in a picturesque courtyard at Lange Nieuwstraat 2.

Now let us look at the **Handelsbeurs** (Exchange). We reach it from Lange Nieuwstraat down the lane called Borzestraat. The building is usually open to the public during office hours, but if for some reason it is closed we will have to skirt it along St Katelijnevest to reach Meir.

Named the Handelsbeurs after the Huize ter Buerze at Bruges where foreign merchants met in the 15th century, it was designed in 1531 by Domien de Waghemakere in Flamboyant gothic style. Although the building we now see is not the exchange that Sir Thomas Gresham knew, which was destroyed by fire in 1868, it is a fairly faithful reproduction of the building. The main difference is that the courtyard of the original exchange was open to the sky, to ensure that all transactions were conducted in the eyes of God, whereas the new building is roofed over. The strange Moorish arcades of the original Handelsbeurs have been carefully reconstructed, but the murals are a 19th-century invention. Now gloomy

179

and deserted, we might nevertheless still be able to imagine the Antwerp exchange in its heyday, when the courtyard rang to the voices of merchants from Italy, Spain, England, Scotland, Holland, France and Germany.

We leave the Handelsbeurs by the south entrance and walk down Twaalf Maandenstraat to reach **Meir**, Antwerp's elegant shopping street. This is a good area to stop for coffee; opposite the **Torengebouw**, built in 1929-32 as Europe's first skyscraper, Locus is an elegant tea room which sells tempting pâtisserie. A few doors down is Cuperus, a shop specialising in coffee, tea and chocolates, where elegant Antwerp ladies perch precariously on uncomfortable stools to enjoy the superb coffee served there.

From the Torengebouw, Schoenmarkt leads to **Groenplaats**, a bustling square surrounded by cafés. My favourite is the old-fashioned De Post, which serves excellent coffee and good lunches. Leaving Groenplaats on the south side, we proceed along Reyndersstraat, then turn right up Hoogstraat, a street lined with a strange mixture of fashionable boutiques and curiosity

shops. The tea room Leonardo at No. 28 is primly elegant, whereas the *frituur* on the corner of Vlas-markt is more down to earth, serving tempting *frites* in a building decorated with a splendid baroque statue of the Virgin standing atop a globe with a snake entwined around it.

We in fact turn off Hoogstraat shortly before Leonardo, proceeding left down Korte Pieter Potstraat then right along Grote Pieter Potstraat. Suikerrui then leads left down to the waterfront, where we can ascend to a breezy promenade to admire the magnificent sweep of the Scheldt. The prints at the beginning of this chapter show the waterfront of Antwerp in 1515, when it was crammed with sailing ships of every description. Even in Baedeker's day the old quays could be described as 'handsome and busy'; nowadays they are empty and forlorn, since ships prefer to berth in the modern docks situated to the north of the old city.

The **Nationaal Scheepvaartmuseum** (National Maritime Museum) is situated in Antwerp's old castle, the **Steen**, which overlooks the river just north of here. The castle was built in the 9th century to protect the western frontier of the German Empire from the troublesome counts of Flanders on the opposite bank of the Scheldt. It can be seen in the detail of the 1515 woodcut shown here, below an inscription that states 'This is the castle where the giant Antigoon lived.' We may be fairly certain that he did not, as Antigoon, if he ever lived, lived long before the 9th century. Nevertheless the printmaker has shown him waving a sword from the balcony.

Examining the woodcut, we will see that almost all the old buildings along the waterfront have now vanished. In the 19th century it was deemed necessary to modernise the port of Antwerp by straightening the harbour front and creating the broad quays that Baedeker admired. This could only be accomplished by demolishing some 600 houses, obliterating eight streets and destroying the old fish market. The only building to survive was the Steen, which now stands on the quayside like a beached whale.

As we ascend the inclined approach to the Steen, we can distinguish two distinct layers of masonry, as if the tide had receded leaving a

high-water mark about mid-way up the walls. The dark lower courses of masonry date from the 13th century, while the lighter upper level was added in 1520, when the Steen was partly rebuilt by the familiar team of Domien de Waghemakere and Rombout Keldermans the Younger. We enter through a gate to emerge on a small terrace, which is all that remains of one of the eight streets destroyed in the 19th century.

After serving for a long time as a prison, the Steen was converted into a museum of antiquities in the late 19th century. It would appear to have been a gloomy place to visit, judging from Baedeker's 1905 guide book, which informed travellers that candles, walking sticks and even umbrellas were available for hire. The collection of antiquities is now in the Vleeshuis (next on the walk), and the stock of umbrellas vanished long ago.

The Steen has been brightened up considerably and its jaunty collection of maritime curiosities is highly entertaining. It is all displayed haphazardly in a maze of little rooms with chronically creaking floorboards, but this casual confusion makes the collection all the more intriguing. A few of the rooms have the added attraction of containing enormous renaissance fireplaces, which were left behind when the museum decamped. The most striking of these is an ornate mannerist fireplace decorated with Biblical scenes, designed by Pieter Coecke van Aalst for the Moelenaere house. Other relics that were rescued from this magnificent renaissance house when it was demolished are now displayed in the Vleeshuis museum.

The maritime museum boasts a large collection of beautifully detailed ship models, figureheads, charts and instruments. Among the curiosities, there are ships in bottles and even one in an electric light bulb. The museum has also amassed a marvellous collection of old photographs of Antwerp harbour. Another feature, in the basement, is a recently excavated cesspit containing detritus from the 16th and 17th centuries.

From the terrace in front of the Steen, we can see our next destination, the step gabled **Vleeshuis** (Meat Hall), flanked by two neo-gothic buildings. We can reach it by an interesting, if somewhat indirect route; after walking along the north promenade, we descend to Jordaenskaai, turn right, then left up Palingbrug, where a flight of ancient steps ascends to the old meat market.

The Vleeshuis is another late gothic work by Domien de Waghemakere's father, Herman, who completed the building in 1503, shortly before his death. Its walls are built of alternating bands of brick and sandstone, a picturesque technique known to Flemish architects as 'streaky-bacon style'. We see the meat hall quite clearly on our detils of the 1515 woodcut. It was then, and still is, one of the tallest buildings in Antwerp, a visible symbol of the power of the medieval guild of butchers. So powerful indeed were they that in 1585, when the Duke of Parma's army was besieging the city, the guild successfully vetoed a plan by the Dutch to flood the polders to the north of Antwerp. This desperate military strategy - successfully employed a few years before to rescue Leiden from the Spanish - would have enabled the Dutch fleet to sail up to the city walls unopposed. But the plan was unacceptable to the butchers of Antwerp because the land to be put under water was where they grazed their beef cattle. The guild of butchers was eventually abolished, as were all the other guilds, during the Napoleonic administration, yet the butchers continued to occupy their guild house for a further seven years before finally quitting.

The Vleeshuis is where we come to learn more about Antwerp's history, for its four floors are crammed with a fascinating miscellany of local antiquities. We begin on the ground floor, a vast vaulted space where the meat was once sold. The heavy baroque doors, fierce oak satyrs and voluptuous Virgins in this room reflect the robust and sensual spirit of Antwerp. Attached to the far wall are two oak brackets decorated with satyrs in a style known, not without cause, as Grotesque. They were carved by Pieter Coecke van Aalst in about 1549 to decorate the loggia of the Moelenaere house. The loggia was faithfully copied by a 19th-century architect in a neo-renaissance mansion at Transvaalstraat 59-61, not far from Cogels Osylei.

Climbing a staircase worn by the footsteps of many generations of butchers, we reach the first floor, which was formerly used by the guild for meetings and banquets. Several furnished rooms are preserved, including the very attractive Raadzaal, where the guild meetings were held. After looking at the exhibits on this floor, which include a gruesome model of a public mutilation, we ascend to the top floor. Here, to our surprise, we find an extensive collection of musical instruments, and a small room devoted to Egyptian relics collected by a 19th-century antiquarian at a time when Egyptology was in vogue. But the main reward for the stiff climb here is the view of the extraordinary medieval roof construction.

To leave the Vleeshuis, we must descend three flights of stairs to the basement and then ascend one flight to return to the ground floor. This lengthy route may seem tiresome, but it is amply rewarded by the lapidarium in the basement. This contains a fascinating variety of sculptural fragments, including façade stones, gravestones and obelisks that marked the boundaries of municipal jurisdiction. Many of the stones are decorated with a hand, the symbol of Antwerp. There are also two renaissance busts of Jan van Eyck and Albrecht Dürer, carved in 1549 to

decorate a house in Antwerp.

As we climbed the spiral stair of the Vleeshuis, we may have glimpsed the **St Pauluskerk** to the north. Let us now visit this church, which we reach by turning left along Vleeshouwersstraat, past some modern dwellings built in imitation of the traditional renaissance houses of Antwerp (such as those in Kaasstraat). **Veemarkt**, the old cattle market, upon which we emerge, is a nondescript square overlooked by the St Pauluskerk, a late gothic church built by Domien de Waghemakere in 1533-71. The church originally belonged to a Dominican friary, and in the 18th century was furnished by the friars with baroque paintings and sculptures. The main painting of interest is a *Scourging of Christ* by Rubens.

The church has a curious little garden which many visitors miss, tucked into the corner of the nave and south transept; we reach it it through a door in the long corridor leading into the church from the street. Two devout Dominican friars laboured here for half a century, from 1697 to 1747, to create a mock Mount Calvary. The artificial hill built up against the church is crowded with baroque statues of saints, angels and prophets in exaggerated poses of ecstasy or grief. At the foot of the hill is a dark cave with a grim vision of Hell. Baudelaire, the irascible French poet, dismissed the work as 'ridiculous', yet the fact that the friars devoted the best part of their lives to the construction of this calvary gives it a certain tragic grandeur.

From the church we turn left along Zwartzusterstraat. A right turn then takes us into Stoelstraat, one of the loveliest old lanes in Antwerp, even if its most picturesque house, at No. 11, is merely a modern reconstruction of a medieval house rather than the genuine article. At the end of Stoelstraat we turn right along Zirkstraat, then left down Hofstraat. During office hours, we can glance into the courtyard of the **Oude Beurs**, at No. 16. This handsome 16th-century palace has an attractive late gothic arcade, and one of the few surviving watchtowers of Antwerp. It is now occupied by the antiquated offices of the local education authority.

We turn right at the end of Hofstraat to reach, on the left, a little alley known as the Spanje-pandsteeg. The 16th-century house at the end of this alley was built for the guild of archers. Named **Den Spieghel** (The Mirror), it was purchased in 1506 by Pieter Gilles (who preferred the sonorous Latin name Petrus Aegidius), Secretary of the City of Antwerp. Gilles was a leading Antwerp humanist whose friends included Erasmus and Thomas More. The inspiration for *Utopia* came to More in 1515 when he was visiting Gilles in Antwerp. As he informs his reader at the beginning of *Utopia*, he had been sent to Bruges by Henry VIII to settle a dispute that was jeopardising the wool trade between Castile and England. While waiting for the Spanish envoy to return from an audience at Brussels, More seized the opportunity to travel to Antwerp to see Pieter Gilles, 'a very fine person and an excellent scholar'. In the opening scene of *Utopia*, More describes his encounter with Pieter Gilles and a certain Raphael Hythlodaye as he was walking back to his inn after attending Mass in the cathedral. Like many young men roaming the streets of 16th-century Antwerp, Raphael Hythlodaye had just returned from a long voyage around

185

the world. As they sit in the garden at More's inn, he tells them of his adventures and of the remarkable island of Utopia.

Utopia was first published in Leuven in 1516 in a Latin edition proof read by Erasmus. One year later Erasmus furnished More with a unique token of their friendship by commissioning the Antwerp painter Quinten Metsys to produce a double portrait of himself and Pieter Gilles (opposite). The portrait of Gilles now hangs in Longford Castle, but there is a copy in Antwerp's Museum van Schone Kunsten. The Erasmus portrait, a favourite book jacket illustration, has been lost, but there are several copies in existence, including a good one in the Palazzo Barberini in Rome.

If Erasmus appears yellowish in his portrait, it is because he was ill at the time. In a letter written to More in 1517, while Metsys was still working on his portrait, Erasmus complained, 'My doctor has taken it into his head to get me to swallow pills to purify my spleen and whatever he is foolish enough to prescribe I am foolish enough to do. The portrait has already been begun, but when I went back to the artist after taking the medicine he said that I didn't have the same physiognomy any more, and so the painting had to be postponed a few days until I looked a little more alive again.'

More was particularly impressed with the uncanny realism of the two portraits by Metsys. On looking closely at the portrait of Gilles, More was delighted to discover that his friend was holding a letter from him, in which the handwriting was clearly recognisable as his own. He subsequently wrote to Gilles asking for the letter to be returned so that he could hang it alongside the painting. 'If it has been lost,' he added, 'I will see whether I in my turn can copy the man who copies my hand so well.'

We now walk back along Oude Beurs and turn right down Wisselstraat, which provides a dramatic approach into Antwerp's main square, the **Grote Markt**. To enjoy the architectural spectacle of this square, let us sit down on one of the café terraces, or at a window table indoors if the weather is bad. Den Engel at No. 3 may well be the best café in Antwerp, but 't Ogenblik at No. 12 has the better view.

Grote Markt is dominated by the renaissance **Stadhuis** (Town Hall), designed by Cornelis Floris in 1561. Its construction marked the end of quaint late gothic architecture and the beginning of an era of disciplined and proportioned public buildings based on Italian principles, and even sometimes Italian materials. The rosy marble of the Stadhuis columns, for instance, are a rare delight in these northern latitudes.

From our café table we can see some of the guild houses on the market square. **Grote Markt 5** (the fifth building on the north side, beginning at the town hall) was built by the guild of coopers in 1579. **Grote Markt 7**, with a statue of St George on the pediment, was erected one year later for the guild of archers.

Now let us turn our attention to the extraordinary fountain which spouts water recklessly over much of the square. Designed in 1887 (and so really very modern when the photograph on the left was taken) the **Brabo Fountain** depicts the legend of Silvius Brabo, a Roman soldier who freed the Scheldt from the tyranny of the giant Druoon Antigoon, whom we met on page 181.

The giant had exacted a toll from every ship sailing down the Scheldt, and severed the hand of any captain foolish enough to resist. Eventually he met his match in Brabo, who is shown holding aloft the hand of Antigoon, just before hurling it into the Scheldt. According to one school of etymology, Brabo throwing the hand gives Antwerp its name; from the Dutch *hand werpen* (to throw the hand). A more prosaic explanation gives Antwerp's root as *aan 't werven* (on the waterfront). The omnipresent hand in Antwerp reveals that the people of Antwerp much prefer to believe the romantic legend of Silvius Brabo.

Visiting Antwerp in 1520, the German artist Albrecht Dürer was solemnly taken to the town hall to be shown the skeleton of Antigoon. 'In Antwerp I saw a bone from the leg of the giant,' he noted in his diary. 'This bone measures five and a half feet in length and is extraordinarily heavy and very thick; the shoulder blade is likewise very broad, like the back of a strong man. This giant was 18 feet tall ...' Dürer seems to have been the victim of a practical joke, however, for the bones he observed were apparently those of a whale.

We leave Grote Markt by the street facing the town hall, Kaasrui, then turn right along Korte Koepoortstraat and left down a narrow lane, Jezuitenrui, so called because it leads to a Jesuit church. And a most splendid Jesuit church it is, known as the **St Carolus Borromeuskerk**. Modelled on Vignola's Il Gesù church in Rome, St Carolus Borromeus was designed by Pieter Huyssens in 1614-21. He was assisted by Rubens, who probably designed the lovely baroque tower and the clustered cherubs above the entrance. John Evelyn wrote, 'The church of the Jesuits is most sumptuous and magnificent, a glorious fabriq without, and within wholly incrusted with marble, inlay'd and polish'd into divers representations of histories, landskips, flowers, &c.' Much of the interior was destroyed by fire in 1718, and little of the original marble remains.

From the attractive square in front of the Jesuit church, we now follow a winding route to reach the house in which Albrecht Dürer lodged for some nine months in 1520. Heading first down

Wijngaardstraat, we then turn right along Hoofd-kerkstraat, and finally right into Wolstraat (Wool Street), so called because of the many English wool merchants who settled here in the 16th century. Notice the splendid baroque portal at **Wolstraat 30** designed by François Duquesnoy. There is a very attractive portrait of this sculptor by van Dyck in Brussels' Musée d'Art Ancien.

Dürer's house is at the end of Wolstraat, on the corner of Minderbroedersrui. In 1520 Dürer travelled from Nuremberg to Antwerp with his wife Agnes and his maidservant Susanna, paying his expenses as he went along by producing woodcuts and sketches of German merchants. He was an acutely observant traveller and filled his notebooks with detailed drawings and descriptions of the curiosities he encountered, from the mansions of Antwerp to the lions in the menagerie of Ghent's Prinsenhof. Through the diaries of Dürer we learn a great deal about the splendour of 16th-century Antwerp. Once he observed a magnificent procession as it rounded the corner into Wolstraat: 'Wagons were drawn along with masques upon ships and other inven-

tions. Behind them came the Company of the Prophets in their proper order, and scenes from the New Testament, such as the Annunciation, the Three Holy Kings riding on great camels, and on other rare beasts, all very well arranged.'

A quiet lane behind Dürer's house, Grote Goddaert, leads us in a gentle curve along the course of the medieval city walls. We emerge on a small square named **Engelse Beurs**, the English Exchange, where a separate stock exchange was established for the English mercantile community. If we turn right here and proceed down Minderbroedersstraat we come upon the neoclassical lodge of the **Academie voor Schone Kunsten** (Academy of Fine Arts), established in 1662 by the artist David Teniers the Younger. In 1810 it moved to its present location in a former Franciscan friary. Exploring the romantically overgrown garden, we come upon a weather-beaten statue of Teniers and some magnificent baroque portals salvaged from demolished buildings.

Stadswaag, where the public weigh house once stood, is our destination now; we reach it by walking up Mutsaertstraat and then turning right. With the weigh house now demolished, a chilly silence has fallen upon this once animated square. Here, as nowhere else in Antwerp, we find that mood of melancholy which so struck William Beckford in 1783: 'No village amongst the Alps, or hermitage upon Mount Lebanon is less disturbed... In its two hundred and twelve streets and twenty-two squares the grass grows in deep silence.' During the day the only sign of life on Stadswaag comes from a specialist beer café called 't Waagstuk, which is tucked away in a secluded courtyard at No. 20. But at night the square becomes more animated, as jazz cafés and bars come to life in the old cellars and abandoned warehouses. Visitors who find themselves at a loose end in the evening might stroll back this way and visit, for example, the curious café De Trein der Traagheid at Lange Noordstraat 33, which is furnished with aged wooden Belgian railway carriage seats from the 1930's.

From Stadswaag we continue along Lange Brilstraat, and right down Venusstraat. The mouldering buildings numbered 11-15 were formerly warehouses used by the English Merchant Adventurers. Later they housed the Berg van Barmhartigheid, a municipal pawnbroking bank founded by Wenceslas Coeberger in the 17th century.

Continuing down Venusstraat, we then turn left along Prinsstraat. An old gateway at No. 13 leads us into the **Hof van Liere**. This splendid late gothic palace was probably built by Domien de Waghemakere in 1515-20 for Burgomaster Arnold van Liere. Visiting van Liere here soon after the completion of the palace, Albrecht Dürer praised the building in his diary and sketched its slender watchtower. In the 1550's the city fathers, who by then owned the palace, offered it to the English Merchant Adventurers as an incentive to remain in Antwerp. It was a successful ploy, if temporary, for the English merchants eventually quit Antwerp in 1611 to resettle in Hamburg. The Hof van Liere was then given to the Jesuits who used it as a religious college, adding two large quadrangles on the north side.

Our explorations in Bruges and Ghent have

perhaps given us a taste for the Begijnhofs of Flanders. Antwerp, too, has a **Begijnhof**, although it is seldom visited by tourists. To reach it, we continue down Prinsstraat, then along Pieter van Hobokenstraat to reach Ossenmarkt, a likeable little square. The Begijnhof, concealed by a high brick wall, is entered through a portal at Rode Straat 39. We discover within its walls the familiar enticing prospect of a simple and secluded community of modest whitewashed houses grouped around cobbled courtyards and leafy squares. It is difficult to imagine a more pleasing place to live, combining as it does the intimacy of village life with the excitement of a metropolis.

We now retrace our steps along Pieter van Hobokenstraat and turn left into Rozenstraat. Our destination is the street named grandly Via Caesarea on the 1565 plan of Antwerp, which we reach by turning right along Kattenstraat, left into Prinsesstraat and then right into Keizersstraat.

Slightly off the beaten track, this street once contained the homes of many prominent Antwerp families. We have come here to visit one of the most splendid of these houses, the **Rockoxhuis** at No. 12, a beautiful Flemish renaissance house bought in 1603 by Burgomaster Nicolaas Rockox. As in the Rubenshuis and the Museum Plantin-Moretus, we discover here the alluring atmosphere of baroque Antwerp.

We have already met Nicolaas Rockox in our wanderings, as captain of the guild of arquebusiers, and a friend and patron of Rubens. Rockox lived here with his wife and thirteen children, all of whom we saw in a painting in the St Jacobs-kerk. When we enter the hall of the Rockoxhuis, we are following in the footsteps of Grotius, Ortelius and Lipsius, all friends of the Burgomaster. The welcome they might have expected can be guessed from the painting opposite, which shows a feast in this very house.

The restoration of the Rockoxhuis has been carried out with impeccable attention to detail: the rooms are furnished in solid baroque style and the walls hung with an interesting collection of Flemish paintings. There is a landscape by Patinir, an astonishing sketch of two old men's heads by Sir Anthony van Dyck, and a view of the fish

market at Antwerp by Frans Snijders, who lived in the house next door to Rockox. But the principal delights of this tasteful little collection are the two works by Rubens. On our walks so far we have seen many, perhaps too many, of Rubens' large-scale religious paintings. In room 2 we get a glimpse of a different style of Rubens altogether. *The Madonna and Child*, executed by Rubens in 1613, is a tender study of his first wife Isabella and their son Nicolaas. There is also a sketch of the *Crucifixion*, drawn in about 1628. Delacroix greatly admired this work, which was owned once by his friend George Sand. The sketch was a preliminary study for a large religious painting, which Rubens was forced to abandon when in 1628 he was called away to mediate in the war between Spain and England. This diplomatic mission was successful and a peace treaty was signed between the two countries in 1630. Rubens received a knighthood from Charles II and an honorary degree from Cambridge University for his efforts.

Room 4, once the picture gallery of Burgomaster Rockox, is the room depicted in the painting reproduced on page 193, the *Feast in the House of Burgomaster Rockox* by Frans Francken the Younger. This *kunstkamer* painting includes allegorical figures representing the five senses; they are gathered around a table laden with food and drink. The painting above the fireplace is Rubens' *Samson and Delilah*, now in London's National Gallery. Two other works in Rockox's picture gallery are now in Antwerp's Museum voor Schone Kunsten: Rubens' painting of *The Incredulity of St Thomas*, seen though the open doorway, though it had been commissioned by Burgomaster Rockox in 1613 to hang above the tomb of his dead wife; and, to the right of the fireplace, Quinten Metsys' diptych of *The Saviour of the World and Mary at Prayer,* one of the most beautiful works by this Antwerp artist.

Antwerp Explored Further

I. The Museum voor Schone Kunsten and its Neighbourhood. The Museum voor Schone Kunsten (Museum of Fine Arts) occupies an imposing neoclassical building in Antwerp's southern quarter. This district was developed in the boom years of the 19th century and it contains numerous splendid buildings from that era. As well as the delights of the relatively unknown Museum voor Schone Kunsten, there are two other interesting museums which have recently opened in this neighbourhood.

My favourite café round here is L'Entrepôt du Congo at Vlaamse Kaai 42. Formerly a brewery, it is simply furnished with wooden tables, a photograph of the late King Baudoin above the bar, and a potted fern next to the expresso machine. Early in the morning there might be one solitary customer leafing through the *Gazet van Antwerpen*, but by the evening we will be lucky to find a table.

On entering the **Museum voor Schone Kunsten**, we are swept into the Great Vestibule, which is decorated with a panoramic frieze by Nicaise de Keyser depicting Flemish art and architecture through the ages. We then ascend a monumental staircase to enter Gallery I, a room devoted to religious paintings by Rubens.

The large panel of the *Baptism of Christ* is, astonishingly, merely a side panel from an early work painted in 1604. In 1600 Rubens set off for Italy, where he stayed for eight years. Soon after arriving in Venice he met Vincenzo Gonzaga the Elder, Duke of Mantua, who offered him employment in Mantua. In 1604 Gonzaga commissioned Rubens to paint a gigantic triptych for the Jesuit church in Mantua. *The Baptism of Christ* is part of this triptych, which is now divided between Mantua, Nancy and Antwerp.

Many of the other works by Rubens in this gallery were commissioned to hang in churches in Antwerp, including *The Adoration of the Magi* (which includes some wonderfully expressive figures), *Christ Crucified between Two Thieves*, *Christ on the Straw* (a tender study painted as an epitaph for his friend Jan Michielsen), and *Christ on the Cross* (a bleak painting commissioned in 1619 by Nicolaas Rockox). *The Incredulity of St Thomas* was also commissioned by Rockox, Rubens' friend and steady patron; we saw the central composition on page 193, and here it is flanked by affectionate portraits of Burgomaster Rockox and his wife Adriana Perez. In the midst of so many monumental works, it is easy to overlook one small painting in a more intimate style. It is a portrait by Rubens of his friend Gaspard Gevartius, town clerk of Antwerp, seated at his desk with his pen poised. A bust of Marcus Aurelius is there to remind us that Gevartius had written

a commentary on the Roman emperor. The study of Gevartius is one of the few portraits by Rubens in Antwerp; because they were easily sold and shipped abroad, the portraits now tend to be in far-off collections, whereas most of the large religious works have stayed in Antwerp.

After we have looked at the works by Rubens in Galleries I and G, it is logical to proceed to Galleries H and F where there are several paintings by his pupils. *The King Drinks* is a work of typically earthy humour by Jacob Jordaens, one of Rubens' many successful followers.

The Flemish Primitives occupy the rooms on either side of the Rubens galleries. Gallery Q is a quiet room containing an exquisite collection of miniature works by Flemish Primitives, including two by Jan van Eyck: a tiny sketch of *St Barbara*, dated 1437, and *The Madonna at the Fountain*, painted two years later. The former adopted a revolutionary approach to its subject. Medieval artists up until then had depicted Barbara holding a miniature tower in her hand to symbolise the building in which she was imprisoned by her jealous father. This is how St Barbara appears in the *Adoration of the Mystic Lamb* in Ghent by Jan and Hubert van Eyck. In the Antwerp sketch, however, as we can see here, van Eyck realistically represents the tower as a full-scale gothic edifice looming above the saint. The tower was modelled upon the north tower of Antwerp Cathedral, which at the time the sketch was done had reached about one-third of its final height. Van Eyck's minuscule study of the cathedral tower contains a plenitude of details concerning medieval construction methods, including a delightful sketch of the architect, who is shouting instructions to the masons at work at the top of the soaring edifice.

Also in this gallery is Roger van der Weyden's *Triptych of the Seven Sacraments* painted in 1445 for Jean Chevrot, Bishop of Tournai. Set in a large gothic church, the Seven Sacraments depicted are, from left to right, Ordination, Marriage, Extreme Unction, Eucharist, Baptism, Confirmation and Penance. Notice the ingenious way that the picture frame has been designed to harmonise with the gothic architecture.

There is also a marvellous portrait by van der

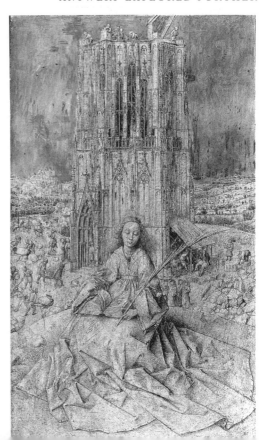

Weyden of Philippe de Croy. This originally formed one wing of a diptych; the other wing - a study of the Virgin and Child - is now in the Huntington Gallery in California. Van der Weyden captures the intelligence and sensitivity of the Burgundian noble, who is dressed entirely in black, against which his face and hands stand out vividly.

In room S we abandon for a moment the Flemish Primitives to look at Simone Martini's four miniatures depicting the Annunciation, the Archangel Gabriel, the Crucifixion and the Descent from the Cross. These four panels originally belonged to a six-part polyptych of the Passion owned by the Charterhouse of Champmol. Founded by the dukes of Burgundy to house their mausoleums, this Charterhouse just outside the city walls of Dijon was endowed with a magnificent collection of gothic painting and sculpture. After the French Revolution the buildings were demolished and this remarkable collection sold off. An Antwerp collector bought these four Martini panels, but the other two were lost to Paris and Berlin. Van der Weyden's *Seven Sacraments* came from the same collection.

This room also contains an enigmatic medieval painting of the *Virgin and Child* by Jean Fouquet. It is strange because of the angels in the background, some painted red, others blue. The colours may symbolize the different realms of heaven, in which case we are looking at a painting of the ascension of the Virgin Mary. This would be an untroubling interpretation if it were not for an inscription on the back of the painting. Signed by an 18th-century French lawyer called Gautier, it says, 'The Holy Virgin is the likeness of Agnès Sorel, mistress of Charles VII king of France, who died in 1450.' The Virgin, then, was no virgin. This woman with her left breast bared was the favourite mistress of Charles VII and one of the most fashionable women in France. The king was so besotted with his loved one that he gave her an estate called Beauté-lès-Paris. She became known as *Agnès, dame de beauté*. We must judge for ourselves if Agnès was beautiful, but she certainly inspired her lover to great deeds. Not known for his valour, Charles set off in 1450 to drive the English out of Normandy. It was during this campaign that Agnès had a miscarriage and died. She was just 28. The painting we see here was commissioned soon after her death by Etienne Chevalier; perhaps it was an attempt to redeem her soul.

Gallery R contains a miniature landscape by Joachim Patinir which we should not overlook. Illustrating Patinir's most cherished Biblical episode, the *Landscape with the Flight to Egypt* is dotted with delightful details such as some tiny rabbits and a goat perched on a mountain ridge. The strange rock formations in Patinir's paintings may look like fantastic creations, but in fact they are based on the extraordinary limestone gorge of the River Meuse between Namur and Dinant.

This gallery contains several beautiful works by the Antwerp painter Quinten Metsys, including his *Triptych of the Entombment of Christ*. Painted in 1508-11 for the carpenters' chapel in Antwerp Cathedral, it shows the dead Christ surrounded by mourners, flanked by panels with the martyrdoms of St John the Baptist and St John the Evangelist. Metsys was particularly gifted as a portraitist, as we might remember from the copy of his picture of Pieter Gilles that we saw above (page 187). Notice here, too, his enchanting *Mary Magdalene with the Box of Spikenard*, reminiscent of Leonardo da Vinci, and his vibrant diptych of *The Saviour of the World and Mary at Prayer*. The diptych was once owned by Burgomaster Rockox; we saw it to the right of the fireplace in the painting of the *Feast in the House of Burgomaster Rockox* (page 193).

In Gallery N, we come upon an unusual work by Hans Memling, *Christ as King of Heaven Surrounded by Angels*, which hung for many years in a Benedictine convent in Spain. Four of the angels are copied from Memling's *St Ursula Shrine* in Bruges: the angel playing a psaltery (far left), the lutenist (third from the left), the angel playing at a portable organ (third from the right) and the viol player (far right). Frans Floris' *Fall of the Rebel Angels*, which hangs in Gallery P, is an example of Antwerp mannerism at its most tormented. Painted in 1554, this crowded composition anticipates the surging baroque style of Rubens.

When we have explored the upper galleries, we

can pause in the museum café at the foot of the back stairs. While we sit beneath a magnificent panorama of Antwerp harbour, let us read about some of the 19th-century and modern paintings in the collection.

Gallery 19 contains a collection of paintings by James Ensor, born in 1860 in Ostend. Ensor's father was a British expatriate and his mother Flemish. *Afternoon at Ostend*, painted in 1881, reflects the solid Victorian milieu in which he grew up. Late in the 1880's, however, Ensor rebelled against this comfortable bourgeois world and his style of painting changed utterly, as is illustrated by *Skeletons Fighting for the Body of a Hanged Man*, painted just ten years after the languid *Afternoon at Ostend*. The dark browns and greys of his early palette are replaced by vivid reds and greens, and instead of solid Ostend citizens we see strange caricatures of people wearing carnival masks. Why Ensor should have changed his style so totally has never been satisfactorily resolved. It may have been that a visit in the 1880's to an exhibition of Turner paintings in London led Ensor in a new direction. This would explain

the almost abstract style of *The Rebel Angels Struck Down*, painted in 1889. The gaudy masks that appear so frequently in Ensor's later works are more easily accounted for, as Ensor's uncle owned a novelty shop in Ostend crammed with Carnival masks.

Ensor's later works caused a furore in the staid Belgian art world when they were first exhibited. Even *Les XX*, the independent group which introduced Impressionism to Belgium, refused to admit Ensor's work to the salons of 1889 and 1890. Though his reputation is now more firmly established, Ensor's greatest work, *The Entry of Christ into Brussels*, was recently sold to the voracious J. Paul Getty Museum in California. Painted in 1888, this large canvas was Ensor's favourite work and it hung in his house at Ostend until his death in 1949. Bought by Knokke Casino, it was then sold to an Antwerp banker, who in 1951 lent it to the Museum voor Schone Kunsten. It remained here until 1983, when it was put up for sale. The Belgian government could not be persuaded to buy the painting, and so *The Entry of Christ into Brussels* exited from Antwerp, one more masterpiece lost in the unending diaspora of Flemish art.

We find several attractive Impressionist works by Rik Wouters in Gallery 21. *Woman Ironing* is a tender domestic portrait of his wife Nel, painted in 1912. During the First World War, Wouters was interned at Amsterdam, and he died there in 1916 after undergoing a series of operations for eye cancer. As we leave the museum, we will see two small cabinets in the Great Vestibule containing mementos of Wouters.

Galleries 8-10 contain an engaging collection of eccentric works by Belgian surrealists. Hanging in room 10 is a melancholy early work by Paul Delvaux, *The Red Bow,* painted in 1937. The streets of a classical city are strewn with black rocks and the walls of buildings are cracked, as if a volcano has recently erupted. Amidst this dark chaos, women wander naked, or with huge red bows over their breasts, their eyes filled with blank despair. In the same room stands René Magritte's impishly irreverent *Madame Récamier.* This sculptural work recalls the portrait by Jacques-Louis David in the Louvre of Madame Récamier reclining on a chaise longue. In Magritte's work an L-shaped coffin has taken the place of Madame Récamier. With this haunting image to ponder, we are perhaps ready for a change of scene, so let us now explore the other two museums in this quarter, which are situated in warehouses in the old docklands.

To reach this area, which at the time of writing was in the throes of redevelopment, we should turn left outside the museum, then right down Verschansingsstraat. At the end of this street stands the **Waterpoort**, or Porta Regia as it was more grandly named in the 17th century. This city gate, the only one still standing in Antwerp, was designed by Hubert van den Eynde and adorned with a splendid sculpture of a river god by Artus Quellin the Elder. Erected in 1624 to commemorate the coronation of Philip IV of Spain, it of course has no business standing in this 19th-century quarter of Antwerp, where it was re-erected in 1937. But the gate does add a nice touch of grandeur to a somewhat desolate open square, which until recently was a dock.

Straight ahead is the **Museum voor**

Fotografie, a museum of photography recently opened in a former warehouse at Waalse Kaai 47. It has a fascinating collection of historic photographs, including many studies of Old Antwerp. A reconstructed photographer's studio is filled with 19th-century gadgets, including a mountain landscape painted on canvas, and a mock egg in which babies were photographed. Other rooms contain antique cameras and a *camera obscura*, but perhaps the most curious exhibit is a 1905 *Keizerspanorama* that was exhibited at the World Exhibition in Liège. The remarkable cylindrical device allowed 25 people simultaneously to view stereoscopic photographs.

From this museum, it is a short walk along the Waalse Kaai, past various promising signs of urban regeneration, to the new **Museum van Hedendaagse Kunst Antwerpen** at Leuvenstraat 32. This museum of modern art occupies an art deco grain silo built in the 1920's. Expect to be amused, teased, tantalised, and bemused by the contemporary Belgian artists exhibited here, who have a delightful talent for assembling quirky surrealist constructions.

Continuing along the Waalse Kaai, we come upon the **Zuiderpershuis**, a severe neo-baroque building with massive rusticated stones, erected in the confident 1880's. This rugged building once housed enormous steam engines that were used to drive hydraulic cranes, operate sluices and even shunt goods trains within the port area. The solemn grandeur of the Zuiderpershuis is typical of the architectural style that developed at Antwerp in the heady years of the *Belle Epoque*. So, too, is an extraordinary monument that stands on Marnixplaats, on the site of the 16th-century Spanish citadel (reached by turning right down Scheldestraat at the end of Waalsekaai). Adorned with glowering sea gods and severed chains, the monument was erected to commemorate the abolition in 1863 of the Dutch right to levy tolls on shipping on the Scheldt.

One last delight in this quarter is appealing house at **Schildersstraat 2**, which we reach by turning right down Zwijgerstraat. Its principal feature is the splendid balcony opposite, modelled exactly on the wooden prow of a sailing ship. This fanciful art nouveau house was designed in 1901 for an Antwerp shipbuilder by Frans Smet-Verhas, who has signed his work in ornate lettering.

II. The Brouwershuis and the Waterfront.

Antwerp's northern quarter is not visited by many tourists, though it has a run-down charm. There is a Russian quarter on Falconplein where shops sell Western goods still not available in Moscow, including plastic dolls, cheap stereos and replacement car headlights. A short stroll to the north brings you to the red light district, where women pose in neon-lit windows for hours on end. Some of them try to look glamorous, but others just flop around in armchairs reading stories in gossipy magazines like *Mijn Geheim* ('My Secret').

The city has tried in recent years to revitalise this area, with the intention of creating a fashionable docklands district. The main effort so far has been the restoration of the empty Sint Felixpakhuis, a crumbling brick warehouse at 30 Godefriduskaai. Not far from here is the **Brouwershuis** (Brewers' House), a sadly forgotten relic

PLAATSNIJDERS

of renaissance Antwerp at Adriaan Brouwerstraat 20. The building was erected in 1553 by Gilbert van Schoonbeke, the founder of the girls' orphanage and promoter of the Friday Market. His most ambitious project was to create a new quarter, the Nieuwstad (New Town), to the north of the old city walls. The streets of the Nieuwstad were laid out according to renaissance principles on a strict grid pattern. Van Schoonbeke planned to build some 24 breweries in this new quarter, but the money ran out and nothing much was ever built except for a few small breweries and the Brouwershuis. The Brouwershuis was later turned into a fascinating museum of brewing, but now the money has run out again, and the museum has closed. The only way to see inside is to arrange a visit through the tourist office. If we do so, we will see the curious mechanism invented by van Schoonbeke to fill reservoirs on the first floor. This used a horse-drawn system of buckets to hoist water drawn from the city moat. The contraption proved so effective that it was still being used to supply a few of Antwerp's breweries in the early years of this century.

After ascending the stairs, we walk along a corridor with walls that are disturbingly askew, to enter a 17th-century room where the guild held its meetings. Hung with gleaming gilt leather, this is one of the most beautiful rooms in Antwerp. It captivated the 19th-century artist Henri de Braekeleer, who painted several mellow studies of this room - one now hangs in Antwerp's Museum voor Schone Kunsten and another in Brussels' Musée d'Art Ancien.

On leaving the Brouwershuis we turn right and then left along a street that leads to the **Bonapartedok**. As its name suggests, this dock was constructed by Napoleon. Turning left along the quayside, we come to the busy Tavenierkaai. Another left turn brings us to a flight of stairs leading up to the north promenade.

Walking along the Schelde waterfront, we cannot help but wonder what lies on the opposite bank. If we are feeling energetic, we can easily satisfy that nagging curiosity. No tourist visiting Antwerp has any idea that it is possible to walk *under* the river. It is, and it is something every born and bred Antwerp citizen remembers doing at least once as a child. We have to go to the Sint Jans Vliet and look for a 1930's brick building in the middle of the square. It isn't well signed, but eventually a creaking wooden escalator similar to those on London's Bakerloo line will appear, which takes us down to a tunnel. Just over half a kilometre long, the **St Annatunnel** takes ten minutes or so to walk through. But why bother? most people would ask. The *Linkeroever,* or left bank, is considered beyond the pale by those who live on the correct side of the river. They are perhaps remembering a time when this side of the river Scheldt belonged to the Counts of Flanders, but it is now part of Antwerp city, and is worth visiting just for the panoramic view back to the city skyline bristling with medieval spires and modern cranes. Artists began coming here by boat in the 16th century to sketch what was then perhaps the most striking urban view in Europe. One of the first artists to do so was the master who produced the 1515 woodcut. Anonymous he might now be, but he is not invisible, for we see him quite clearly to the left of the cottages in the foreground, sitting on the river

bank with his sketch book (page 149). That is not the only reason to come here. A patch of wasteland on the waterfront has been turned into an open-air maritime museum, filled with rusty seafaring relics such as anchors, cannon and ship's bells. From this spot, a riverside walk signposted *Wandelweg* meanders along the water's edge for a couple of kilometres, past derelict slipways and abandoned trucks. Finally, and this you will not believe, you come to Antwerp beach. The Sint Annastrand may not be in any tourist guide, but it is a genuine stretch of sand with a few beach cafés painted jaunty pink and blue colours. It was a popular resort in the 1930's, but now looks` out over a giant oil refinery. It isn't beautiful, but it is certainly fascinating.

III. Cogels-Osylei. The 19th-century residential area of Cogels-Osylei is crammed with extravagant architecture. We will find fake gothic castles next to mock Venetian palaces, and Belgian art nouveau mansions rubbing shoulders with neat English Tudor façades. This quarter used to be a well-kept secret, but word has got around. Dutch and German coaches now crawl along Cogels-Osylei as the guides point out the art nouveau flourishes on 'The Sunflower' house (No. 50) or the convoluted iron balconies of No. 80 (p 154).

Amid all the rampant individualism, it is refreshing to find four houses built in perfect harmony. They stand at the crossroads of Water-loostraat and Generaal van Merlenstraat, and are decorated with tile pictures of the four seasons. A tea room called Mellaneys at 16 Cogels-Osylei serves tea and cakes from Thursday to Monday. The interior is a marvellous 19th-century confection of moulded cornices, swags of fruit and chandeliers.

Mechelen

Mechelen

With its old houses and languid river, the beautiful Flemish town of Mechelen has something of the appeal of Bruges. Yet it remains virtually undiscovered by tourists, despite being favourably situated mid-way between Brussels and Antwerp. Mechelen is still a secret city where we can wander along quiet, cobbled streets overlooked by crumbling renaissance houses and ancient baroque convents built of mellow brick and soft white sandstone. Not that it is totally dead; there are elegant shops on Bruul and crowded cafés on Grote Markt, and the town is surrounded by factories mass-producing oak furniture of medieval proportions. But when we stray away from the centre, especially into the areas once occupied by the Begijnhofs and convents, we quickly become immersed in the peaceful mood of this old Catholic town.

Originally under the sway of the Prince-Bishop of Liège, Mechelen (Malines in French) passed in 1213 to the Berthoud family. In 1333 it was captured by Louis de Male, Count of Flanders, and so passed to the dukes of Burgundy when Louis died in 1384. By the middle of the 15th century, the city was sufficiently prosperous to embark on the construction of a church spire that was planned to be the tallest in the world.

Mechelen assumed an important role in medieval politics in 1473, when the Grote Raad, the supreme court of the Burgundian Netherlands, was established here by Charles the Bold. As a result, numerous lawyers, councillors and

advisers settled in the city. When Charles the Bold died in 1477, his widow, Margaret of York, settled in Mechelen. Following the tragic death of her daughter in 1482, Margaret of York brought up her grandchildren here. One of them, Margaret of Austria, returned to Mechelen on being appointed Regent of the Netherlands in 1507. Her court became a centre of art and learning, drawing to Mechelen numerous northern renaissance scholars and painters, such as Erasmus, Albrecht Dürer, and Bernard van Orley.

When Margaret of Austria died in 1530, her successor Mary of Hungary moved the court back to Brussels. This proved as disastrous for Mechelen as the silting of the Zwin had been for Bruges. The decline of the city after 1530 can be gauged by the many 16th-century buildings left unfinished, such as the cathedral tower and the palace of the Grote Raad on Grote Markt. One would not guess it from the print above, but this is a dying town.

In the First World War Mechelen had the bad luck to be bombarded both by the retreating Belgians and by the advancing Germans. It also suffered badly in the last war, yet it has weathered these misfortunes and is today a very pleasing and picturesque city.

Mechelen is best visited as a day excursion from Antwerp or Brussels. A fifteen-minute train journey and a short walk, brings us into the heart of this historic old city. The two walks described below will pleasantly fill a complete day.

209

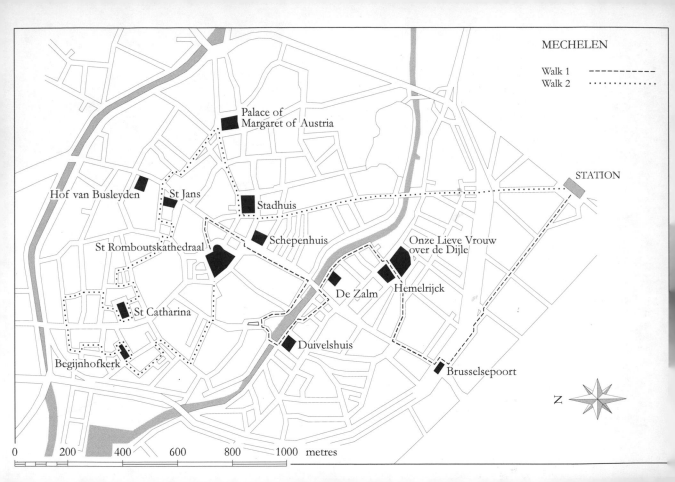

MECHELEN

Walk 1 ------------
Walk 2 ....

Palace of Margaret of Austria

STATION

Hof van Busleyden

St Jans

Stadhuis

Schepenhuis

St Romboutskathedraal

Onze Lieve Vrouw over de Dijle

De Zalm

Hemelrijck

St Catharina

Duivelshuis

Begijnhofkerk

Brusselsepoort

N

0   200   400   600   800   1000   metres

Along the River Dijle

On our first walk in Mechelen, we will find out about the Devil's House, the Beethoven family, and a failed attempt to build the world's tallest spire.. We begin at the mighty **Brusselsepoort** (which we reach from the station down Léopold-straat, then left along Van Benedenlaan). This city provides us with a striking impression of Mechelen's medieval grandeur. The curious baroque domes were added in the 17th century.

We now enter the old city and proceed down Hoogstraat, where we obtain our first beguiling glimpse of the cathedral tower. The busy street we are on leads straight into Grote Markt, the main square, but we take a less direct route there, since it is quite often in the quiet side streets of Flemish cities that we discover the most interesting and unusual details. So we turn right along Milsenstraat, soon to see the tower belonging to the church of **Onze-Lieve-Vrouw over de Dijle** (Our Lady Across the Dijle). Seen from Milsen-straat, this church appears as a harmonious Gothic edifice built of an attractive white sandstone, but from the rear it is a very much more complex composition. The north portal is a delicate late gothic addition designed by Rombout Kelder-mans the Younger, and the choir a baroque embellishment added in the 1640's by Jacob Franckaert. If we are able to enter this church, which I have found generally to be locked, we will see a large work by Rubens called *The Miraculous Draught of Fishes*. He painted this in 1618 to hang in the guild house of the fishermen, a building we will shortly have an opportunity to admire.

At Onze-Lieve-Vrouwstraat 64, opposite the north portal of the church, stands a once hand-some house, now mouldering, called **Hemelrijck**

211

(The Kingdom of Heaven). A bas relief showing Adam and Eve in Paradise gives this house its name. Dating from about 1525, Hemelrijck is designed in an intriguing transitional style that combines elements of late gothic and early renaissance. Seen from afar it looks like a gothic house, but examined in detail it proves to be decorated with renaissance arabesques and griffins.

We now head down to the River Dijle by 't Plein, a narrow lane opposite this house. A quiet quay called **Zoutwerf** (Salt Quay), where salt for curing fish was once unloaded, leads along the waterfront. This used to be a bustling quay, but it is now rare to see even a rowing boat on the Dijle. Some attractive quayside buildings have survived, however, including at Nos. 7 and 8 two early 16th-century houses with jettied wooden façades. The magnificent guild house of the fishermen at No. 5 dates from 1530-35. A beautiful gilded carving of a salmon above the entrance gives this house its name, **De Zalm**. One of the earliest and most beautiful renaissance buildings in Flanders, its most striking feature is the superimposition of three architectural orders. This arrangement of columns is entirely in accordance with Italian theories of architecture, although the overcrowded decoration betrays the hand of a northern renaissance architect. We also see a lingering attachment to the gothic, for example in the tall, narrow gable. Once again we are looking at a transitional style of building, neither quite free of the gothic, nor entirely at ease in the renaissance style.

On reaching the 13th-century Grootbrug, we turn left down Guldenstraat to enter **Korenmarkt**, the corn market. No. 8 was the home in the 16th century of a wine merchant, who gave it the enticing late gothic watchtower at the rear. In the 17th century the house was bought by the guild of crossbowmen, and a symbolic iron crossbow was added to the tower, together with gold-tipped arrows on the façade. The figure above the splendid baroque portal is St George; he was, for no very obvious reason, the patron saint of the crossbowmen. Korenmarkt 6, a weather-beaten baroque building, is nowadays occupied by a carillon manufacturer.

There is little else to detain us on this square,

so let us retrace our steps, then turn left down Van Beethovenstraat. A large brewery looms over the narrow street, filling the air with a warm yeasty smell. We may wonder why this dingy street is named after the German composer. The reason is that Beethoven's grandfather was born in Mechelen: hence the name is van Beethoven, not von. There is said to be a stone tablet with Beethoven's death mask on it, somewhere on the brewery wall, but I have failed to find its whereabouts. The one memento I have seen is an abandoned night club called the Beethoven.

This street brings us back to the River Dijle, here overlooked by a ragged fringe of decaying buildings. At the time of writing there were nevertheless some promising signs of renovation along the water's edge.

We want to look at three houses in particular that have survived in this quiet corner of Mechelen. They overlook the revolving iron bridge at the end of **Haverwerf** (Oats Quay). The house at No. 23 is a most remarkable building called the **Duivelshuis** (Devil's House). It was constructed in 1519 in the curious transitional style that we have already encountered. Its jettied wooden façade, pierced by leaded glass windows, is unmistakably Gothic. But look now at the twelve wooden satyrs decorating the window mullions. Whoever carved these strange goat-like figures was obviously in touch with the ideas of the renaissance. Originally this house was called the Prodigal Son after the scene decorating the wooden frieze on the door lintel. But later it became known as the Devils' House, which is indeed a far more fitting title for this dark and mysterious dwelling. The name also contrasts nicely with that of its neighbour to the right, which is called **Paradijs**. Recently repainted in vivid medieval colours, Paradijs is another example of transitional architecture from the 1520's. It takes its name from the two splendid, though much weathered, bas reliefs showing the Tree of Knowledge, and Adam and Eve in Paradise. This house is almost contemporary with Hemelrijck, which illustrated the same theme, clearly a popular notion then.

Our wanderings along the Dijle end here, and we now cross the iron bridge and turn right along

213

Persoonshoek. No. 9, the former 16th-century refuge of the Cistercian abbey at Villers, was in a sad state of decay the last time I passed this way. Refuges - of which there are several in Mechelen - were built by rural abbeys and monasteries as safe havens for monks in troubled times.

Turning right along Drabstraat brings us to the **Vismarkt** (the fishmarket), where fish is still very much in evidence. Ijzerenleen (Iron Avenue), upon which we emerge, derives its name from the double row of iron railings that once, centuries ago, enclosed a canal. We eventually turn left up this elegant street, but before doing so I recommend a short detour straight ahead down Lange Schipstraat to obtain a magnificent view of De Zalm on the opposite quay.

Back on Ijzerenleen, we will see an attractive gothic building at the far end, formerly the **Schepenhuis** (Town Hall). Standing opposite the flight of stairs, we can distinguish the original 13th-century town hall to the left from the ornate 14th-century Brabant gothic town hall added on at right angles. The Grote Raad met in this building from 1474 to 1618.

Standing where we are, we need only turn and look left to see a third town hall on the opposite side of Schoenmarkt, begun in the 14th century but not completed until the 16th century. The present town hall - Mechelen's fourth - occupies a beautiful building on Grote Markt that we will look at later; its predecessor on Schoenmarkt is now the main post office.

Before entering the cathedral, which is our next concern, we might pause on a café terrace to prepare ourselves for the visit. To our right lies Grote Markt, where the most convivial cafés in Mechelen are situated. The café 't Voske at No. 36 enjoys the best view of the cathedral, but any other would do just as well.

From Grote Markt, I suggest that we take an indirect route to the cathedral for a succession of striking views of its majestic medieval architecture. Leaving Grote Markt on the north side along Frederik de Merodestraat, we turn left along Schoolstraat, passing the 16th-century **Koraalhuis**, once a school for choristers. Upon emerging on St Romboutskerkhof, formerly a cemetery, we head down the attractive lane at the back of the choir to enter the cathedral by the south portal.

Begun in the 13th century in an early gothic style, **St Romboutskathedraal** was completed by the 14th century. However, a fire in 1342 destroyed the building, and it was subsequently rebuilt in Brabant high gothic style by Jan van Osy. Its west tower is one of the most beautiful works of late gothic architecture in Flanders. It was planned as the tallest spire in the world and, had it been completed, would have reached a height of 167 metres. However, construction came to a standstill in the 1520's, when the tower had only got to 97 metres. Even in its unfinished state, some 26 metres lower than the cathedral spire at Antwerp, Mechelen's west tower is a magnificent architectural achievement, once praised by Vauban, Louis XIV's military architect, as the eighth wonder of the world. Its construction, which was funded by donations from pilgrims who flocked to the city to receive indulgences, was carried out by three successive generations of architects of the Keldermans family of Mechelen. Andries Keldermans the Elder

began this great work in 1452, laying down a massive buttressed base. Anthonis Keldermans took over from his father in 1481, and in 1488 was succeeded in turn by his son, Rombout Keldermans, who supervised the building work until about 1520, when the project was suddenly abandoned. The construction of the third tier had by then already started. The reason for the stoppage has never properly been understood; but whether for lack of funds or some other reason, it must have struck the younger Keldermans a bitter blow. The unused stone shipped to Mechelen remained in the masons' yard at the foot of the tower until 1583, when the troops of William of Orange carried it off for use in the construction of the new Dutch citadel town of Willemstad.

The interior of the cathedral is extraordinarily spacious and lofty, especially the nave, which is built of a gleaming white sandstone. The intricate patterns of stonework in the clerestory of the choir are strikingly beautiful. There are, as always in Belgium, baroque additions which we might prefer not to be there, but the spirit of the Counter-Reformation is fortunately restrained here. The pulpit, though, is an outrageously inappropriate baroque intrusion brought here from a Norbertine monastery in Mechelen. The work of Michiel van der Voort, it illustrates St Norbert's dramatic conversion, with animals scattering in terror as the lightning flashes.

The principal painting in the cathedral is a *Crucifixion* by Sir Anthony van Dyck. Painted in 1627, it hangs in the south transept on a large altar that partly conceals an intriguing Gothic fresco. Born in Antwerp in 1599, van Dyck was a pupil in Rubens' atelier. Although he lived intermittently in Antwerp, van Dyck worked mainly in England, where he painted numerous portraits of English monarchs and nobles, including a famous equestrian portrait of Charles I which hangs in London's National Gallery.

The interior of this great cathedral tells much about Mechelen's past. A chapel in the ambulatory, for example, contains a memorial to several local priests who died resisting the Germans during the First World War. Another chapel in the north aisle commemorates the Malines Conversations organised by Cardinal Mercier in the 1920's in an attempt to reconcile the Church of England and the Catholic Church.

After exploring the cathedral, we will find numerous places in the neighbourhood for lunch. *Boerenbrood hesp*, a local speciality consisting of an open sandwich with ham and salad, is served in 't Voske and other cafés on Grote Markt. The farms around Mechelen grow most of Belgium's vegetables, including crisp, yellowish-white *witlof*, the Belgian version of endive, which features in local specialities such as *witlofsoep*, a herby cream of endive soup, and *prelaatshaantje*, chicken with endive. This delicacy was apparently discovered quite by accident during the Belgian Revolution in 1830. A farmer who had fled the country leaving some chicory roots in a dark cellar returned home after the fighting was over to discover that the chicory had sprouted shoots. As food was scarce, he fed these to his family, and they lapped them up. The countryside around Mechelen is also dotted with farms cultivating plump, white Belgian asparagus, which is briefly in season in May and June.

Late Gothic Architecture

Fortified by lunch, let us begin our afternoon walk by exploring the pleasant quarters to the west and north of the cathedral, where we come upon quiet cobbled streets and crumbling brick houses. Standing at the base of the cathedral tower, we will see a pretty little chapel opposite, the Heilig Geestkapel, dating from the end of the 13th century. From here Minderbroedersgang, takes us past a former Franciscan chapel. Continuing down Arme Clarenstraat, then right along Nieuwe Beggaardenstraat, we then turn left into Nonnenstraat. This street was once was closed off by one of the gateways of the **Groot Begijnhof**, a convent built in 1259. Though the walls of the Groot Begijnhof have gone, the streets once within its confines still preserve much of the atmosphere of a Begijnhof, with quaint bell-pulls, ancient iron lamp brackets, rose bushes trained up whitewashed walls and tiny statues of saints set in niches (such as a St Ursula smitten by an arrow in Twaalf Apostelenstraat).

If we turn left down Conventstraat, then right into Hoviusstraat, we come upon a captivating street with several splendid baroque portals, such as No. 16. At the end of the street, overshadowing a convent founded in 1620, the brewery Het Anker lends a distinctive smell of hops to the neighbourhood. Built on the site of the Begijnhof infirmary, Het Anker has been brewing strong, dark Mechelen ales since 1421. Nowadays, it produces excellent traditional bottled beers such as *Gouden Carolus* and *Mechelschen Bruynen*, both of which can be sampled in the cafés on Grote Markt.

At the end of Krankenstraat we come upon the weathered baroque frontage of the **Begijnhof-kerk**, built by Jacob Franckaert between 1629 and 1647. The majestic figure of God the Father at the top of the gable was carved by Luc Fayd'herbe. Following Moreelstraat, which runs to the right of the church, then turning left behind the choir, we pass the romantic ruins of a monastery built in the 15th century by the Order of St Alexis, which cared for plague victims. We then walk along St Begga-straat, turn right on Cellebroedersgang and left into Acht Zalighe-denstraat. This quiet Begijnhof lane whose name means 'Street of the Eight Beatitudes' has much the same atmosphere as a Georgian mews. On emerging from it, we turn right along Twaalf Apostelenstraat and again right down Schrijn-straat, which leads out of the precincts of the Groot Begijnhof.

Thereafter we continue straight ahead down Nokerstraat, past a large baroque monastery built by the Order of St Alexis after they had aban-doned the medieval building behind the Begijnhofkerk. Turning right down Gulden-bodemstraat, we pass an interesting enclave of modern architecture, then follow Bornstraatje, turn right on Heembeemd and left along Schutte-vee. This leads to the **St Catharinakerk**, an attractive white sandstone Gothic church with a simple wooden roof. There are several fine details within, including 17th-century baroque confes-sionals and a remarkable pulpit in the form of an overgrown classical ruin. This was designed by Thomas Verhaegen in 1774 and cost, according to a small brass plaque attached, 1,554 guilders.

If, on leaving the church, we turn left along St Katelijnekerkhof, we come upon a lane called Kerkstraatje that leads us to Kanunnik de Decker-straat. There we turn left, then again left at the Maria Magdalenakapel, to enter a little square. A small portal on the right leads into the **Klein Begijnhof**, an unexpected and delightful convent. But it is indeed *klein* (small) and we soon emerge once again on Kanunnik de Deckerstraat. Oppo-site is a handsome 15th-century building designed in late gothic style, with alternating courses of bricks and white sandstone. It was built as a refuge for monks from the Norbertine monastery of Tongerloo, which lies to the east of Mechelen. The building is now occupied by the Gaspard de Wit tapestry workshop, which can be visited on Saturdays at 10.30am.

Continuing down Schoutetstraat, we pass another refuge, built in the 16th century by the Benedictine abbey at St Truiden. There is a striking view, like a Flemish Primitive painting, from a bridge a few steps to the right on Goswin de Stassartstraat. The ivy-clad brick walls overlook a stretch of stagnant water resembling thick pea soup, and called, accordingly, Groen Waterke (Green Water).

We now cross the road and turn down a narrow passage called Klapgat that leads to the **St Janskerk**. This simple white sandstone Gothic church contains a triptych painted by Rubens in 1616-9 of the *Adoration of the Magi*. Isabella Brant, Rubens' first wife, posed for the Virgin.

On St Janskerkhof we turn right, soon to come upon an attractive garden overlooked by a late gothic palace. If the weather is mild, we might enter the garden and sit on one of the benches in the corner on the right, which will give us another glimpse of the beautiful cathedral tower.

When we leave the garden, we should turn left into Frederik de Merodestraat. This takes us past the **Koninklijk Beiaardschool** (Royal Carillon School) on the corner. Sometimes a student can be glimpsed within practicing on the carillon keyboard, which is operated by hammering the wooden keys with one's fists. The school has its own set of bells hung in a 16th-century octagonal watchtower.

Our next destination is the municipal museum at Frederik de Merodestraat 65. This is situated in the **Hof van Busleyden**, a late gothic town house begun in 1503 by Anthonis Keldermans the Elder and completed by his son Rombout in 1508. It was commissioned by Hieronymus van Busleyden, who trained as a lawyer at the universities of Leuven and Bologna, and moved to Mechelen after being appointed by Philip the Fair to serve on the Grote Raad. Van Busleyden was a leading Flemish humanist whose friends included Erasmus, Thomas More and Pieter Gilles. Thomas More, who stayed here in 1515, was so impressed that he wrote three poems in praise of the house and its collections of books and musical instruments. More's *Utopia*, first published in Leuven in 1516, begins with a dedication to van Busleyden written by Pieter Gilles.

In 1517 Erasmus, who was a frequent guest here, persuaded van Busleyden to provide in his will for the foundation of a *Collegium Trilingue* in Leuven, that would offer a humanistic education in Latin, Greek and Hebrew. This came to pass sooner than expected, since in the same year, while on a diplomatic mission to Spain on behalf of Charles V, van Busleyden fell ill in Bordeaux and, much to the distress of Erasmus, died there aged 47.

In 1620 the Hof van Busleyden was converted by Wenceslas Coeberger into a Mons Pietas, one of the charitable lending banks established in Flemish cities under the Archduchess Isabella. The quaintly named Berg van Barmhartigheid (Mountain of Charity) was still in operation in the early years of this century. After being badly damaged in the First World War, it was rebuilt to house the municipal museum.

Fortunately, the renaissance dining room (No. 12) has survived more or less intact. This lovely little room, where van Busleyden may have entertained Erasmus and More, was decorated with murals by Bernard van Orley and Michiel Coxie the Elder in 1507-17. Tragically, the murals were badly damaged by the bombardment, but copies made in 1916 give some impression of their strange beauty. One of them depicts Belshazzar's Feast, at which the king of Babylon, entertaining his wives and lascivious concubines, is suddenly terrified by the message of doom written on the wall by a disembodied hand.

The collection of paintings, architectural fragments and furniture in this museum provides some interesting insights into Mechelen's history. A painting in room 5, for example, depicts an incident, perhaps apocryphal, in which the townspeople mistook the moon shining through the tracery of the cathedral tower for a fire, and promptly attempted to extinguish it. A 17th-century painting in the same room depicts the Groot Begijnhof, with 46 miniature scenes illustrating the works of the Beguines, which ranged from lace-making to caring for the sick. In room

6 we see a set of six remarkable 16th-century consoles from the guild house of the swordsmen, and some plans and views of the town.

One of the highlights in the collection is the series of sixteen panels of the *Legend of St Victor* painted by an anonymous master in 1510-20 for a convent in Mechelen. The scenes from the life of this minor saint of the second century are set amidst fantastic architecture, with beautiful costumes and expressive faces. The last painting of the series, in which angels receive the martyred body of St Victor, is particularly moving.

Room 11 is decorated with modern stained glass windows depicting historical episodes, including Erasmus and Thomas More visiting the house. Notice also the fragments of gilt leather and the renaissance fireplace rescued from the palace of Margaret of Austria. The upstairs rooms, though containing little of great importance, are nevertheless worth poking around in.

After exploring the museum, we head down Biest, the street opposite the carillon school, to the **Veemarkt**. At No. 3, next to the baroque church of St Pieter en Paulus, stands the **Palace of Margaret of York**, or what is left of it. The palace was renovated in 1480 for Margaret of York, who retired to Mechelen after the death of her husband in 1477, and it was here that she raised Mary of Burgundy's children. Facing us is the 16th-century **Palace of Margaret of Austria**. If we now walk through to the second courtyard of this beautiful building, we will find a bench in the gothic arcade to sit and read about the palace.

Margaret of Austria was one of the children of Mary of Burgundy raised in Mechelen. Only two years old when her mother died in 1482, Margaret was immediately ensnared in the complex web of medieval politics. In 1483, under the terms of the Peace of Atrecht, this tiny toddler was married off by her father, Maximilian of Austria, to the future Charles VIII of France. Margaret spent the next eight years in the château of Amboise on the Loire, but when political allegiances altered the marriage was dissolved to permit Charles VIII to marry Anne of Brittany. Margaret was sent back to the Netherlands, and her father then married her off to Don Juan of Castile in the hope of combining the Austrian and

221

Spanish Hapsburg territories. Margaret, then aged 17, was sent by ship to Spain for the wedding. But this scheme, too, failed when Don Juan died nine months later. Undeterred, Maximilian arranged a third marriage with Philibert the Handsome, the Duke of Savoy. Margaret, who had known Philibert since her childhood days at Amboise, spent three happy years at the château of Pont d'Ain in Burgundy. However, tragedy struck again in 1504 when the handsome duke died of pleurisy at the age of only 24. One year later, Margaret commissioned the Flemish architect Loys van Boghem to build a church in memory of Philibert at Brou, on the outskirts of Bourg-en-Bresse. It is one of the most beautiful churches in France, built in a florid late gothic style with hints here and there of the renaissance. Much could be said elsewhere in praise of its choir stalls and its memorial effigies.

In 1506 Margaret was compelled to leave Brou and return to the Netherlands because of the death in Spain of her brother, Philip the Fair. Having inherited the Hapsburg territories upon the death of Maximilian in 1494, Philip had married Joanna of Castile two years later, thereby realising his father's ambition of uniting the Spanish and Austrian Hapsburg possessions. After his death, Margaret - who by that time had abandoned all hope of finding a faithful or robust husband - took charge of her nephews and nieces. In 1507 she was appointed Regent of the Netherlands on behalf of the eldest son of Philip the Fair, the future Charles V.

Margaret chose to establish her court at Mechelen, rather than Brussels, and moved into the palace of Margaret of York, where she had spent the first two years of her life. Four years later, she commissioned Rombout Keldermans to design a new palace in ornate late gothic style. However, only the rear wing, where we are now sitting, was built. It seems that Margaret became fascinated with renaissance art and architecture in the second decade of the 16th century, and in 1515 she commissioned an outsider, Guyot de Beaugrant, to complete the palace in the most modern style. It was one of the earliest renaissance buildings in the Netherlands, and symbolised the end of the Keldermans' late gothic.

Margaret's palace in Mechelen became a centre of northern renaissance art and music, and here she was visited by many of the great artists of the day, including Albrecht Dürer, Pieter Coecke van Aelst, Jan Gossaert, Jan Mostaert and Bernard van Orley, who painted this melacholy portrait of her.

Margaret died in 1530 of gangrene of the foot and her entrails were buried in Mechelen, while her heart was taken to a convent in Bruges. Two years later her body was carried to Brou to be buried in the exquisite chapel she had built in memory of Philibert. With the death of Margaret, Mechelen's brief period of splendour was over; the city became another Bruges, another dead city of Flanders. Philip II attempted to save Mechelen by elevating the city to an archbishopric in 1559. Antoine Perrenot, the first Archbishop, lived for the next two years in Margaret of Austria's palace, but was then recalled to Spain to assist Philip II in his campaign of religious terror and never returned to Mechelen. The palace was occupied by the Grote Raad from 1618 to 1794, and is now used as a court of law.

We can leave by the rear portal, turning right and again right to reach Keizerstraat, then returning to Grote Markt along Befferstraat. It is worth pausing in the long gothic arcade on Befferstraat for a marvellous view of the cathedral tower soaring above a cluster of baroque gables.

It is now perhaps time for a coffee or a beer at one of the cafés on the square. We might choose **In de Beer** (At the Bear) at No. 32 for its historical associations. A tavern formerly stood here called 'At the Angel', which Charles V once visited to slake his thirst after a day in the saddle. The Emperor was so dirty, however, that the landlady refused to admit him, until a passing soldier intervened on his behalf. Charles V decided that the tavern didn't deserve the name 'The Angel' and ordered the landlady to change it to 'The Bear'.

While sitting here, sipping perhaps a dark Mechelen beer, we can study the interesting range of buildings on the east side of the square (photographed opposite in about 1911). In the middle we see the remains of a 14th-century cloth hall, modelled on the Halle in Bruges. The building was gutted by fire in 1342 and the planned belfry abandoned, leaving just the sad stump we see here. The two pepperpot corner turrets and the gable window were added in the 16th century in an attempt to jolly up the hall's appearance.

The florid building to the left of the belfry, whose arcade we have already walked down, is now the **Stadhuis** (Town Hall). It was originally commissioned by Charles V to serve as a new palace for the Grote Raad, which at that time was still convening in the old town hall at the end of Ijzerenleen. Designed by Rombout Keldermans the Younger, the grand building in the photograph was begun in 1526 on the site of the north wing of the gutted cloth hall. All did not go according to plan however, and all is not as it seems. Work was suddenly halted in 1534 owing to financial difficulties, and the palace was left unfinished. How very unfinished is clear from the photograph on page 226, taken only about eleven years before the other.

For Rombout Keldermans it must have been a very disheartening experience. For the third time

Malines — Hôtel de Ville et anciennes Halles aux draps.
Mechelen — Stadhuis en oude Lakenhallen.

MALINES. — L'ancien Parlement ND Phot.

in this brief day in Mechelen we have come across Keldermans hard at work on projects that were to be suddenly taken away from him. His tower for St Romboutskathedraal was abandoned for reasons we can only guess at, with only a third of it built. Fashion dictated that he be replaced as architect to Margaret of Austria at an early stage in the construction of her palace; one wing only was built. It must have seemed to him that only the shadow of his Stadhuis would ever be seen. What he could hardly know, however, is that with this building at least he would be vindicated - though not until some 380 years after his death.

We can see what actually happened from this photograph. In 1551 the abandoned building was divided into shops, and by the end of the 19th-century it had become a dilapidated ruin, apparently serving as a shabby inn. This was clearly undignified, given Belgium's new position in the world. In an astonishing campaign of restoration, Rombout Keldermans' original architectural drawings were used to construct the beautiful white sandstone edifice we see today.

Who is to say that this is not the original building, or that it is not a true example of medieval architecture? Many medieval buildings took generations to complete. In the Burgundian Netherlands, as indeed in Germany, much was left unfinished as the glory of the middle ages was tarnished by the terrible history of the 16th and 17th centuries. What more natural, one might suppose, than to celebrate the growing wealth and self-confidence of Léopold's Belgium by bringing to fruition the plans of that earlier golden age of Belgian history? We have seen other examples already in our walks, and there are plenty of parallels elsewhere: the spires of Cologne Cathedral, for instance, were only topped out in 1876.

On leaving Grote Markt, we can make our way back to the station down Bruul, past the imposing baroque frontage of **Onze-Lieve-Vrouw van Leliendaal**, a Norbertine convent designed by Luc Fayd'herbe in 1662-72. If there is time, we might stroll into the **Kruidtuin** (Botanical Gardens), once the site of a monastery belonging to the Order of Teutonic Knights. There are not many botanical specimens to be seen, but it is a pleasant spot by the River Dijle, with an interesting view of the baroque church of **Onze-Lieve-Vrouw van Hanswijk** opposite. We then cross an attractive neoclassical square and five minutes later are back at the station.

Brussels

Brussels

Of all the market squares in Flanders, none is more beautiful than Grand'Place in Brussels, with its splendid entourage of baroque houses laden with gilded sculptures. Brussels also boasts numerous convivial Flemish restaurants warmed by blazing fires, where we can feast on hearty slabs of steak or overflowing pots of steaming mussels.

Yet Brussels is not at all a typical Flemish city. Nor is it truly French, despite the fact that most of the population are French speaking. Brussels is a unique city, whose identity has been shaped by numerous European cultures: the Burgundians, who made Brussels a city of artistic excellence in the 15th century; the Spanish, who built many of its baroque churches and guild houses in the 17th century; and the Austrians, who

laid out elegant squares and parks in the 18th century. The confluence of so many cultures gives Brussels a fascinating diversity of buildings, parks, cafés and restaurants. Even in the most unpromising of streets, we will often encounter an unexpected delight, such as Cirio, a beautiful café reminiscent of old Vienna in Rue de la Bourse, or the secret, nameless park below the Rue du Parme, with its strange mock-classical ruins.

As in the case of so many Flemish cities, the name Brussels has an etymology that refers to its watery origins. **Brucsella**, as the city was originally called, means 'dwelling on the marsh' in Old Dutch. According to popular legend, the city was founded in the 6th century by St Géry, a French missionary who built a chapel on an island in the River Senne. The 'dwelling on the marsh' prospered because of its favourable location on the important medieval trading route between the North Sea and the Rhine. This route, now followed by the E40 motorway and the Hans Memling Eurocity train, linked the cities of Bruges, Ghent, Brussels, Leuven, Liège, Aachen and Cologne.

In the late 10th century Duke Charles of Lower Lorraine built a castle on the site of St Géry's chapel. The lands of Lower Lorraine later passed to the counts of Leuven, who in the 11th century erected a new castle on the heights to the south of the valley of the Senne. This move marked the beginning of the social division of Brussels: craftsmen and shopkeepers lived in the Lower Town, while the dukes and nobles inhabited the Upper Town.

Brussels became particularly important under the dukes of Burgundy, whose possessions included the former lands of the counts of Leuven. In 1430, Philip the Good decided to move the Burgundian court from Dijon to the Upper Town of Brussels. The knights and officials of his court were all French speaking, and so the Upper Town became an enclave of French culture and manners. But in the Lower Town, in the guild houses and markets around Grand'Place, Dutch continued to be spoken. The fatal frontier between Latin and Germanic cultures therefore cut straight through the city of Brussels, roughly along the line of the Boulevards de l'Empereur, de Berlaimont and Pacheo.

During the brief but spectacular period of Burgundian rule, the economy of the Lower Town was increasingly devoted to the production of luxury goods, as the Burgundians had an insatiable appetite for flamboyant gothic architecture, rich tapestries, exotic costumes and gargantuan feasts. Unfortunately not much Burgundian gothic architecture has survived in Brussels; we have to go to Bruges for that. But the museums of Brussels contain some exquisite works of Burgundian gothic art, such as the paintings of Roger van der Weyden at the Musée d'Art Ancien and the sculpture in the Musée d'Art et d'Histoire.

Charles V's formal abdication in 1555 proved a decisive turning point in the history of the Low

Countries. Philip II, Charles V's son, inherited his father's territories in Spain, the Netherlands, Italy and the New World. Austere and devout, he soon embarked on a pitiless policy of religious persecution in the Low Countries, which eventually sparked off the Dutch Revolt.

The prolonged war against Spain began in 1566 as a mild protest at the wedding in Brussels of Alexander Farnese, then Prince of Parma. Several hundred nobles soured the festivities by petitioning his mother, Margaret of Parma - Charles V's sister and the Governor of the Netherlands at the time - to adopt a more tolerant approach to the Protestants. This petition stung Philip II into ordering the execution of Counts Egmont and Hoorn in Grand'Place in 1568, and the Dutch Revolt erupted soon afterwards.

At first Brussels was held by the Protestant rebels led by William of Orange, known as 'the Silent', but in 1585 the city fell to the Spanish army led by Alexander Farnese. From then on Brussels was the capital of the Spanish Netherlands. However, it was in no sense a sparkling capital under Spanish rule, except for a brief period from 1596-1621 under the Archduke Albert and Archduchess Isabella.

The period of Spanish rule finally ended in 1706 in the War of the Spanish Succession, when the city was captured by the Duke of Marlborough. Under the terms of the Treaty of Utrecht of 1713, the former Spanish Netherlands passed to the Austrian Hapsburgs. The new governors were at first unpopular, and provoked an uprising in 1719. This was crushed, and Frans Anneessens, the leader of the guilds of Brussels, was beheaded on Grand'Place. A new era of prosperity began in 1744 when Charles, Duke of Lorraine, was appointed Governor by his sister-in-law, the Empress Maria Theresa. He embarked on an ambitious plan to restyle Brussels as a northern Vienna, and several elegant neoclassical schemes were completed, such as the Place Royale and the Parc de Bruxelles in the Upper Town, and the square now known as the Place des Martyrs in the Lower Town.

In 1795 the French Republican army entered Brussels. All the street names were translated into French, often erroneously. The French were driven out of Brussels in 1814, although one year later Napoleon came close to recapturing the city. He was defeated by the combined forces of Wellington and Blücher at Waterloo, some twelve miles south of the city. Under the terms of the treaties of Vienna and London, the Kingdom of the Netherlands was established under King William I. This led briefly to the reunification of the old Burgundian Netherlands, but the two Netherlands had developed quite differently since the 16th century and the match soon proved disastrous. The event that sparked off the Belgian Revolution was, surprisingly, a performance of the opera *La Muette de Portici* by Auber. As a duet about patriotism was being sung, some members of the audience stormed out of the Théâtre de la Monnaie and began to riot in the streets. It was a curious beginning to 'that little Biedermeier slapstick war', as the Dutch writer Jeroen Brouwers once described the Belgian revolution.

Prince Léopold of Saxe-Coburg, the noble chosen to rule the new state of Belgium, was a German prince and a favourite uncle of Queen Victoria. In his efforts to create a prosperous Belgian state he looked particularly to Victorian Britain for inspiration. His achievements were widely approved there; a character in Thackeray's *Vanity Fair* praises Brussels as 'one of the gayest and most brilliant little capitals in Europe'.

Léopold I was succeeded by his son, the Duke of Brabant, who became Léopold II in 1865. He seems to have been an unpromising future king, judging from Madame de Metternich's description of his marriage to Marie-Henrietta of Austria as the union of 'a stable boy and a nun, and by nun I mean the Duke of Brabant'. Yet Léopold II (seen overleaf later in life) proved to be an exceptionally vigorous, if not entirely virtuous ruler. He developed the Belgian Congo as a virtual private colony and used the profits from his ventures there to rebuild Brussels on a truly heroic scale. The great picture galleries and museums of Brussels, the boulevards and arcades, the Palais de Justice and the Parc du Cinquantenaire, were all built during his 44-year-long reign. Most of these projects benefited the Upper Town, the aristocratic French quarter of the city. Indeed,

it is quite likely that the old Flemish areas of Brussels would have vanished altogether had not Burgomaster Charles Buls campaigned strenuously for their preservation. Without these Flemish quarters the character of Brussels would now be quite different; it would be a dull and disappointing city of formal neoclassical buildings, like the cities painted by Paul Delvaux.

Léopold's Brussels provided an attractive refuge for exiled French writers, as its boulevards, cafés and arcades gave it something of the allure of Paris. Many French exiles in Brussels were political refugees from Napoleon III, including Victor Hugo and Pierre-Joseph Proudhon. They were carrying on a tradition initiated after 1815 by the French revolutionaries exiled by the Bourbon restoration, most famous of whom was the painter Jacques-Louis David, who died in Brussels, and whose famous painting of Marat murdered in his bath now hangs in the Musée d'Art Ancien. Others fled here from France for less laudable reasons, such as Alexandre Dumas, who simply used Brussels as a convenient bolthole from his creditors.

By the end of the 19th century Brussels had become one of the most scintillating cities in Europe, rivalling Paris and Vienna for glamorous cafés and dazzling art nouveau architecture. However, Brussels' *Belle Epoque* came to a sad and sudden end when the German army occupied the city in the First World War. The Burgomaster of Brussels, Adolphe Max, was deported for stubbornly resisting the Germans, and in 1915 the courageous British nurse Edith Cavell was executed by the Germans for helping Allied soldiers to escape to the neutral Netherlands. The firing range where Edith Cavell was shot can still be visited, down a cobbled lane off Rue Colonel Bourg, not far from the Belgian broadcasting tower.

Brussels regained some of its cosmopolitan sparkle in the 1920's and 1930's, when many apartment blocks in art deco style were built on the grand boulevards. The most imposing of these was the Residence Palace at 155 Rue de la Loi, a luxury apartment complex built in 1926, complete with a restaurant, swimming pool and theatre. After the Second World War, however, Brussels was again in the doldrums. The 1958 World Fair gave a boost to the economy, and one year later Brussels became the capital of the recently founded European Economic Community (now the European Union), an organisation created in 1967 by the fusion of the European Economic Community, the European Coal and Steel Community and Euratom. The Berlaymont Building, overlooking Rond Point Schuman, used to house the offices of the European Commission but now lies empty while asbestos ceiling panels are removed. The European Parliament has its Brussels base nearby in a magnificent new complex overlooking Parc Léopold. Officially known as the European Congress Centre, the building has been dubbed the Caprice des Dieux on account of its alleged resemblance to a distinctive French cheese. Thus Brussels continues to prove its preference for food over politics.

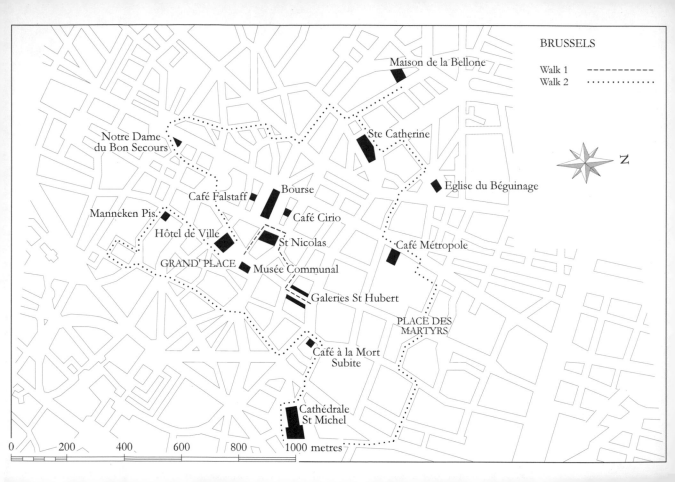

BRUSSELS

Walk 1 ————————
Walk 2 ··············

Maison de la Bellone

Ste Catherine

Notre Dame
du Bon Secours

Eglise du Béguinage

Café Falstaff   Bourse

Manneken Pis.   Café Cirio

Hôtel de Ville   St Nicolas   Café Métropole

GRAND' PLACE   Musée Communal

Galeries St Hubert

PLACE DES
MARTYRS

Café à la Mort
Subite

Cathédrale
St Michel

0   200   400   600   800   1000 metres

Grand'Place and its Neighbourhood

For our first glimpse of this convivial and likeable city, I propose that we stroll to **Grand'Place**. The finest approach to this square is, I think, down Rue des Harengs (next to the tourist office at 61 Rue du Marché aux Herbes), then right along Rue du Poivre, and left into Rue Chair et Pain. The advantage of this convoluted and secret route is the thrilling view it offers of the medieval spire of the town hall framed by the tall buildings on Rue Chair et Pain.

We will cross Grand'Place several times during our peregrinations in Brussels for, just as Brussels is (as it boasts) the crossroads of Europe, so Grand'Place is the crossroads of Brussels. The square is a source of inexhaustible pleasure, its character changing at different hours and in different seasons. Grand'Place is particularly enchanting at twilight on a crisp winter's evening, when the last rays of the sun touch the gilded details of the gables, and the cafés lure us inside with their blazing fires, gleaming brass fittings and rich red cherry-flavoured *kriek* beers. Once darkness has fallen, floodlights transform the square into a magnificent theatre. Here, according to John Motley, the 19th-century American historian of the Dutch Revolt, 'so many tragedies, so many scenes of violence have been played out'. On Sunday mornings, Grand'Place is filled with the unexpected sounds of cocks crowing and geese cackling. This is when the weekly bird market is held, and locals browse around the cages hoping to pick up a green parrot, a brace of grouse or even a pet swan. The man to look out for deals in Harz canaries, which are (or so he claims) the only birds in the world that can sing without opening their beaks. These maestros - descended from the 17th-century singing canaries of Nuremberg - are bright yellow in colour, though you do not buy a Harz canary for its colour. Good grief, no. That would be like buying a Stradivarius because it matched your carpet. You buy a Harz canary for one thing only and that is the song. Each canary is sold complete with a small report card on which are listed its accomplishments in nine different skills. There is a hint of the Eurovision song contest here, combined perhaps with the more tasteful episodes in a Miss Belgium award. The judges give points for such achievements as whistling, trilling, warbling and general deportment. The higher the score, the more the bird is worth. A virtuoso warbler, with above-average trilling and the deportment of a supermodel, is likely to cost more than a thousand francs. You could very probably buy a box of quails for the same money, but you do not get much of a song out of a quail.

The magnificent architecture of Grand'Place is the proud creation of the guilds of Brussels. The majority of the houses on the square were rebuilt soon after 1695, when much of the Lower Town was devastated by Louis XIV's artillery, commanded by Marshal de Villeroi. Some 3,630 houses and 16 churches in the Lower Town were destroyed in this attack. The print opposite shows the sorry state of Grand'Place after the bombardment. To the left is the Hôtel de Ville, which miraculously survived the attack, while opposite is the side wall of the badly damaged Maison du Roi.

The guild houses were rapidly rebuilt in a vivacious Italo-Flemish baroque style, reminiscent of the buildings in Antwerp designed by Rubens in the early 17th century. But the buildings on Grand'Place are even more ostentatious, flashing with gilded details, and bristling with pinnacles and statues.

The best place to begin an exploration of Grand'Place is the **Hôtel de Ville** (Town Hall), which is some three centuries older than the guild houses. In 1402 Duke Wenceslas of Luxembourg laid the first stone of the wing to the left of the belfry, designed by Jacob van Thienen and Jan Bornoy in an ornate Brabant gothic style. The wing to the right of the belfry was not originally

planned and the constraints of the site meant that it had to be shorter than its counterpart. Charles the Bold, Duke of Burgundy, laid the first stone in 1444 and it was completed a mere four years later. In 1455 the town hall was embellished with a slender, elegant belfry designed by Jan van Ruysbroeck. Victor Hugo, who had the enviable good fortune to lodge in a hotel at 27 Grand'Place, praised the belfry in 1837 as 'a jewel comparable to the spire of Chartres'.

The town hall is encrusted with effigies of dukes and duchesses, and the upper tier is trimmed with a delicate border of masonry. The effect, especially at night, is like a lace screen; so fragile is the appearance that we might imagine a puff of wind blowing away the entire edifice. Yet we know from our 1695 print that the building survived the French bombardment, and so it cannot be as flimsy as it appears.

The arcade to the right of the belfry is particularly delightful to investigate; the 15th-century masons have decorated the capitals with amusing little scenes, the most enigmatic of which shows people busily shovelling three-legged stools. The preliminary drawing for the capital - probably produced in Roger van der Weyden's studio in about 1450 - is now owned by New York's Metropolitan Museum of Art. The curious scene is probably a whimsical play on the name of a local building, De Scupstoel, which literally means 'the shovel chair'. Another building known as De Papenkelder (The Pope's Cellar) is treated to a similar gentle mockery.

Let us now walk around the square in a clockwise direction, beginning with the row of six houses to the right of the Hôtel de Ville. We are lucky enough to be able to see the square as it was in 1737, thanks to a set of drawings by a local artist F. J. de Rons. Reproduced opposite is his view of these six guild houses, Nos. 1 to 7, and very little seems to have changed since then. The house on the far left (No. 7), known as **La Maison du Renard** (The House of the Fox), was designed in 1699 for the guild of haberdashers and pedlars, whose patron, St Christopher, is perched atop the gable. The trading activities of this guild are amusingly illustrated by the cherubs in the four bas reliefs on the ground floor, while their far-

het brouwers huijs   het cuijpers huijs   het ant schutgulden huijs   het timmermans huijs   het vettewariers huijs   het bakers huijs

flung travels are alluded to by four caryatids on the second floor. They represent the Continents then known to exist; Africa is shown carrying ebony and ivory, Asia bears incense and ivory, America is symbolised by gold, while the figure of Europe is laden with a cornucopia of riches. The fifth figure represents Justice.

A certain furniture-maker named Antoon Pastorana designed two of the most remarkable buildings on Grand'Place, at Nos. 4 and 6. A bas relief above the doorway of No. 4 gives **La Maison du Sac** (The House of the Sack) its name. This building was commissioned by the guild of joiners and coopers in 1696. Named Het Timmermans huijs (the carpenters' house) on the drawing, its most impressive feature is a decorative top resembling an ornate baroque cabinet. The following year, Pastorana designed the eccentric **Maison du Cornet** (House of the Horn) at No. 6 for the guild of boatmen. If we turn again to the drawing, we can see that the building is surmounted by an elaborate confection resembling the stern of a 17th-century ship. A bust commemorates the sickly Charles II of Spain,

who was ruler of the Spanish Netherlands at this time. Sea horses and lions add further animation to this extraordinary building.

La Maison de la Louve (The House of the She-wolf) at No. 5, third from the left on the drawing, belonged to the guild of archers. Its name derives from the bas relief above the entrance showing Romulus and Remus being suckled by a she-wolf. Four baroque caryatids on the second floor represent the paired opposites of Truth and Falsehood, Peace and Disorder. The pediment is surmounted by a phoenix rising from the flames, which recalls the repeated rebuilding of this house in the 17th century. It was twice destroyed by fire, but the third building, designed by Pieter Herbosch in 1691, proved sufficiently robust to survive the French artillery bombardment four years later; we can see its four-floor frontage standing amidst the ruins in the 1695 engraving (page 239).

La Brouette (The Wheelbarrow) at No. 3, second from the right on the drawing, is the simplest in this row of six houses. Rebuilt in 1697 by Jan Cosyns, it was once the guild house of the tallow merchants, who traded in candles and oil. The wheelbarrow above the entrance gives the building its name, while on top of the gable is a statue of St Giles, patron saint of the tallow merchants.

La Maison du Roi d'Espagne (The House of the King of Spain) at Nos. 1-2, on the far right of the drawing, was also rebuilt by Jan Cosyns in 1697. Commissioned by the guild of bakers (and hence named Het Beckers huijs on the drawing) it is a palatial building surmounted by a dashing cupola on which the figure of Fame is delicately perched. Six figures on the balustrade represent Energy, Grain, Wind, Fire, Water and Prudence, while above the door is a bust of St Aubert, the patron saint of bakers. The relief in the upper floor again honours Charles II of Spain, who is flanked by Turkish flags and chained prisoners. This magnificent building now houses Brussels' largest café, Le Roi d'Espagne. In contrast to the splendid baroque exterior, the café is convivial and cluttered, with a blazing fire, solid wooden tables and a moth-eaten, stuffed horse. If we decide to visit Le Roi d'Espagne - a favourite with Brussels students and, indeed, almost everyone - we should try to obtain a window table on the mezzanine to enjoy a very attractive view of Grand'Place through the tiny barred windows.

The side of Grand'Place facing the Hôtel de Ville is dominated by the **Maison du Roi** in which the excellent Musée Communal is situated. The museum, devoted to Brussels' art and history, occupies a building known in Flemish as the Broodhuis (Bread House), but in French by the grander title of the Maison du Roi (King's House). The Flemish name is the more accurate, as this site was once occupied by the guild house of the bakers, whereas it was never a royal residence. Early in the reign of Charles V, it was rebuilt in late gothic style, probably by Rombout Keldermans and Domien de Waghemakere, assisted by Hendrik van Pede and Lodewijk van Bodeghem. After being badly damaged in 1695 by the French bombardment, the Maison du Roi was hurriedly rebuilt by Jan Cosyns. By the 19th century the building had fallen into such disrepair that the city authorities resolved to rebuild it. Using historical sources supplemented, where

243

necessary, by conjecture and imagination, Victor Jamaer erected the present building in 1873-95. We see it in this photograph of about 1900, when it was more or less brand new.

The **Musée de la Ville de Bruxelles** - established in the rebuilt Maison du Roi in 1887 - is a marvellous place to while away a rainy afternoon. The ground floor rooms contain a fine collection of Brussels paintings, tapestries, altarpieces, sculpture, furniture and porcelain. The most charming painting is Pieter Bruegel the Elder's *Marriage Procession*, which wonderfully portrays the group of guests attending a country wedding, with an ashen-faced father at the head of the procession glancing back ruefully to his beaming daughter.

The first floor is devoted to a fascinating collection of scale models, maps, topographical paintings and photographs of Brussels, which enable us to grasp something of its complex development. Brussels' history is dominated by destruction, unfortunately, as is vividly illustrated by the series of engravings showing the sorry state of the Lower Town after the bombardment in 1695. We also see a nostalgic series of water-colours of the River Senne threading its way through the old town, before it was buried below the streets like a sewer. Another series of paintings show the Ducal Palace on the heights of Coudenberg, which burned down in 1731, while a watercolour depicts the beautifully named Rue Nuit et Jour, which has also vanished. We also glimpse Brussels as it might have been in an art nouveau drawing illustrating a bold scheme to build an elevated arcade between Boulevard Anspach and Rue Royale. Notice, too, the amusing series of satirical sketches from *Charivari* magazine ridiculing the grandiose schemes of Léopold II. One delightfully irreverent drawing represents the Palais des Beaux-Arts by a group of artists working in an empty space.

If all this conveys a negative impression of destruction and planning disaster, we can immediately restore our faith in Brussels by glancing out of the first-floor windows of the Maison du Roi to see, through a veil of neo-gothic tracery, the rich architecture of Grand'Place. After we have visited the top floor of the museum to look

at the costumes worn by the Manneken Pis, the famous bronze statuette of a urinating boy which stands in the Rue de l'Etuve, we can sit down on the worn stone bench outside the Maison du Roi to admire, as many generations have done, the exquisite spire of the Hôtel de Ville.

Continuing a clockwise tour of Grand'Place, we come to the row of six houses illustrated in the next drawing by de Rons, overleaf. **La Chaloupe d'Or** (The Golden Caravel) at No. 24-25, third from the left on the drawing, was designed in 1695 for the guild of tailors by Willem de Bruyn, architect of several houses on Grand'Place. It is built in a marvellously heavy and unabashedly opulent baroque style which is thrilling to behold on even the greyest of Belgian days. The figure poised on the gable top represents St Bonifacius holding aloft a pair of tailors' scissors, while the guild's patroness, St Barbara, occupies a bull's-eye window above the entrance. A pleasant café named La Chaloupe d'Or now occupies this building. I suggest that we settle ourselves in this café to read the remainder of this chapter. Should we be fortunate enough to secure a table by a

al de huijsen van aen
den hoeck van de
keerijackstraet, tot
aen den hoeck van de
keijserstraet, op de
groote meet,

16 97

window, we may admire the remaining houses on Grand'Place as we sip our coffee.

Two doors down from this café is a **Godiva chocolate shop** (at Nos. 21-22, second house from the right on the drawing). The Godiva Company, founded by Joseph Draps in the 1920's, has recently become an international success, opening glamorous shops in capital cities of the world, where Belgian chocolates are displayed amidst silk and lace as if they were precious gems. About one-third of Godiva's chocolates are still hand-made, and many are flavoured with a generous dash of alcohol.

The adjacent side of Grand'Place is dominated by the **Maison des Ducs de Brabant** (House of the Dukes of Brabant), designed by Willem de Bruyn in 1695. Named after the busts decorating the façade, this magnificent building creates an illusion of grandeur by concealing six guild houses, each three bays wide, behind a monumental baroque frontage. Tucked away in a corner to the right of this house is a tiny building known as 'Fame'. Appropriately enough, the figure of Fame blowing a trumpet, which gives

this house its name, now adorns the entrance to the Brussels Jazz Club.

Maison des Brasseurs is boldly emblazoned in gold letters on the frieze of the brewers' guild house at No. 10. It can be seen in a third drawing by de Rons, on page 249, where it forms the centrepiece of a row of five houses. This portly pile, also designed by Willem de Bruyn, is a masterpiece of baroque gusto, crowned with a staggering weight of ornamentation, including an equestrian statue of Charles of Lorraine hoisted up in 1752. If we look closely at the drawing, which was made 15 years earlier, we will see that the building was then surmounted by a different figure, that of Maximilian Emanuel II of Bavaria, who was Governor of the Spanish Netherlands from 1692 to 1711. Maximilian Emanuel II contributed to the diaspora of Flemish painting by acquiring numerous works by Rubens, which now form some of the highlights of the collection in Munich's Alte Pinakothek.

La Maison du Cygne (The House of the Swan) at No. 9, to the right of the Maison des Brasseurs, was the guild house of the butchers. It was built in 1698 as a private house in a French baroque style, but in 1720 the butchers bought the building and added the bulbous, almost Parisian, mansard roof above the pediment, creating a most unsettling effect. Karl Marx frequented a tavern located in this building during his three years of exile in Brussels, which ended with his expulsion from Belgium in 1848.

The little house at No. 8 named **L'Etoile** (The Star) on the far right of the drawing, surmounted by a star, was once occupied by the city magistrates. If we compare the drawing with the present building, we will see that its former ground floor has been replaced by an open arcade. This represents an elegant solution to a pressing problem that arose in the 19th century, when the lane between this house and the town hall became so thronged with traffic that L'Etoile had to be demolished in 1852. A few years later Burgomaster Charles Buls proposed this ingenious reconstruction, thereby appeasing both the hawks of progress and the doves of conservation.

The arcade contains some curious memorials, including an elaborate monument to Everard 't Serclaes designed in 1902 by Julien Dillens. Three bas reliefs illustrate a famous episode in the 14th century during the Brabant War of Succession. In the uppermost tablet, Everard and his men are scaling the city walls to expel Count Louis de Male, who had staked his claim to Brussels and installed himself in the magistrates' house on Grand'Place. The second scene shows the citizens of Brussels welcoming Duke Wenceslas of Luxembourg, while the bottom tablet illustrates the assassination of Everard some thirty years later by hirelings of the Lord of Gaasbeek. Six centuries have passed since Everard died, yet he is still revered as a saintly martyr. According to a local legend, it brings luck to touch the right arm of the recumbent figure of Everard, which explains the highly polished lustre to his arm. Not everyone, apparently, follows this tradition to the letter, for we can also see a very shiny dog, a gleaming cherub and even a glowing mouse concealed in a garland.

Having looked at Grand'Place, we might think of exploring the streets in the neighbourhood in search of a restaurant or café. One of the most

van aen den hoeck van de
koeijmaeckers straedt, tot
aen den hoeck van de
sterstraedt op de groote
meert· 1729

engaging restaurants in Brussels is Chez Jean, just off Grand'Place at 6 Rue des Chapeliers. Chez Jean has been serving steaks drenched in butter, accompanied by enormous servings of *frites*, since 1931.

The tangle of medieval lanes to the east of Grand'Place known as the **Quartier de l'Ilot Sacré** is the liveliest area of Brussels after nightfall. It is also the most European quarter of the city, for here there are restaurants, cafés and bars from virtually every member state of the European Union (apart, I think, from Luxembourg). This is an area so exclusively devoted to food that (paraphrasing Emile Zola's description of Les Halles in Paris as 'le ventre de Paris') it might be called 'the Belly of Europe'. Even the street names in this old quarter of Brussels make a direct appeal to the stomach; there is a Rue au Beurre (Butter Street), Rue des Harengs (Herring Street), Rue des Bouchers (Butchers' Street) and Rue Chair et Pain (Meat and Bread Street).

Many of the restaurants in the old quarter of Brussels tend to be traditional Flemish establishments where the emphasis is placed on simple, substantial cooking at a moderate price. Brussels' restaurants have long been renowned for their generous portions; the 1905 Baedeker guide warned travellers that, 'A single portion of soup or beefsteak or *filet de boeuf* is enough for two persons, and a single portion of any of the other dishes is enough for three.' The most popular dishes in these restaurants are *steak-frites* (steak with french fries) or overflowing pots of *moules* (mussels). To add to their appeal in winter, many of these restaurants have blazing open fires.

Following Rue au Beurre from the Roi d'Espagne, we pass **Dandoy** at No. 31, an attractive old shop specialising in *spekulaus*, a spicy biscuit cut in the shape of human figures using moulds of 17th-century design. Straight ahead is the Bourse (Stock Exchange), which is surrounded by attractive cafés, such as Le Falstaff (described on page 302) and Cirio (page 312). Turning right along Rue de Tabora, we pass the **Eglise St Nicolas**, a church now so hemmed in by houses that it is almost hidden from sight. Nor does it now have a tower to give it prominence; the first one collapsed in 1367, a second tower was destroyed in the bombardment of 1695, while the third collapsed in 1714. Once the church of Brussels' merchants, St Nicolas is dedicated to their patron saint, Nicolas of Myra (who is also Santa Claus).

Several attractive 19th-century taverns are hidden in the narrow alleys of this old quarter. Opposite St Nicolas, a neon sign at 11 Rue de Tabora points down an alley to **La Bécasse** (The Woodcock), an inn dating from 1877. When crowded, the upstairs room of La Bécasse becomes particularly Bruegelian and merry.

On turning right up Rue Marché aux Herbes, we pass two more taverns tucked away in narrow lanes. The Impasse St Nicolas at No. 12 leads down to **Au Bon Vieux Temps**, and the Impasse des Cadeaux at No. 6 descends to **A l'Imaige Nostre Dame**. Although these *estaminets* bear French names, they have much of the atmosphere of a 17th-century Flemish tavern. My own favourite is A l'Imaige Nostre Dame, which has a rustic old Flemish interior of uncertain age.

Rue de la Fourche, the first street on the left, takes us into the heart of the Ilot Sacré. Strains of bozouki music spill out of the many Greek restaurants on this street. To add to the Mediterranean atmosphere, tables are set out in the street even on days when a light dusting of snow covers the tablecloths. A passage on the right leads through to Petite Rue des Bouchers, past Actor's Studio, a small cinema with an interesting programme of international films. Turning left brings us to Rue des Bouchers. Aux Armes de Bruxelles at No. 13 is an elegant and reliable old Brussels restaurant, while directly opposite, at No. 18, stands Chez Léon, where enormous potfuls of steaming mussels are served with *frites* and beer. Chez Léon began in 1905 as a tiny restaurant named after its founder Léon Vanlancker. The restaurant has now expanded to occupy a row of eight old houses which can accommodate about 500 patrons at one time. The kitchen is open from midday to midnight throughout the year, and on an average day will serve some 1,000 kilograms of Zeeland mussels. Chez Vincent, just around the corner at 8 Rue des Dominicains, was established in the same year as Chez Léon. Again the emphasis is on solid,

251

substantial cooking. If not deterred by the giant slabs of butter piled high in Vincent's window, we enter this restaurant through the kitchen, which is adorned with a gleaming tile tableau depicting a herd of grazing cattle. The rear room is decorated with another painting on tiles of a small Flemish fishing boat battling against the North Sea, while the adjoining room is furnished in an attractive old Flemish style with shiny brass cooking utensils strung from the ceiling.

We may be amused to note, not far from Vincent's, a narrow alley with a curious name. Situated opposite 28 Rue des Bouchers, the alley is so narrow that we might easily pass by without noticing it. Its name is the Rue d'une Personne (One Person Street), for the obvious reason that no more than one person may walk down it at a time. Indeed, after a hearty meal in Brussels, even one person may find Rue d'une Personne a tight squeeze.

The Lower Town

On our second walk in Brussels we venture into the old Flemish quarter of the city, following streets that W. H. Auden described as 'tangled like old string'. In this interesting area visited only by the most adventurous of tourists, we will come upon a rich diversity of architectural styles bearing witness to the complex evolution of Brussels. Old Flemish houses stand next to elegant French arcades, gleaming skyscrapers overlook weather-beaten baroque churches, and secret squares are concealed behind modern office blocks. Nowhere else in Brussels do we receive such a vivid impression of the many conflicting forces that have shaped and shaken this city, be they Flemish, Spanish, Austrian, French, British or American. Admittedly, the contemplation of this clash of cultures is not always an agreeable experience, but it offers, I believe, a fascinating insight into the tumultuous history of which Europe is made.

We begin this walk *(see page 236 for map)* on **Grand'Place**, and where better than a café table? I am fond of La Brouette at No. 3, with its browned old Brussels posters and heavy wrought-iron lamps. There is a small table next to the window, which can sometimes be found unoccupied in the early morning. With a coffee and some biscuits served on a tray, we can watch the flower sellers from the Pajottenland setting out boxes of marigolds and geraniums. The price of a coffee may be slightly higher here, but we are paying for the privilege of sitting in one of the most beautiful squares in Europe.

Once we have finished our coffee, we should enter the courtyard of the **Hôtel de Ville** through the portal below the belfry. The vaulting in the portal is decorated with eight prophets' heads, copies of originals, dating from about 1405, which are now safely protected from the elements in the Musée de la Ville de Bruxelles opposite. In the courtyard beyond are two 18th-century fountains picturesquely overgrown with ivy. They are adorned with reclining figures representing the river gods of the Scheldt and the Meuse, the two principal rivers of Belgium.

We leave the courtyard by a gateway on Rue de l'Amigo and turn right. The building opposite stands on the site of the old town jail, known as the Amigo - an obsolete Southern Netherlands word for a prison. History has taken an ironical turn here, for the Amigo is now a very luxurious hotel. We now turn left along the Rue du Marché du Charbon, a winding street where picturesque old haberdashers are being turned into chic night bars. A good example is Au Soleil at No. 86, an abandoned shop converted into a lively café that spills out onto the street on summer evenings. The neighbourhood has become much more lively in recent years, though we may sometimes regret the passsing of an establishment where one hundred types of string were stocked alongside jars of boiled sweets. Just beyond Au Soleil we come to the baroque façade of **Notre-Dame du Bon Secours,** designed by Willem de Bruyn, the architect of La Chaloupe d'Or and the Maison des Brasseurs on Grand'Place. Its pleasingly compact and harmonious interior is the work of Jan Cortvriendt.

On reaching Place Fontainas, we take Rue de la Grande Ile, which begins on the far side of Boulevard Anspach and swings off to the right. Romantic though it sounds, we will find no trace of any Grande Ile (Great Island) here any more. The island vanished when the River Senne was ignominiously buried under the streets in the 19th century. The river now disappears into a tunnel near Ruisbroek and emerges some ten miles to the north-east, not far from the Gare de Schaerbeek, following the line of boulevards running from Gare du Midi to Gare du Nord. At the unveiling of this momentous urban project in 1871, Burgomaster Anspach boasted that he had 'replaced the dangerous and dreary river with the most important and arguably the most beautiful boulevards in our city'. Baudelaire, however, grumbled about 'the sadness of a city without a river'.

Rue de la Grande Ile takes us from here past the **Eglise Notre-Dame aux Riches Claires**, designed by Luc Fayd'herbe in 1665. The choir of the convent church is a highly unusual composition with numerous tiny apses surmounted by scrolled gables and picturesque turrets. It is just visible in the background of the print reproduced overleaf.

Soon we come to the 19th-century meat hall on **Place St Géry**, once the heart of the Grande Ile. It was on this site, according to legend, that St Géry, Bishop of Cambrai, established a church in the 6th century. Not a whisper of the church remains. Although Brussels, like Paris, began as a settlement on a river island, it has developed quite differently: the two islands in the Seine in Paris have flourished, whereas those once in the Senne in Brussels have been left to decay. As we look at the crumbling houses in this historic neighbourhood, we may find ourselves for once nodding in agreement with G.K. Chesterton, who complained that: 'Except for some fine works of art, which seem to be there by accident, the City of Brussels is like a bad Paris, a Paris with everything noble cut out, and everything nasty left in.'

The print overleaf shows Place St Géry as it was in the early 19th century. Notice the small carriage being drawn by dogs, a curious form of transport which John Evelyn commented on when he visited the Flemish cities in 1641. Travelling from Brussels to Ghent, he noted 'divers little wagons prettily contrived and full of pedling merchandises, drawne by mastive-dogs, harnessed compleately like so many coach-horses, in some 4, in others 6, as in Brussels itselfe I had observed. In Antwerp I saw, as I remember, 4 dogs draw 5 lusty children in a charriot: the master commands them whither he pleases, crying his wares about the streetes.'

Another interesting detail in this print is the large obelisk standing in the middle of the square. This was a renaissance fountain, and when the Marché St Géry was erected here in 1881, a proposal was put forward to save the fountain by placing it inside the market. As a result of this

pleasing conservation measure, it now dominates the central aisle of the former meat hall.

At the time of writing, the Marché St Géry was being restored to create a small scale version of London's Covent Garden, with shops, restaurants and cafés. Opposite, some old Flemish brick houses have been attractively restored and, to the delight of local historians, a short stretch of the River Senne has been uncovered in the courtyard beyond (reached through an archway at 23 Place St Géry). If enthusiasm does not wane, as it sometimes does in Brussels, this old quarter should become increasingly animated.

We now wander down Rue du Pont de la Carpe; the street name sounds promising but proves doubly disappointing for we will see neither a bridge nor any carp. Before the Senne was tidied away below the streets of Brussels, there was at least a *pont* here, but it seems very unlikely that *carpe* ever flourished in the murky river. We then cross the busy Rue Van Artevelde and turn left down Rue Antoine Dansaert. L'Archiduc, at No. 6, is a chic art deco jazz bar dating from the 1920's; the liveliest sessions do not really begin until well after most of Brussels has retired to bed. We also find some fashionable boutiques in Rue Dansaert, with striking interiors designed by young Belgian architects. We turn right into the Rue du Vieux Marché aux Grains, a quiet, leafy street that leads to the Rue de Flandre. This street may look fairly unpromising, but it contains one remarkable, virtually forgotten building hidden down a long passage at No. 46. Overlooking a secret courtyard is the splendidly ornate **Maison de la Bellone**, designed in Italo-Flemish style by Jan Cosyns in 1697. Military accoutrements decorate the façade of this house, which was built soon after the bombardment of Brussels, and named after Bellona, the Roman goddess of war. The Maison du Spectacle now uses the building for exhibitions on French theatre in Brussels.

We now carry on to **Place Ste Cathérine**, once the site of the fish market and still the best place in town for seafood. There is usually a stall in the square where we can eat mussels or oysters, when in season, washed down with a glass of Muscadet. Or we can visit one of the many excellent fish restaurants in this neighbourhood, such as La Belle Maraîchère at 11 Place Ste Catherine, a comfortable, traditional Brussels restaurant where the emphasis is rightly placed on cooking and service, rather than frills.

The weather-beaten **Eglise Ste Cathérine** looks as if it has been looming over the old fish market for several centuries, but it is in fact something of a parvenu, for it was designed in 1854 by Joseph Poelaert, the architect of the Palais de Justice. The mysterious baroque tower standing nearby once had a small chapel to justify its existence, but this was demolished in the 19th century. There was even talk in the 1950's of demolishing the church itself, but it has so far been spared.

We now walk down the **Quai aux Bois à Brûler**, formerly a quay overlooking a bustling harbour on the River Senne. But the harbour has been filled in to create a bleak and windswept square. Turning right off this square down Rue du Peuplier, we come upon the beautiful, billowy **Eglise du Béguinage**. Its 17th-century baroque façade is divided into three bays, each topped with a curlicued Flemish scroll gable, giving the church the appearance of a row of three houses. The secluded religious community of Béguines was shattered in 1579, when a Protestant mob broke into the church and plundered its treasures. The Béguinage was dealt a further blow in the 19th century when most of the 60 or so houses belonging to the sisterhood were demolished.

Let us leave this sad corner of the old city along Rue des Augustins, which brings us to the animated **Place de Brouckère**. We can pause for coffee in the magnificent Café Métropole (described on page 291). At the very least, we should enter the lobby to admire the aged iron lift, now a protected monument, and the photograph next to the porter's desk showing Albert Einstein and Marie Curie attending a conference at the Métropole. To reach our next destination, Place des Martyrs, we continue along Boulevard Adolphe Max, then turn right down the Passage du Nord, an elegant 19th-century arcade where 30 dusty caryatids gaze down on us with a look of mild contempt. On Rue Neuve, we should turn left, unless tempted by the thought of an English pork pie, in which case a short stroll in the opposite direction will bring us to Marks & Spencer's. Rue Neuve was once a street of aristocratic allure, to which the Marquis of Spinola moved in 1675, but modern shops have put an end to its pretensions of grandeur. However, we should not overlook the baroque **Notre-Dame de Finistère**, which is especially pleasing because it manages, amidst the glittering distractions of Rue Neuve, to retain an atmosphere of piety. Perhaps it succeeds because it is itself crammed with glittering distractions, including grey stucco, baroque paintings and ornately-carved confessionals. It also boasts a splendid carved pulpit decorated with cherubs struggling to secure a canopy using a complicated system of ropes and pulleys. In the small chapel on the right there is a 16th-century statue of Notre-Dame de Bon Succès, apparently shipped to Brussels in 1625 from Aberdeen.

On leaving the church we return briefly to the crush of Rue Neuve and turn right, then left down Rue St Michel, one of the narrow streets leading into the **Place des Martyrs**. Even without its martyrs' monument - a subterranean shrine to the 445 rebels who died in the Belgian Revolt of 1830 - Place des Martyrs would be a ghostly square. It was designed in the 1770's by Claude Fisco in the cool, white neoclassical style imposed on Brussels by the Hapsburgs. The first time I walked across the cobblestones the buildings around lay derelict and empty, but they have recently been splendidly restored by the government of Flanders to provide prestigious offices in the heart of the city. The government of Wallonia, with its capital in Namur, may feel a pang of envy now that the Belgian national monument is surrounded on all sides by Flemish institutions.

We leave the square on the opposite side along Rue du Persil, a winding medieval lane lined with disconcertingly futuristic buildings. Turning left and then right, we climb Rue des Sables, where there are some attractive early 20th-century buildings, including **Magasins Waucquez** at No. 20, designed by Victor Horta in 1903. This is Horta's only surviving department store, the others having been destroyed over the years. Now beautifully restored, it provides a scintillating setting for the Belgian museum of comic strips. Anyone with a soft spot for Tintin or Lucky Luke cartoons should spend some time among the whimsical memorabilia displayed on the upper floors. Even if you decide to give the museum a miss, go inside to admire the lofty entrance hall and glance briefly at the little exhibition devoted to Horta's vanished architecture. The museum has a shop selling cartoon books and postcards, a specialised library of comic strips and a lively brasserie full of French tourists who flock here to rediscover forgotten childhood heroes.

We now ascend a flight of steps and cross the busy Boulevard Pachéco. Perched on the hill above is the **Colonne du Congrès**, designed in 1850 by Joseph Poelaert to commemorate the drafting of the Belgian constitution in 1831 by the National Congress. It stands on a square offering an interesting view of the Lower Town, but it is a bleak, windswept site, and besides is difficult to reach from here, so let us leave it until another day and proceed now up Rue de la Banque to reach the street enchantingly named **Rue du Bois Sauvage** (Wild Wood Street). The origin of this name may serve as a cautionary tale to the large community of translators now working in Brussels. Originally it bore the Dutch name, Wout de Wildestraat, after a certain Wolter de Wilde, but during the French occupation, when the Napoleonic administrators altered all the street names from Dutch to French, the translator mistook Wout for *woud* (a wood) and so gave the street its beguiling, but quite inaccurate name. Curiously, the Dutch name for this street is now Wildewoudstraat, which is a straight translation of the French! No. 14 in this lane is an attractive late gothic town house with a slender turret. Photographers tend artfully to conceal the fact that this house has lost half of its step gable to No. 13, but I think that the juxtaposing of these two different styles creates an interesting curiosity. Let us now enter the cathedral and sit down to read a little about the building.

The **Cathédrale St Michel**, now rather forgotten, has been the scene of many momentous events, including the spectacular chivalric ceremonies of the Order of the Golden Fleece held in the 15th century by Philip the Good and

Charles the Bold. Among the many tombs we come across here are those of Duke John II of Brabant and his wife Margaret of York, daughter of Edward I of England, who are buried in the mausoleum of the dukes of Brabant behind the high altar. The late gothic chapel attached to the north side of the choir contains the tombs of the Archduke Albert and Archduchess Isabella, and Charles of Lorraine. Roger van der Weyden, City Painter of Brussels, is also buried somewhere in St Michel, though the only indication of this is a mildewed reproduction of his *St Luke Painting the Virgin.* This marvellous work is now in Boston, but there is a good copy in the Groeningemuseum in Bruges.

The oldest part of the cathedral is the choir, an early 13th-century gothic structure, to which the nave and transepts were added in the 14th century, probably to designs by Jan van Ruysbroeck and Jacob van Thienen. The west front of the church was then splendidly terminated by twin towers, completed in 1451 and 1475 (and seen opposite about 1900, before large-scale clearance of the surrounding streets). The beau-

tiful late gothic Chapelle du St Sacrement de Miracle, appended to the north side of the choir in 1534-9, commemorates an unpleasant anti-Semitic legend of the 14th century. The story relates how a consecrated Host allegedly stolen by a Jew miraculously spurted blood after being stabbed by the congregation in a synagogue. The Host was subsequently venerated as a holy relic in St Michel.

From here we head back down the slope and into the Lower Town along Rue d'Assault. Turning left along the curiously named Rue Montagne aux Herbes Potagères brings us to the **Café à la Mort Subite** at No. 7. The café takes its name, which means literally 'sudden death', from a dice game once played by its regulars that involved reckless drinking bouts. Designed in 1910 by Paul Hamesse, this marvellous neoclassical café has been in the hands of the same family since the 1920's. The owners have preserved the interior intact and virtually the only sign of progress is a gleaming chrome espresso machine. The café specialises in family-brewed Mort Subite beers. These are traditional

ales from the Pajottenland, a rural area to the west of Brussels where Bruegel found inspiration in the 16th century for many of his scenes of peasant weddings and village fêtes.

Our walk is now almost over, but we have one important sight still to visit: the Manneken Pis fountain, which we must see if our visit to Brussels is to be considered complete. From Mort Subite, we turn left up Rue d'Arenberg, then right along Rue de la Montagne. After passing a statue of Charles Buls, the conservationist Burgomaster of Brussels from 1881 to 1899, we proceed down Rue des Eperonniers, where we can buy nostalgic old tin toys at La Trottinette (No. 4), art and architecture books at Postscriptum (No. 37) and attractive art and architecture postcards at Plaizir (No. 50). We then cross Place St Jean to reach Place de la Vieille Halle aux Blés. Still continuing straight ahead, we follow Rue de Dinant (or what is left of it), then turn right into Rue de Villers. To our left is a fragment of Brussels' oldest fortifications, which enclosed the city from 1267 to 1357. Other sections of this wall crop up in unexpected locations: a tower and a length of wall at the foot of the picturesque Rue de Rollebeek, and another tower, saved by Charles Buls from demolition, just off Place Ste Catherine. Brussels' second city wall was more efficiently disposed of in the 19th century and all that now remains is the stalwart Porte de Hal at the end of Rue Haute.

But we are forgetting our purpose; once we have looked at this ancient stone wall, we should continue to the end of Rue de Villers, then turn left down Rue du Chêne to reach the **Manneken Pis**. Baedeker's 1905 guide warned travellers that this statue of a boy urinating was 'a great favourite with the lower classes', but conceded that 'the figure is not without considerable artistic excellence'. The present statue, which replaced an older version, was cast in bronze in 1619 by the sculptor Jérôme Duquesnoy.

From the Manneken Pis we can return to Grand'Place along Rue de l'Etuve, a narrow street with the well-trodden look of a pilgrimage route. The shops along this street have given up selling bread or cheese and have dedicated themselves with alarming single-mindedness to the sale of Manneken corkscrews, Manneken beer-dispensers and the like.

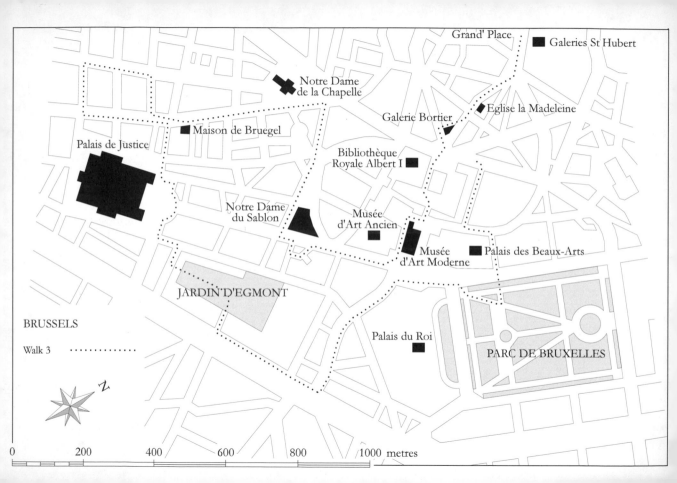

Grand' Place

■ Galeries St Hubert

Notre Dame
de la Chapelle

Galerie Bortier

◆ Eglise la Madeleine

Maison de Bruegel

Palais de Justice

Bibliothèque
Royale Albert I ■

Notre Dame
du Sablon

Musée
d'Art Ancien

Musée
d'Art Moderne

■ Palais des Beaux-Arts

JARDIN'D'EGMONT

BRUSSELS

Walk 3 ···········

Palais du Roi

PARC DE BRUXELLES

N

0   200   400   600   800   1000 metres

WALK 3

The Upper Town

Let us now explore the heights of the Upper Town, where the dukes and nobles of Burgundy erected their splendid gothic palaces in the 15th century. Sadly, little now remains of this chivalric court apart from a solitary town house and one tiny chapel. The elegant architecture of the Upper Town now mainly dates from the 18th century, when impressive neoclassical houses were built around parks and squares. Boulevards of the 19th century and 20th-century shopping arcades add further allure to the Upper Town, yet the main attractions of this walk are the two magnificent collections of paintings housed in the Musée d'Art Ancien and the Musée d'Art Moderne, collectively known as the **Musées Royaux des Beaux-Arts** (closed on Mondays). On this walk, we will look at the Madonna of the Porridge Spoon, climb the Mountain of Vegetables, and discover the price of a fork with one prong.

To plan our peregrinations in the Upper Town, I suggest that we familiarise ourselves with the route over coffee in Mokafé, a well-preserved 1930's café at 9 Galerie du Roi. This introduces us to the **Galeries St Hubert**, a magnificent glass-covered shopping arcade situated off Rue du Marché aux Herbes. Designed by Jean Pierre Cluysenaer in 1847, the neoclassical arcade comprises three intersecting wings with the appropriately grandiose names of Galerie du Roi, Galerie de la Reine and Galerie des Princes.

The Galeries St Hubert proved particularly popular in the 19th century with the exiled French community in Brussels. During his stay in Brussels in 1864, Baudelaire sullenly paced the long arcade every day as he worked on *Pauvre Belgique,* a bitter diatribe against Belgium. Another French habitué of the arcade was Verlaine, who bought the pistol with which he shot his friend Rimbaud in a shop here.

The arcade has scarcely changed since its construction, and it still has old wrought iron lamps, marble pilasters and lithe statues set in little niches. We may while away an hour or two here on a rainy afternoon, looking at the elegant shops, of which the best-preserved is Neuhaus at 25 Galerie de la Reine, whose chocolates have been tempting the Belgian sweet tooth since 1857. Another attractive shop to browse in is the Librairie des Galeries at 2 Galerie du Roi, which stocks sumptuous art books, including thick tomes on Burgundian art and elegant little guides to the architecture of Brussels. The attractively modernised neo-renaissance interior of the French bookshop Tropismes at 11 Galerie des Princes is also worth a glance.

We can explore another arcade, designed by the same architect but now rather forgotten, when we ascend to the Upper Town by Rue de la Madeleine. On the way there we pass the attractive 15th-century **Eglise La Madeleine**, which was carefully transplanted during the construction of Gare Centrale to a site some fifty yards from its original location. The houses that once surrounded this church did not receive such charitable treatment and have all vanished, leaving La Madeleine looking somewhat isolated.

Entered by a neoclassical portal at 23-5 Rue de la Madeleine, **Galerie Bortier** was erected by Cluysenaer very soon after the Galeries St Hubert, but seems never to have enjoyed the same fashionable appeal. A short passage leads into a curving glass-roofed arcade, with the back of an old market opposite a row of shops, most of which are now bookshops specialising in second-hand French paperbacks.

From the entrance on Rue St Jean we turn left to reach the windswept Boulevard de l'Empereur, which marks the broad swathe cut by the railway tunnel linking Gare du Nord with Gare du Midi. Begun in 1911, this scheme was finally completed in 1952 with the opening of Gare Centrale, designed by Victor Horta in art deco style. The tunnel, which runs from the botanical gardens to a lovely baroque chapel dedicated to St Bridget, has left Brussels permanently scarred.

As we wait for a pause in the traffic, we can look across to the **Mont des Arts** opposite. This series of stepped terraces was created in the 1950's to link the Lower and Upper Towns. There are several interesting features of this complex, including a modern glockenspiel programmed to chime Flemish and Walloon folk tunes alternately. Hidden on the rear wall of the building that bridges the road to our left, it plays every 15 minutes, though seldom to an audience.

Our route to the summit proceeds straight ahead up a flight of steps leading to the **Bibliothèque Royale Albert I**, the national library. Built in a sober neoclassical style in 1954-69, it houses many beautiful illuminated manuscripts from the Burgundian court. The manuscripts are sometimes exhibited in the **Nassau Chapel**, an exquisite late gothic chapel buried in the fabric of the new library building. The outside wall of the chapel is visible from the upper arcade, just beyond the library entrance. The chapel - the most curious Burgundian memento in Brussels - once formed part of the Nassau palace. It was built in the late 15th century for Engelbert of Nassau, who served as Governor of the Netherlands under Philip the Fair, Duke of Burgundy. William the Silent later inherited the palace, but it was confiscated by the municipal authorities when he sided with the Dutch rebels. When the palace of the dukes of Burgundy was destroyed by a fire in 1731, Governor Maria-Elisabeth took up residence in the Nassau palace. A later Governor of the Austrian Netherlands, Charles of Lorraine, rebuilt it in 18th-century neoclassical style, but fortunately spared the 15th-century Nassau chapel. Nor, miraculously, did it perish in the 1950's, when much of Charles of Lorraine's neoclassical palace was demolished to make way for the royal library. So it still stands today, an intriguing relic of Burgundian Brussels and the perfect setting for exhibitions of rare manuscripts.

Let us now climb up to the breezy terrace situated on the flanks of the aptly named **Coudenberg** (Cold Hill). From here we obtain a panoramic view of the guild houses and spires of the Lower Town. Ignoring one or two unfortunate modern intrusions, this is very much the view of Brussels which the Burgundian nobles would have enjoyed from the gothic windows of their palaces. From this vantage point, Brussels seems a remote and unreal city, like the distant clusters of city gates and spires that we see in the backgrounds of 15th-century paintings.

Behind us is the **Rue Montagne de la Cour** (Mountain of the Court Street), one of the streets whose names intrigued Gérard de Nerval on a visit to Brussels in the 1840's. 'Imagine in the middle of the flattest country on earth,' he wrote in a letter, 'a city consisting almost entirely of mountains: Montagne du Parc (Mountain of the Park), Montagne de la Cour (Mountain of the Court), Montagnes des Larmes (Mountain of Tears), Montagne aux Herbes Potagères (Mountain of Vegetables); horses and dogs are exhausted after a ten-minute trot, and anyone on foot soon runs out of breath.'

We now ascend Rue Montagne de la Cour. To our left, the Delacre chemist at 64 Rue Montagne de la Cour is an imaginative revival of Burgundian gothic architecture designed by Paul Saintenoy in 1897. The tile tableau at the top is particularly attractive, reminiscent of a scene from an old illuminated manuscript. Two years later Paul Saintenoy switched to art nouveau when he designed the beautiful **Old England** department store perched on the slope at No. 94. This wistful six-floor building lay empty for many years, but the fabric is now being restored to provide a fine setting for the Museum of Musical Instruments. Until the work is completed, our only opportunity to see the interior is to visit one of the temporary art exhibitions held in the half-finished rooms. The main attraction for many people is the rooftop café (only open to those who buy an entrance ticket). This was once a fashionable tea room where Old England customers would meet for lunch and exchange gossip about the girlfriends of King Léopold II. We can now sink into an ancient battered sofa, or lounge on a deck chair on the terrace, gazing down on the cathedral spires through the frail curtain of art nouveau ironwork seen in the photograph opposite. Nowhere else does Brussels seem so romantic.

A flight of steps on the right-hand side of the

street leads into the former courtyard of the Nassau palace. The **Ancien Cour**, a striking neoclassical building on our right, is one of the last vestiges of the palace built in the 1760's for Charles of Lorraine. The most astonishing feature of the quiet neoclassical square is the subterranean court of the Musée d'Art Moderne, which a too-hasty tourist might easily overlook. We spy the semicircular gallery through small oval windows in the parapet surrounding the court. Before visiting this gallery, let us look first at the Flemish Masters in the **Musée d'Art Ancien**, which we reach up Rue du Musée, then right along Rue de la Régence, entering by a giant portico flanked by massive columns of Scots granite.

It is fitting that this museum should stand on the heights of Coudenberg, for it owns many paintings linked to the Burgundian court that once flourished here. As City Painter of Brussels from 1436 to 1464, Roger van der Weyden provides many clues as to the characters and customs of the vanished court of the dukes of Burgundy. He vividly portrays the sharply-chiselled features

of the *Man with an arrow* (room 11), who is depicted wearing the collar of the Order of the Golden Fleece and carrying an arrow. Also by van der Weyden is the attractive portrait of Laurent Froimont. About the life of Laurent Froimont we know nothing, but we may assume that he was a member of the aristocracy, as his motto, *Raison l'ensaigne* ('reason giveth knowledge'), is written in French rather than Dutch. We may also surmise that he was a devout Christian, as this painting was originally part of a diptych; the portrait of the Virgin which once accompanied it now hangs in the museum in Caen.

There are several 15th-century portraits from Bruges in the museum. Two by Memling show Burgomaster Willem Moreel and his wife (room 14), painted some six years before they reappeared in the triptych by Memling in the Groeningemuseum in Bruges. In the tiny triptych by the Master of 1473, we see Jan van de Witte, Burgomaster of Bruges, and his second wife Maria Hoose. According to the Latin inscription at the base of the frame, this painting was completed in 1473 and shows the Burgomaster aged 30, with his 16-year-old bride. Behind the child bride is a small white dog, the familiar Flemish symbol of marital fidelity.

Dirk Bout's *The Justice of the Emperor Otto* (room 13) was commissioned in 1468 by the councillors of Leuven to hang in the court room of the beautiful gothic town hall. It illustrates the cautionary tale of a young noble unjustly accused by the Emperor's wife. In the panel to the left, we see the arrest of the young man and his execution, observed by the Emperor and his scheming wife from behind a wall. In the second panel, the wife of the executed nobleman, shown carrying her husband's head, is subjected to an ordeal by fire before the Emperor. Having thereby proved the nobleman's innocence, the Emperor Otto orders the Empress to be burned at the stake; we see the sentence being carried out on a distant hill. An odd feature of this diptych is the tracery at the top of the wooden frame, which matches the pattern of tracery in the doorway in the right-hand painting, a technique that adds to the illusion of depth.

Hieronymus Bosch's *Christ on the Cross* (room

17) illustrates the artist's eccentric religious imagination. The summery blue sky and the gaily striped trousers worn by one of the onlookers seem altogether incongruous in the context of the Crucifixion. The walled city in the background has been identified as Bosch's home town of 's-Hertogenbosch, in the Netherlands.

The paintings by Bernard van Orley portray Flemish figures of the early 16th century, such as Margaret of Austria (room 26), and Dr Georges de Zelle, a young doctor who lived close to Bernard van Orley in the Place St Géry. The pattern of crossed hands on the hanging behind de Zelle probably indicates that the artist and his sitter were close friends, but the meaning of the interlocked letters remains mysterious. We will also see here van Orley's dramatic *Triptych of the Virtue of Patience*, commissioned by Margaret of Austria to give to a friend. The work illustrates a poem written by the thrice-widowed Margaret on the sufferings of Job. It is often arguable whether a painting was executed by van Orley or his workshop, but here there can be no doubt, for the artist has added his name twice - once on the edge of the step at the bottom of the painting, and again in a tiny inscription on the pillar to the left. If we peer closely, as we are so often required to do by Flemish artists, we will also see on the pillar the motto '*Elx syne tyt.*' ('A time for everything'). The painting's date - 1521 - can also be read here.

Portrait of a Man by Jan Mostaert (room 24) is another painting to tempt us into speculation. Its subject is a bony faced, anxious man - perhaps a scholar - who is resolutely facing away from a scene of bizarre architecture and strange events. A group of people are gazing up at the sky, where a Madonna floats mysteriously in the clouds, surrounded by angels. The chained ape sitting on a ledge suggests that the painting may be an allegory of folly.

Quinten Metsys' *Triptych of the Life of St Anne* (room 22) also repays close scrutiny. Painted in 1509 for the St Pieterskerk in Leuven, it treats the lives of Joachim and Anne in a pleasingly unorthodox manner. In the left-hand panel we see Joachim being told by the angel that Anne is to bear a child, the future mother of Christ. A miniature scene in the background shows a shepherd tending his flock - an allusion to the legend that Joachim was living with shepherds in the desert when the angel appeared. The beautiful figure of Anne holding the Virgin Mary reveals Metsys' skill as a portraitist. Notice, too, the little child seated at the bottom left-hand corner of the centre panel solemnly reading a book upside down.

One of the most appealing paintings in the collection is Gerard David's *Virgin and Child* (room 21). Also known by the intriguing title of *The Madonna of the Porridge Spoon*, this miniature painting shows the Virgin feeding porridge to the Christ Child with a wooden spoon. The setting and the sentiment are typically Flemish, and the quiet domesticity anticipates 17th-century Dutch masters such as Vermeer. Another painting of great tenderness is *Child with a Dead Bird* (room 22), painted by an anonymous artist.

The Musée d'Art Ancien is particularly proud of its collection of paintings by Pieter Bruegel the Elder, which includes the famous *Fall of Icarus*, opposite, painted in the 1550's when Bruegel was still living in Antwerp. In the beautiful poem *Musée des Beaux-Arts*, ('How right they were, the old masters') Auden dwells on this painting as an illustration of the way that suffering 'takes place/While someone else is eating or opening a window or just walking dully along'. At first, we do not see Icarus at all; our eye falls first on the figure of a daydreaming ploughman in the foreground, and then on a sailing ship. Only upon examining the painting closely do we see a tiny splash in the water and a leg about to disappear below the waves. Auden suggests that Icarus is ignored because 'the expensive delicate ship that must have seen/ Something amazing, a boy falling out of the sky,/ Had somewhere to get to and sailed calmly on'.

In Bruegel's *Census at Bethlehem*, painted in 1566 after he had moved to Brussels, the main characters are again difficult to find. The scene is a Flemish village of the Pajottenland on a crisp winter's day. Looking at this work, one's attention constantly shifts, from the charming scenes of children playing on the ice to the construction of a house, and from the dilapidated village to the red

ball of the setting sun. The Census is just one more detail in this bustling scene, as are the figures of Mary, seated on a mule, and Joseph.

The other important work here by Bruegel, *The Fall of the Rebel Angels*, was painted at about the same time as *Dulle Griet* in Antwerp, and it is an equally disturbing work, crowded as it is with bloated fish and winged monsters. Yet I think that *The Census at Bethlehem* has an underlying horror which is far more powerful, for it tricks us into smiling at the happy children engaged in various games, until the terrible thought occurs to us that the census which is quietly taking place in a corner of the scene will be followed all too soon by the Massacre of the Innocents. Bruegel's own *Massacre of the Innocents*, incidentally, is now in Vienna's Kunsthistorisches Museum, but the Musée d'Art Ancien has a copy made by Pieter Bruegel the Younger.

Once we have seen the Bruegels, we should look at the Rubens collection one floor higher. Interestingly, this includes a sketch of the *Fall of Icarus* which, unlike Bruegel's, captures the full drama of the tragedy. The sketch is one of a series of mythological scenes ordered by Philip IV of Spain in 1636 to decorate the Torre de la Parada, a royal hunting lodge near Madrid.

Of the 19th-century paintings in the museum, the most famous is Louis David's *Dead Marat* (room 71), painted in 1793. It depicts the murder of the revolutionary Jacobin journalist Marat, who suffered from a debilitating skin disease that could only be alleviated by long hours in a bath, where he did most of his writing. He was in this vulnerable position when Charlotte Corday, a beautiful young woman from Normandy, burst in and stabbed him to death. Marat is shown holding the letter dated 13 July 1793 that Corday wrote as a ploy, asking for the charity that she knew Marat would give her. In the next room (No. 70) we see David's *Mars Disarmed by Venus*, a late work painted in Brussels the year before he died. Louis David had chosen exile in 1816, and lived in Brussels until his death in 1825.

Room 69 contains the preliminary study by Antoine Wiertz of *The Apotheosis of the Queen*. This painting, commissioned to commemorate the Belgian Silver Jubilee in 1856, was to have been 150 feet high! Had it been executed, it would have been taller than the Colonne de Congrès on Rue Royale. Also in this room is Gustave Wapper's painting *Day in September 1830*, showing Belgian rebels hoisting the flag at Grand'-Place during the 1830 revolution. A small room opposite is devoted to Henri Leys, whose 19th-century paintings nostalgically evoke Flemish cities under the Burgundians and Hapsburgs.

Many of the most interesting 19th-century paintings in the Musée d'Art Ancien are hidden away in rooms 72-91. As an antidote to Leys' Flemish patriotism, we should search out the drawings by Ensor displayed on the mezzanine level above room 83. Ensor we meet in our tour of Antwerp, though he lived in the beach resort of Ostend. His drawing of *The Battle of the Golden Spurs*, dating from 1891, is a marvellously irreverent depiction of the 14th-century conflict between the French knights and the Flemish workers. In room 80 we see the rich, heavy renaissance interiors of Antwerp in paintings by Henri de Braekeleer. The interior of the Brouwershuis, with its glowing gilt leather walls,

particularly attracted this quiet, nostalgic artist. Notice also in room 88 the works by Henri Evenpoel, including some attractive portraits of children and a marvellous still life titled *White Dress*.

The **Musée d'Art Moderne** can be entered directly from the Musée d'Art Ancien, or from 1 Place Royale, an 18th-century town house where Alexandre Dumas wrote much of an almost forgotten novel called *La Comtesse de Charny*. A fascinating collection of modern art is displayed in a subterranean gallery sunk eight floors below the level of the Place Royale. At level minus 3 we come upon Vic Gentils' *Rua de Amor*, a macabre wooden sculpture depicting two unattractive women and a male client in a seedy Spanish brothel.

The next level down contains many more works by the eccentric Ostender James Ensor. A portrait of his father, an Englishman who lived in Ostend, illustrates Ensor's early Impressionism, which used the same melancholy brown and grey tones as the Dutch Impressionists. His style then changed dramatically in the 1880's, as we see from the explosive *Carnival on the Beach*, painted in 188, or Antwerp's *The Intrigue*, opposite.

On the same floor is Rik Wouters' affectionate portrait of his wife Nel as *The Woman in the Red Necklace*, and his Cézanne-like *Flautist*, painted shortly before the outbreak of the First World War. The felicitous pre-war period of Belgian history is reflected, too, in Louis Thevenet's alluring paintings such as *Honeymoon*. Thevenet retained his optimistic outlook throughout the war years, or so his 1917 painting *Hat-stand* seems to suggest.

Six floors below Place Royale, we come upon an eerie collection of surrealist paintings. The works by Paul Delvaux date mainly from his melancholy middle years in Brussels; they are chilling paintings depicting skeletons, night trains, empty trams and statuesque nude women. Occasionally we detect the echo of a famous Old Master, as in *Vox Populi* painted in 1957. Set in a melancholy street of Brussels' Upper Town, it shows a group of strait-laced ladies, widows perhaps, gazing sternly at a reclining nude in the style of Titian. Another work reinterprets the story of Pygmalion, the King of Cyprus who fell in love with a statue that was then brought to life by the goddess Venus. Delvaux alters the roles so that the statue is male and the lover female. There is also a strange study by Delvaux of the *Crucifixion,* painted in 1951, in which all the human figures are replaced by skeletons.

In the paintings by René Magritte, to whom a room is devoted, we see unexpected images depicted with the objectivity of photographs. In one, *Empire of Light*, a clear blue sky is juxtaposed with a benighted suburban street illuminated by a solitary lamp. In another painting the body of a nude female on a beach has become partially blue, the colour of the sea.

It is important to descent to the deepest level, eight floors underground; this is where the most bizarre art is to be found. You will see playful surrealist works by Marcel Broodthaers that feature mussels, broken eggshells and a bone painted with the Belgian colours. I urge you then to search for Wim Delvoye's *Installation with 2 Gas Cylinders and 29 Saws*. Words fail me at this moment.

On leaving the museum we should cross Place Royale and turn right along Rue de la Régence. Soon we turn off this busy street into the surprising Rue des Six Jeunes Hommes, where we discover a nook of attractive old houses which have tenaciously survived the redevelopment of this quarter. The lane emerges on **Place du Petit Sablon**, an intimate square created in 1890. Weather permitting, we can sit on a bench here to read about the sixty or so statues that surround us. The main figures are Counts Egmont and Hoorn, proudly placed on a lofty pedestal. These two nobles were executed by order of the Duke of Alva in 1568 for alleged treason. The statue of the two friends on their way to the scaffold originally stood on Grand'Place, where the execution took place, following their imprisonment in the Maison du Roi. They are surrounded by a miscellany of 16th-century Flemish figures, including William the Silent, Bernard van Orley, and the geographers Mercator and Ortelius. A hedge has been clipped to create niches for these statues; at night when the figures are floodlit the effect is decidedly romantic. A further set of 48 bronze figures representing Brussels' 16th-century guilds stand atop the neo-gothic columns surrounding this park, ensuring that statues far outnumber people in this quaint retreat.

The park overlooks the attractive **Eglise Notre-Dame du Sablon** (opposite), founded in 1304 by the guild of crossbowmen. Pilgrims flocked to this church in the middle ages after a statue of the Virgin, brought here by boat from Antwerp in 1348, proved to have miraculous qualities. A tapestry in the Musée de la Ville de Bruxelles depicts this legend. The miracle was later celebrated in the annual Ommegang procession, which culminated in a competition to shoot a wooden bird from the roof of the Sablon church. When the Archduchess Isabella won this competition in 1615, the event was meticulously recorded by Antoon Sallaert in a painting now hanging on the main staircase of the Musée d'Art Ancien.

To cope with the huge influx of pilgrims, this church was rebuilt in the 15th and 16th centuries in Brabant late gothic style. Its most ornate feature is a small sacrarium appended to the outside of

the choir on the north side. Built in 1549, it eventually fell into decay (as late gothic architecture is wont to do). The architect who restored it at the turn of the century added an ornate upper tier of his own invention, where once had been a small cupola.

It is worth venturing into the church to enjoy a harmonious late gothic interior without the customary clutter of second-rate baroque sculpture. What baroque there is tends on the contrary to be first-rate, particularly the twin chapels flanking the choir, erected by the von Thurn und Taxis family, who founded Europe's first postal system in the late 15th century. Von Thurn und Taxis was one of many aristocratic families residing in this quarter of Brussels, but of their palace nothing now remains.

As its name suggests, the **Place du Grand Sablon** was originally a sandy hill. Several inns were established on the square in the middle ages to serve the needs of pilgrims. Now there are numerous cafés and restaurants here and in the quiet side streets nearby, such as Rue Ste Anne, Rue des Pigeons and Rue de Rollebeek. What-

ever buildings are not devoted to restaurants tend to be occupied by exclusive antique shops, some of which are situated in attractive arcades opened up in the courtyards behind the houses. A Sunday morning in Brussels can be enlivened by a visit to the antique and book market here.

We now descend from the aristocratic heights of the Sablon quarter to explore the picturesque streets and narrow alleys of the Marolles. The Rue de Rollebeek plunges down to the Marolles from the bottom end of Place du Grand Sablon. At the foot of the lane, we turn left along Rue Haute. Before crossing Rue Joseph Stevens, we should pause to look at the grey skyscraper to the left. It stands on the site of Victor Horta's Maison du Peuple, a spectacular art nouveau building erected in the 1890's and torn down, despite cries and pleas from every quarter, in the 1960's.

A happier story can be told about the church on the other side of Rue Haute, whose white Brabant stonework now gleams in the sunlight following a recent restoration. The **Eglise Notre-Dame de la Chapelle** presents us with a baffling diversity of styles to unravel. Its transepts are romanesque, the choir dates from the early gothic period, and its nave and aisles were rebuilt in late gothic style following a fire. The tower is a baroque embellishment, replacing a slender spire which the French bombardment brought down in 1695. It was designed by Antoon Pastorana, the architect of the bizarre guild house of the boatmen at 6 Grand'Place.

It was in this church, in 1563, that Pieter Bruegel the Elder married Maria Coecke, the daughter of Pieter Coecke van Aelst, a leading Flemish artist of the day. Bruegel, who died in his early forties, only six years after the marriage, was probably buried here, although no grave survives. The only hard evidence is a memorial in the church erected in honour of his father by Jan Bruegel in 1625. It once incorporated a painting by Rubens of *Christ Handing the Keys of Heaven to St Peter*, which he presented as a token of his admiration for Bruegel. Unfortunately the church authorities sold this painting to a private collector in the 18th century, replacing it with a copy.

Bruegel probably lived in the house now known as the **Maison de Bruegel** at 132 Rue Haute.

The attractive step-gabled building was certainly owned by the artist's grand-daughter Anne Bruegel, who bequeathed it to her son, David Teniers III. However, the assumption that Anne inherited it from her father, Jan Bruegel, and he in turn from Pieter Bruegel the Elder, is not proven. The house now contains a museum devoted to Pieter Bruegel the Elder, but it has been closed for as long as anyone can remember. It was while he lived here, if he ever did, that Bruegel painted two works now in the Musée d'Art Ancien - *The Census at Bethlehem* and the tiny portrait *Yawning Man.*

Bruegel's house stands in the heart of the **Marolles**, a quarter settled by weavers in the middle ages. The weavers of Brussels, like those of Ghent, were a notoriously unruly crowd, giving the Marolles its enduring reputation for lawlessness; even Baedeker felt it necessary to warn his readers in 1905 that the streets of the Marolles 'exhibit many drastic scenes of popular life'. Nowadays we relish scenes of popular life, as long as they are not too drastic, and the Marolles as a result has experienced a certain revival of

281

interest. It is the only quarter left in Brussels where we might, on a rare moment, come upon a scene evoking a painting of children's games by Bruegel. Eating out in a restaurant in the Marolles may likewise recall the convivial mood of Bruegel's paintings of wedding feasts. One of the most atmospheric bistros in this quarter is L'Idiot du Village at 19 Rue Notre Seigneur. Situated near the attractive baroque chapel of a vanished convent, this bustling restaurant has an appealingly festive mood, with dried roses hanging from the ceiling and an old post office counter.

We now continue along Rue Haute, past a curious old-fashioned hatter's shop at No. 158, and turn right down Rue St Gisleins. The kindergarten at No. 40 was designed in 1895-9 by Victor Horta. Examining the façade closely we can discern any number of delightful details such as the tiny leaf-like decoration at the tops of the windows and the eccentric little turret. Notice, too, to the left of the name 'Jardin d'Enfants', Horta's ingenious treatment of a horizontal gutter's intersection with a vertical shaft, the effect like ivy entwined around a post.

To continue our exploration of the Marolles, we must retrace our steps a short distance to Rue Blaes, where we turn right to reach the **Place du Jeu de Balle**. Named after a ball game traditionally played here, the square is now the scene of a popular daily flea market. Every morning at first light, dealers drive battered vans down to the Marolles, and spread threadbare carpets over the cobblestones to display their spoils. You can find just about anything here: a stuffed bird, a solitary size 44 ski boot, a rusty dentist's drill, crates of mildewed ledgers, scratched LP records featuring forgotten French singers, a marble memorial to 'My Husband, Dearly Missed,' sets of pre-war hair curlers, a sepia photograph of someone's great-grandfather setting off for the trenches, a bakelite television set, a tattered 1953 Ghent phone book cover, a cocktail cabinet disguised as a globe, a half-used packet of Chinese noodles, a mirror cracked from side to side, perhaps even a box of used toothbrushes.

As the day wears on, objects get trampled on, soaked by the rain, lodged between the cobblestones, until eventually the square looks like one vast rubbish dump. Yet locals still keep sifting through the debris in search of treasures. Will anyone ever buy that tarnished fork with one prong? you ask yourself. The answer is probably yes. I have even seen one enterprising trader selling old copies of one of the city's free newspapers.

Even if we are too late to catch the market, which peters out in the early afternoon, the curio shops on Rue Blaes provide us with an equally entertaining variety of bizarre bric-à-brac. Once you have had your fill of gilded ballroom chairs and broken telephones, you might glance at the little food stand at 2 Place du Jeu de Balle called *Hommage à Mafritte*. I couldn't believe my eyes when I first saw this place. Where else in the world would you find a humble *friterie* dedicated to a famous artist? The walls of this tiny eatery are decorated with scenes from Magritte paintings, in which *frites* appear among the familiar images of briar pipes and giant combs. There is even a little framed painting of a *frite* labelled *Ceci n'est pas une frite,* which, as any Magritte fan will tell

you, is a parody of *Ceci n'est pas une pipe.* The Mafritte joint is run by an amiable couple who also do sandwiches and various forms of fried meat, but it is the *frites* that merit a pause. On balmy summer days , you can plant yourself on a plastic chair in the doorway and watch the world go by, which, in the case of the Marolles, means watching a beat-up Renault van drive past with a damp sofa strapped to the roof and a stuffed giraffe poking out of the back door.

A café at 50 Place du Jeu de Balle has the odd name of De Skieven Architek. Market traders come here at dawn for coffee and rolls and the one thing you must not call them is *skieven* as this is local slang for someone crooked. The *skieven architek* is Joseph Poelaert, thanks to whom the word 'architect' is just about the worst insult you can hurl at anyone in Brussels. The building which earned Poelaert his villainous reputation is our next destination.

After perhaps one quick last look at the flea market, we head up the steep, cobbled Rue des Renards, turn left along Rue Haute and then right up Rue de l'Epée. Looming above us now is the monstrous **Palais de Justice**, on the construction of which Joseph Poelaert toiled from 1866 until his death, from exhaustion, in 1879. Finally completed in 1883 (and so visible in our photograph on page 279, taken around 1900), the building is one of the most potent symbols of the reign of Léopold II, who once declared his ambition to be 'to make Belgium greater, stronger and more beautiful'. Poelaert helped Léopold to achieve the first two of these aims, though perhaps not the third, by modelling the Palais de Justice on the massive monumental temples of Egypt and Assyria. The elevated site on Galgenberg (Gallows' Hill) was deliberately chosen to strike terror into the lawless folk of the Marolles.

We ascend to the main entrance of the Palais de Justice by a series of ramps reminiscent of the temples of the Nile. As we enter the building between colossal statues of Cicero, Demosthenes, Lycurgus and Domitius Ulpian, we may spy a ghostly floodlit head of a Sphinx gazing down from a window above. I suggest that we do no more than glance into the cavernous and echoing *Salle des Pas Perdus* (Waiting Room), for it is a chilling place, which I think does not really belong in this country of miniature paintings, intimate interiors and eccentric details.

From the terrace in front of the Palais de Justice we obtain another panoramic view of northern Brussels, this time too crowded with modern architecture to recall the paintings of the Flemish Primitives. Northern Brussels is dominated by two gigantic eccentricities. The nearer one is the **Basilique Nationale du Sacré-Coeur**, situated in the *commune* of Koekelberg. Léopold II laid the first stone of a planned neo-gothic church on this site in 1905, but the project was abandoned in 1914 with nothing more than the foundations sunk. In the 1920's, however, an art deco church designed by Albert van Huffel was begun. Work was halted by the Second World War, but it was later resumed and the church finally completed in 1970. The other bizarre structure looming in the distance is the Atomium, a 120-metre-high building representing the nine atoms of an iron crystal (described on page 304).

We can retreat into the secluded **Jardin d'Egmont** by crossing Place Poelaert, turning left along Rue aux Laines and then right into Rue du Grand Cerf; the park is down a lane on the left. The 27-floor Hilton Hotel, which overlooks this park, proves to be a useful aid to navigation in this quarter of the Upper Town.

The Jardin d'Egmont is named after the 18th-century palace next to the park. The late gothic precursor of this palace was built by the mother of the executed Count Egmont in 1548. Diving into the mysterious park, we discover a lovely 15th-century well-head which stood on the flank of Coudenberg until redevelopment necessitated its removal to this leafy spot. Leaving by a cobbled lane on the far side brings us to the Boulevard de Waterloo, a busy thoroughfare following the course of the second city wall. All that remains of the fortifications is the massive Porte de Hal, a grim and gloomy 14th-century city gate at the end of Rue Haute, which has been restored to accommodate a museum of folklore.

We now turn right along the boulevard, past the Hilton doorman and the Hermès boutique, to reach two attractive old cafés highlighted by a gaudy assortment of neon signs. Both are tempting places to pause; Waterloo is the more formal, its waiters dressed like luxury liner stewards; Le Nemrod next door is owned by the same family as Le Métropole, La Chaloupe d'Or and La Brouette, and possesses the same distinctions as these Lower Town cafés. Le Nemrod's blazing fire will certainly tilt the balance in its favour on a chilly winter's day. After coffee, we may wish to explore the elegant shops along Avenue Louise and in the nearby arcades. Once shopping has been done and the services of a guide are again required, I suggest that we head along the Avenue de la Toison d'Or to the Porte de Namur, which may provide a good occasion to stop for coffee and cake. Though the Porte de Namur quarter has lost much of its fashionable allure, one splendid tea room called Au Flan Breton at 54 Chaussée d'Ixelles continues to do a roaring trade. Unlesss you are on a very strict diet, it is perhaps worth sneaking down the Chaussée d'Ixelles to sample one harmless cake. I should warn you that this is not a spacious tea room, but Belgians are seldom deterred by such worries. Even an elegant woman laden with six Kookaï bags and a dog will somehow manage to squeeze behind a row of chairs to the one unoccupied table that remains.

The steep Rue de Namur descends from the Porte de Namur to **Place Royale**, an elegant neoclassical square designed by Barnabé Guimard in the 18th century. Guimard's original plan achieved a pleasing intimacy by linking the individual aristocratic residences by neoclassical arcades, but Rue de Namur is the only street to retain this unusual feature.

Not many people are aware of the existence of several vanished streets and buildings underneath Place Royale. When this formal square was laid out in 1775, the steep old streets that plunged down the hill were preserved below the cobblestones, forming a secret network of passages which were used, apparently, by King Léopold II to visit his mistress and, in the Second World War, as an escape route for allied airmen. At the time of writing, archaeologists were excavating the foundations of the Aula Magna, the great hall, built by Philip the Good in 1452-60. The scene of Charles V's coronation in 1515, and forty years on, of his abdication, the hall was destroyed when the royal palace burned down in 1731. A vague plan existed at the time of writing to turn the labyrinth of underground streets and buildings into a museum.

Turning right at Place Royale we cross the road to the **Parc de Bruxelles**. 'The trees offer us shade,' states an antiquated iron sign at the park entrance. 'Along with the plants and the flowers, they are the joy and the beauty of the countryside. Anyone who damages the trees and the plants causes damage to himself.' Mindful of this stern warning, let us sit on a bench to read about the park.

Despite the sign we have just read, the trees offer us very little shade, for they have been ruthlessly trained on trellises. Indeed this park may well strike us as an object lesson in geometry rather than botany. Designed in 1787 by the Austrian landscape gardener Joachim Zinner, the avenues of the Parc de Bruxelles are laid out in the form of a compass - a masonic conceit best appreciated by studying a map.

The park is dotted with a curious miscellany of

statues, including Roman Emperors, Venus, Diana and Narcissus. There is also a statue of Peter the Great, who visited Brussels in 1717. Wandering down the straight alleys of the Parc in 1844, Thackeray complained that: 'Numbers of statues decorate the place, the very worst I ever saw. These cupids must have been erected in the time of the Dutch dynasty, as I judge from the immense posterior developments.' Robert Louis Stevenson was a more enthusiastic visitor, lyrically describing the pleasures of the park at night in a letter to his mother in 1872. 'If any person wants to be happy I should advise the Parc. You sit drinking iced drinks and smoking penny cigars under great old trees. The band place, covered walks, etc., are all lit up. And you can't fancy how beautiful was the contrast of the great masses of lamplit foliage and the dark sapphire night sky, with just one blue star set overhead in the middle of the largest patch. In the dark walks, too, there are crowds of people whose faces you cannot see, and here and there a colossal white statue at the corner of an alley that gives the place a nice *artificial*, 18th century sentiment.'

Before being prettified by Zinner, these woods were a ducal hunting estate dating back to the 14th century. In the 16th century, Charles V converted part of the woods into a tilting yard. Behind it stood the late gothic palace of the dukes of Burgundy, which was gutted by fire in 1731. It was within this palace that Margaret of Parma received a petition in 1566 calling for the abolition of the inquisitorial courts. During this historic audience, Count Berlaymont whispered to Margaret, 'Madam, it is nothing but a gang of beggars.' The following day, when several hundred nobles met in Count Kuilemburg's palace on Rue des Petits-Carmes to toast the success of their petition, they proudly declared themselves *Gueux* (beggars). Berlaymont's casual insult later prompted the Dutch rebels to dub themselves Sea Beggars and to equip themselves with a symbolic beggar's bowl.

The quarter around the park is now very definitely Viennese, rather than Burgundian, in tone. Barnabé Guimard, the creator of the Place Royale and Rue Royale, designed the neoclassical **Palais de la Nation** which attractively encloses the northern end of the park. Originally the seat of the Council of Brabant, this building has been home to the Belgian Parliament since 1831. The **Palais du Roi** which faces it across the formal parterres was erected on the site of the old Palais du Coudenberg in the early 20th century to provide Léopold II with a suitably grandiose town residence.

To return to Grand'Place, I recommend an indirect descent by two little-used flights of steps. The first leads down from Rue Royale to Rue Baron Horta, and permits us to glance at the programme of the **Musée du Cinéma** at 9 Rue Baron Horta, where three different films are screened daily, together with two classic silent films with piano accompaniment. The cinema museum is tucked away in a corner of the **Palais des Beaux-Arts**, built by Victor Horta on a tricky sloping site in the 1920's. By then, his art nouveau adventure was ended and he had fallen in line with the international art deco style. We can enter at 23 Rue Ravenstein to pick up a programme and perhaps visit the pleasant café.

The Palais des Beaux-Arts occupies the site of the garden of the Pensionnat Héger, where Charlotte and Emily Brontë stayed as students in 1842. It was quite common for wealthy British families to send their daughters to a finishing school in Brussels during the reign of the Anglophile Belgian monarch Léopold I. Charlotte returned alone the following year to teach here, and based *Villette* on her experiences as a single woman in Brussels. An evocative passage in the novel describes the lonely heroine wandering through the garden at sunset listening to the bells of the Eglise du Béguinage 'peal out with their sweet, soft, exalted sound'.

Left along Rue Ravenstein brings us to the **Hôtel Ravenstein** at No. 1. Built in the 15th century for Count Adolphe Cleve, it was restored in 1899 by Paul Saintenoy, the architect of the Delacre pharmacy and the Old England department store on the nearby Rue Montagne de la Cour. The Hôtel Ravenstein is now the sole surviving aristocratic town house in Brussels from the Burgundian period. An ancient flight of steps in front of the residence known as the Jodentrap, or Jews' Stairs, once linked the Lower and Upper Towns through the former Jewish quarter. When the Jews were driven out of this quarter in the 14th century, many fashionable new town houses such as the Hôtel Ravenstein were built here.

Let us now descend the steps to Rue Terarken, a dark alley overshadowed by this enormous town house. If we look right at the bottom we will see two splendid, but forgotten, late gothic bay windows projecting from the blackened stone walls. A tunnel below Rue Ravenstein leads to Rue des Sols, past a European Union office identifying itself in nine languages. On reaching Cantersteen, we are back on familiar ground and should have no difficulty making our way back to Grand'Place.

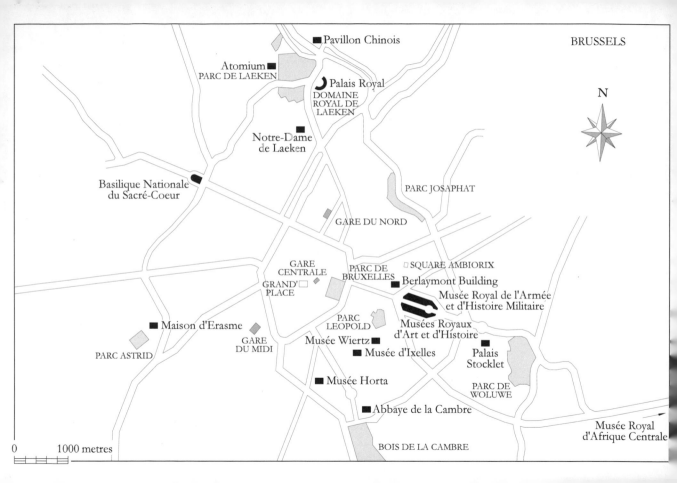

Brussels Explored Further

If you still have time to spare in Brussels, an enjoyable day or two can be spent exploring the suburbs of the city by tram and metro. The **Café Métropole** at 31 Place de Brouckère is a convenient place in which to plan an excursion, as it is close to De Brouckère metro station. The Hôtel Métropole was designed in 1894 by a French architect, Alban Chambon, who had made his reputation in the previous decade by designing numerous Victorian theatres in London, Brussels and Amsterdam. The Métropole, too, is designed in a theatrical spirit, with gleaming brass, large mirrors and chandeliers. Its old-fashioned charm is enhanced by waiters in long white aprons, excellent coffee served on a silver tray with a small chocolate, and a terrace on the bustling boulevard. So let us sink into a plump sofa in the Métropole to study the six excursions suggested below.

I. Museums in the Parc du Cinquantenaire. To commemorate the 50th anniversary of the foundation of the Belgian state, Léopold II created the Parc du Cinquantenaire in 1880. The park - reached by taking the metro to Mérode - once contained two large exhibition halls built by Gédéon Bordiau, who also designed the lovely Square Marie-Louise nearby. The south hall was destroyed by fire and rebuilt in a sober late art deco style, but the north hall has survived intact. The huge triumphal arch linking these two buildings was designed during the 75th anniversary celebrations in 1905 by Charles Girault, the

French architect responsible for the Congo Museum in Tervuren.

The rarely visited **Musées Royaux d'Art et d'Histoire** (Royal Museums of Art and History) share the south hall of the Cinquantenaire palace with a museum of motor cars. It used to be that you could wander through this vast museum for an hour and the only other person you would encounter would be an embalmed Egyptian mummy. In the past few years the mood has changed; some fifty new rooms have been opened to the public, and hundreds of treasures have been brought out of storage. A few rooms are still sometimes roped off, but the staff at the information desk are now happy to show you any room you wish to visit.

A new museum café is one of the delights recently introduced. Located just off the entrance hall, it occupies a light and airy set of rooms decorated in Flemish style with romantic 18th-century landscapes. I suggest we find a table to read about some of the treasures amassed here. When the time comes to explore the museum, a plan on sale at the information desk will help us to get around the vast collection with the minimum of wrong turnings.

Room 52, perhaps the best place to begin, contains some beautiful examples of Mosan art. With its extraordinary detail and liveliness, this early medieval art of the Meuse valley prefigures the miniature perfection of the Flemish Primitives. One of the most fascinating works is the *Portable Altar of Stavelot*, which a 12th-century traveller carried on his journeys. Notice the delightful seated figures of the Four Evangelists that form the feet of the altar, each of them holding a book in which the opening words of his gospel are inscribed.

An oval hall (room 18) contains a number of 18th-century carriages. Another little room contains two magnificent 17th-century globes. A dazzling collection of art nouveau jewellery and sculpture is displayed in a shop interior designed by Victor Horta for the Wolfers department store in Brussels (room 50).

A large hall in the depths of the museum (room 53) contains a magnificent series of eight Flemish 16th-century tapestries. Flemish tapestries were highly prized in the courts of renaissance Europe, which is why today the best examples are found in such far-flung places as Prague and the Vatican. The eight tapestries here, together with another two which have been lost, were sold to Cardinal Lorenzo Cambeggi, who shipped them to his palace at Bologna. The series was recently repatriated and restored at the De Wit tapestry workshop in Mechelen.

Based on cartoons by Bernard van Orley, the tapestries were woven by Willem de Kempeneer in the 1530's. The letters B.B. in the margin signify that they were produced in Brussels, in the province of Brabant. The series illustrates the story of Jacob, who deceived his father into bestowing his fortune upon him rather than his brother Esau. As was customary in 16th century art, the various scenes from Jacob's life are set in Flemish interiors. If we look at the tapestry illustrating Jacob's vision of a ladder ascending to heaven, we can see that the floor tiles are decorated with the Hapsburg double eagle.

The neo-gothic cloisters beyond the hall of tapestries contain several interesting tombs of medieval knights and abbesses. There are also curious fragments of stained glass from Brussels Cathedral, showing human faces and angels. The rooms beyond contain a number of large retables, such as the *St Joristafel* from Leuven, which depicts an unpleasant catalogue of cruelties, and the more appealing *Retable of Claude de Villa and Gentine Solaro*, dating from 1470.

If you can hunt it out, pause to admire the bronze font resting on six lions that was cast in 1149 for the church of St Germain in Tienen; its rim is decorated with fourteen Biblical scenes. Other rooms are devoted to Rome, Greece, Egypt, Islam, Polynesia and America. There is a remarkable scale model of ancient Rome in room 20 and a collection of antique cameras in room 75. It would take at least a day to see it all, but even a short visit is worth the effort.

The **Musée Royal de l'Armée et d'Histoire Militaire** (Royal Army and Military History Museum) occupies the building on the opposite side of the arch. Old wooden display cases are crammed with rusty horseshoes and worn saddles, cannon that pounded Flemish cities in the

15th century and dented Spanish armour, not forgetting the two stuffed horses - the oldest in the world, they say - on which the Archduke Albert and Archduchess Isabella cantered into Brussels almost four centuries ago. A glass case in the Salle Historique contains memorabilia of King Léopold II, including his umbrella, dumb-bells and pince-nez. There is also a British-made tricycle on which, one must presume, the bespectacled monarch intended to lead his army to victory.

Perhaps it is fortunate that Léopold died before the outbreak of the First World War, as this event shattered forever the innocent belief in progress of his age. A vast gloomy hall of the army museum is crammed with relics of this appalling conflict. You can almost smell death as you wander among stretchers stained with blood, battered howitzers and mud-spattered uniforms. No attempt has been made either to glorify or to condemn; the museum has merely gathered anything it could lay its hands on - machine guns, tanks, uniforms, first aid kits, torn maps, fragments of crashed aircraft and wreckage from sunken ships. It all looks as if it has only recently been dredged from the mud of Flanders.

Waterloo was a different story. This battle fought just to the south of Brussels in 1815 was a classic boy's adventure. Several cabinets in the entrance hall contain objects found on the battlefield, including rusted horseshoes, Prussian sabres, coins, buttons, guns and a portrait of an unidentified soldier. Perhaps the most interesting relic is Napoleon's satchel (or at least what remained after a fire in Madame Tussaud's in London, where it was once on display) which was discovered by Prussian soldiers in Napoleon's carriage, along with his hat and sword. Another interesting memento is a fragment of shrapnel that served Victor Hugo as a macabre paperweight.

The one-day battle in 1815, at which some 40,000 soldiers died, seized the imagination of all Europe. To novelists, it provided an irresistible backdrop, with episodes of heroism and tragedy to satisfy the most demanding of romantic readers. In 1816, when the battlefield was still littered with boots, buttons and bullets, Lord Byron was taken there by Major Lockhart Gordon. After casting an approving eye over the scene, Byron 'galloped across the fields of Waterloo', the Major recalled, 'cloak flying out behind, eyes fixed ahead.' On returning to his lodgings at 51 Rue Ducale, opposite the Parc de Bruxelles, Byron drafted several stanzas on the battle to incorporate into *Childe Harold*. His poem *The Eve of Waterloo* vividly captures the excitment in Brussels: 'There was a sound of revelry by night,/And Belgium's Capital had gathered then/Her beauty and her Chivalry.' Thackeray penned a marvellous description of the battle in *Vanity Fair*, based on eye-witness accounts. Waterloo also features in several French classics, such as Victor Hugo's *Les Misérables*, part of which he wrote while staying at the Hôtel des Colonnes in the village of Mont St Jean, the site of the British field hospital. Stendhal's *Charterhouse of Parma* includes a Waterloo episode, which magnificently captures the confusion of battle.

The romantic obsession with Waterloo was not confined to novelists, for Britain is dotted with obelisks and other miscellaneous monuments to the battle. A peculiar practice of the day was for landowners to lay out plantations of trees to represent the formation of their regiment on the eve of the battle. There is one at Peniel Heugh in Roxburghshire and another near Hadnall in Shropshire.

Unfortunately, the battlefield itself has lost much of its romance. Surrounded now by souvenir shops and coaches, we are very unlikely to sense 'horror breathing from the silent ground', as Wordsworth did on his pilgrimage there in 1820. It is perhaps better therefore to give it a miss, and to let the relics here evoke the events of that decisive day in European history.

The other departments of the museum may be antiquated and cluttered, but they have a musty charm. The uniforms worn by 19th-century armies are particularly fascinating to pore over. The Second Cavalry Regiment of the French army (room 8, cabinet 8) would appear to have trotted into battle with a sabre in one hand and a hat-box in the other. The helmets they wore seem to have been the last word in military haute couture: made of gleaming silver and polished brass, they were surmounted by something that resembles a large feather duster.

The Belgian army was no less immune from the demands of fashion. In the 1830 Revolution (room 2), the rebels sported a pale blue smock and a twelve-inch stove-pipe hat topped with a red pompom. For the ill-fated Mexican campaign of 1864-67 (room 8, cabinet 34), the Belgians deployed a fetching dark blue jacket with green trim, charcoal grey plus-fours and their favourite stove-pipe hat, topped this time with a clutch of feathers which look as if they may have been plucked from a dead blackbird. Despite this careful dressing for success, the Belgians were defeated by the Mexican Republicans, and the unfortunate Archduke Maximilian of Austria, Emperor of Mexico, was shot by firing squad. Manet's famous painting of the scene shows him wearing just a plain white shirt.

The Salle des Provinces Réunies was recently added to the museum to display a collection of shiny armour and artillery from the middle ages to the 17th century. As well as hefty pieces of jousting equipment, there is a miniature suit of armour made for the young Joseph-Ferdinand of Bavaria.

We may be exhausted by now, but there is one last hall to visit. It contains a collection of 130 aircraft, ranging fom flimsy biplanes that dropped bombs on the Ypres Salient to a streamlined Lockheed Starfighter. Several salvaged relics of aircraft are displayed, including the battered wing of an American B-17 bomber shot down in Liège province, which was used until recently by a local farmer to enclose his chicken shed.

After exploring this museum, we leave the park on the south side and turn left along the Avenue des Nerviens, pausing at Rue des Francs to admire the **Maison Cauchie** at No. 5, built by Paul Cauchie in 1904 as his home and studio. The business sign by the door gave callers an indication of Cauchie's skills, as did the sgraffito murals, which are designed in a willowy Pre-Raphaelite style. The oval studio window which pierces this art nouveau composition looks as if it may have been inspired by the marvellous Maison de Saint-Cyr at 11 Square Ambiorix, but the rest of the façade seems more like early art deco.

If we continue along the Avenue des Gaulois,

we reach the busy Porte de Tervuren. The most cosmopolitan café hereabouts is La Terrasse at 11 Avenue de Tervuren, where we can settle into fabulously plump sofas in art nouveau partitioned compartments.

II. Museums in Ixelles. The *commune* of Ixelles contains two museums that are worth exploring if we find ourselves with an afternoon to spare. The **Musée d'Ixelles** at 71 Rue Jean van Volsem, founded in 1892, boasts a splendid and varied collection of paintings and sculpture, from a drawing by Dürer to various contemporary Belgian works. Several rooms contain paintings by French Impressionists, including an extensive collection of Toulouse Lautrec posters. The emphasis is mainly on modern Belgian paintings, however, and there are marvellous surrealist works by Magritte and Delvaux. *The Dialogue*, painted by Delvaux in 1974, illustrates the serene style of his later years; it shows two nude women in a mysterious setting that suggests an unbuilt classical city. One of the most enjoyable works in the collection is Philippe Vindal's *The Brothel*, a precisely detailed model of a derelict house used as a brothel, crammed with an extraordinary miscellany of domestic rubbish.

Ixelles' other museum is the secluded **Musée Wiertz** where, as an art student, Delvaux discovered the strange nude studies of Antoine Wiertz such as *La Belle Rosine*, a voluptuous Rubensian woman confronting her own skeleton. The Ostend painter James Ensor was also drawn to this haunting art collection at 62 Rue Vautier.

In a leafy setting at the top of a hill, the Musée Wiertz looks almost like an artist's villa in Rome. This is quite fitting, for Antoine Wiertz, like his hero Rubens, had spent some years in Rome, and retained a fond attachment to Italy and its art. Three small rooms of the house contain numerous delightful little studies by Wiertz of festive Italian scenes. But the paintings that prompted Thomas Hardy to write in *Tess of the D'Urbervilles* of 'the staring and ghastly attitudes of a Wiertz Museum' are found in the huge atelier adjoining the house. On the back of its door is written a definition of modesty as 'a mask that flatters the vanity of others to draw praise to oneself'.

297

Antoine Wiertz certainly could not be accused of modesty, for his works are among the largest ever painted. The *Revolt of Heaven Against Hell*, the largest work in the museum, is 11.5 metres high and 7.9 metres wide! The canvas has been tilted forward to improve visibility, and the cleaning staff, irreverently, have used the space behind to store their mops and brooms.

The Musée Wiertz is perhaps not a museum for a dark winter's day, for many of the paintings are deeply pessimistic, such as *The Suicide*, which captures the terrible moment when a melancholic, with a book named *Matérialisme* lying on the table, blows out his brains. Reproduced opposite is another typically gruesome work, *Premature Burial*, in which we see a man's blind panic as he tries to escape from a coffin.

Now considered only a minor artist, Antoine Wiertz was immensely popular in mid-19th-century Belgium. In 1850 he even managed to solve the obviously difficult problem of storing and selling his giant works by persuading the government to build this house and studio for him on condition that they became a state museum after his death. Under the terms of this peculiar agreement, all the paintings that he completed after 1850 also became the property of the state. The house has changed very little since then, and the studio is still lit by natural light; but one intriguing feature described in Baedeker's 1905 guide has unfortunately disappeared: 'In the corners of the room are wooden screens, through peep-holes in which paintings hung behind them are seen. The effect is curiously realistic.'

Not far from the Musée Wiertz is the **Parc Léopold**, a romantic 19th-century retreat dotted with interesting old buildings. Another more extensive park in Ixelles is the **Bois de la Cambre**. 'The alleys of this park are thronged with fashionable equipages,' Karl Baedeker informed his readers in 1905. Now they are thronged with fancy dogs and red-faced joggers, but it is still a very pleasant place for wandering on a Sunday afternoon. Once part of the Forêt de Soignes, the Bois de la Cambre was imaginatively landscaped in the 19th century. Its most beguiling feature is an artificial lake with an island, which can be reached by rowing boat or

by a quaint mechanical ferry.

Lying in a hollow to the north of the Bois de la Cambre is the attractive **Abbaye de la Cambre**, a Cistercian abbey founded in the 12th century in what was then an idyllic river valley in the Forêt de Soignes. Most of the abbey was rebuilt in the 18th century in baroque style, but the attractive 14th-century church still survives.

An afternoon in Ixelles would somehow seem empty without at least a cup of coffee. There is the famous Nihoul at 300 Avenue Louise, where elderly ladies sit with dogs on their laps, but I prefer Passiflore at 6 Parvis de la Trinité. Possibly it is the flamboyant oriental decor that appeals to me, but I suspect it may be the cakes. A single Passiflore chocolate cake might seem like the ultimate temptation. But, no, you can sink deeper into sinfulness by ordering a selection of three types of pâtisserie.

III. Art Nouveau architecture. The nervous and flowing style of art nouveau, inspired by the sinuous lines of flowers and trees, originated in Britain in the 1880's, but it flourished particularly in the great Continental cities of Paris, Vienna, Brussels and Barcelona. The finest art nouveau buildings in Brussels were built at the turn of the 19th century by Victor Horta, who once confessed that 'the warmth of stone has made my happiness'. Tragically, many of his buildings have been demolished, but thankfully one has been preserved as a museum: the **Musée Horta** at 23-5 Rue Américaine, which can be reached by taking tram 81, 91 or 92 to Place Janson. The house, which was Horta's home and studio from 1898 to 1919, contains a wealth of delightful art nouveau details, such as the magnificent staircase which ascends through the interior like an exotic tropical plant, with its polished wooden banisters tightly intertwined like creepers. In the attic, an extraordinary illusion of infinite space is created by means of mirrors. Notice also the radiator cleverly concealed behind a sofa on the staircase.

Despite exuding a warmth and exhilarating beauty, the Horta family home was not entirely harmonious, for Madame Horta was uninterested in art nouveau and treated Horta's architectural associates coldly. In 1919 Horta sold the house and atelier because he needed more space to work on the large-scale projects that were then coming his way. The departure from this house effectively marked the end of Horta's art nouveau period and a shift to a chilling art deco style, as evidenced by Brussels' Gare Centrale and Palais des Beaux-Arts.

There are a number of attractive art nouveau houses in the neighbourhood, including one, the **Hôtel Hannon** at 1 Avenue de la Jonction, which is now occupied by the Contretype photography gallery. It was designed in 1903 by one of Horta's students, Jules Brunfaut, for Edouard Hannon. Hannon had been employed as an engineer by the industrialist Ernest Solvay, for whom Horta designed a house at 224 Avenue Louise. As well as holding temporary exhibitions of contemporary photography, the gallery houses a small collection of early 20th-century photographs taken by Hannon on his travels.

A house at 85 Rue Faider has splendid, if faded, frescoes featuring languid Pre-Raphaelite women. It faces down Rue Paul Emile Janson, where Horta built his first art nouveau house - the Hôtel

Tassel - in 1893. At 48 Rue Defacqz is another attractive art nouveau house built in 1897 by Paul Hankar for the symbolist painter Albert Ciamberlani. Its decorated frieze is sadly too far gone for us to make out what it is about.

The big round windows of Ciamberlani's studio face down Rue Veydt. The café-restaurant Amadeus is at No. 13, in a rambling set of rooms which in the 19th century housed a sculptor's workshop. Glossy Dutch magazines discovered this artistic hideaway years ago, but fame has not entirely destroyed the atmosphere. It is worth a visit just to look at the blue courtyard walls and the dusty statues of Greek gods lurking in dark corners. The mood is best caught in the early hours of the afternoon, when you might have the entire place to yourself, apart from a couple from Rotterdam smooching under a potted fern. By the early evening, the oyster bar is mobbed with beautiful people.

Perhaps the most spectacular art nouveau restaurant in Brussels is **De Ultieme Halluci-natie** (The Ultimate Hallucination), concealed behind a drab 19th-century façade at 316 Rue

Royale (reached by taking tram 92, 93 or 94 to Ste Marie). Paul Hamesse - a pupil of Paul Hankar - remodelled the interior of this mid-19th-century town house in 1904. The Dutch name of the restaurant alludes to the dream-like mood of the interior, with its painstakingly restored murals and gleaming brass fittings. Perched upon third-class Belgian railway carriage seats in a winter garden filled with ferns and statuary, we can eat a simple omelette or a *plat du jour*. Alternatively, we can eat a full dinner in the beautiful former dining room.

On the same street, the **Maison Isabelle de Backer** at 13 Rue Royale is a handsome art nouveau florist's shop designed by Paul Hankar in 1899. Its mahogany frontage seems as delicate as the exotic orchids displayed within.

Situated in the Lower Town opposite the Bourse, **Le Falstaff** at 17-23 Rue Henri Maus, is another art nouveau café, designed in 1903 by E. Houbion, one of the architects who worked in Victor Horta's studio. Its large round windows are a familiar motif of Belgian art nouveau, although some of the other features such as the signs outside seem more in the geometrical style of art deco, and the woodwork and stained glass windows inside look more like lingering Victorian eclecticism. What makes Falstaff Brussels' most popular café is not merely its interior design, however, but also an excellent menu, good selection of beers and virtual 24-hour service.

IV. Laeken. To the north of Brussels, on the heights of Laeken, we find a strange ensemble of buildings from the reign of Léopold II. Taking tram 52 or 92 from De Brouckère to the stop named Araucaria, we see a **Japanese pagoda** looming above the trees. The tower was one of Léopold II's gifts to the city. The idea of building a pagoda next to the royal palace came to the elderly king during a visit in 1900 to the Universal Exhibition in Paris. Léopold had been particularly impressed by a Japanese pagoda he had seen which formed part of an exhibition called 'The World Tour'. The king set his heart on constructing something similar in northern Brussels. His original plan was to erect a whole string of buildings in various exotic styles, but even Léopold's vast funds could not realise more than a part of his dream. In the end only the Japanese pagoda, a Chinese pavilion, and a reproduction of the 16th-century Flemish-designed Neptune Fountain in Bologna were built. We reach the pagoda through a tunnel under the road, emerging in a quiet Japanese garden with water trickling from bamboo pipes and a pond stocked with goldfish. Inside, the pagoda is sumptuously decorated with carved wood, red lacquer and gold. Wooden cabinets contain a few carefully spotlit examples of wafer-thin Imari porcelain.

Back on the other side of the road, we find the **Chinese Pavilion**, an exquisite replica of a Chinese temple decorated inside with gilt mirrors and rococo landscapes. Léopold intended it to be a restaurant, but that alluring prospect was never realized; it currently provides a scintillating setting for a collection of Chinese porcelain.

The Chinese pavilion is now unfortunately surrounded by a tangle of busy roads. Watching the international trucks rumble by, we can meditate on the disadvantages which stem from being

'the crossroads of Europe', as Brussels is often dubbed. Léopold's Bolognese fountain can be glimpsed, marooned on a traffic island. On reaching the far side of the road, we turn right and skirt the edge of the **Park de Laeken** to reach the entrance. Once in the park, we will see, crowning a summit on the left, a neo-gothic monument erected to Léopold I in 1881. From there we can look down upon the 18th-century **Palais Royal**, where Napoleon signed the fateful order in 1812 that sent his armies into Russia.

No directions are needed to reach our next destination, the **Atomium**, whose ghostly aluminium spheres loom above the trees. This strange memento of the 1958 World Fair is very much a creation of the 1950's, standing in the middle of a traffic roundabout like a space craft in a boys' comic. Representing the nine atoms of an iron crystal, the Atomium rises to a height of 120 metres and dominates the northern skyline of Brussels, especially at night when the spheres are picked out with lights. A high-speed lift takes us up to the topmost sphere, where we can enjoy a panoramic view of Brussels, although skyscrapers tend to blot out the older and more interesting buildings. We then descend through various other spheres by very long escalators, or staircases located in the tubular arms linking the spheres. The Atomium was recently renovated, and dusty old display boards describing atomic energy were replaced by a more catchy exhibition devoted to human biology. Even if the idea of entering a giant blood cell does not appeal, you may still enjoy exploring the Atomium, which remains one of the most bizarre structures ever built.

The main building we see from the observation deck of the Atomium is the art deco **Palais du Centenaire**, built in 1930 for the centenary celebrations of the founding of the Belgian state, and now part of a sprawling exhibition centre. To the left is the Bruparck, which contains a sophisticated swimming pool, a 23-screen cinema complex, and a park laid out with several hundred scale models of European buildings. Restaurants, cafés and taverns occupy mock old Flemish houses, similar to those built for the 1958 World Fair.

The metro takes us straight back to the centre, but if we still have time to spare we might visit one more curiosity. Taking tram 81 to Royauté, then turning left along Rue du Champ de l'Église, we come upon a huge neo-gothic church bristling with pinnacles, **Notre-Dame de Laeken**, where the Belgian kings and queens are buried. We should not worry too much if the church is closed, as it is the exterior which is impressive, especially when seen from the cemetery behind.

The **Cimetière de Laeken** contains an extraordinary collection of 19th-century tombs of eminent Belgians. As well as neo-gothic and neoclassical monuments, there are several eccentricities, including a mosque, an Egyptian temple and the tomb of a general symbolically decorated with a shattered cannon. The most famous Belgian buried here is the architect Joseph Poelaert, who designed Notre-Dame de Laeken in 1870. His face betrays the exhaustion he suffered in the struggle to complete the Palais de Justice. Tucked away in a corner of the cemetery is a fragment from a 13th-century church built of an attractive honey-coloured stone. Old Baedeker

guides also refer to underground catacombs, but these I have never managed to find. Once we have explored this fascinating cemetery, we can take a tram back to the centre.

V. Tervuren and the Forêt de Soignes. One of the most beguiling excursions from Brussels is by tram 44 to the Flemish village of Tervuren. We can easily do this trip in a half day, but if the weather is pleasant then it is worth devoting a whole day to the expedition. We can then have lunch in one of the restaurants in Tervuren and spend the afternoon walking in the beautiful woods nearby.

We first take the metro to Montgomery station, where tram 44 begins its 20-minute journey to Tervuren. The tram returns to street level on the elegant Avenue de Tervuren, which Léopold II built to connect the Parc du Cinquantenaire with the village of Tervuren. Just beyond the stop Père Damien, look out on the right for the splendid **Palais Stocklet**, designed by the Austrian architect Josef Hoffman in 1905 for the rich Belgian industrialist Mons Stocklet. The pure geometric lines of this building illustrate the principles of the Wiener Werkstätte, which Hoffman founded with Koloman Moser in 1903. The battle-cry of this movement clearly implied a rejection of art nouveau aesthetics. 'We will use ornament where appropriate,' they declared, 'but without compulsion and not just for its own sake.' As we can see in the photograph, even the trees in front of the Palais Stocklet have been trimmed into neat geometric shapes. The interior contains some murals by Gustav Klimt but, to the chagrin of enthusiasts of the Vienna style, the house remains firmly closed to the public.

Tram 44 then rumbles on past the gently rolling **Parc de Woluwe**. If we are tempted to stretch our legs in this attractive park, we should leave at a stop curiously named Chien Vert. However, Tervuren offers even better walks, so perhaps we should leave Woluwe's park to another day.

Soon we leave the city behind and plunge into the **Forêt de Soignes**, a wonderfully wild forest of oak and beech which stretches in a wide sweep around the southern edge of Brussels from Tervuren to Waterloo. One of the delights of Brussels, especially on a crisp autumn day, is to head off into the wilderness of the Forêt de Soignes, all that remains of the great forest which once covered most of present-day Belgium. Known to the Romans as the Sylva Carbonaria, the Charcoal Forest, it still contains a few charcoal kilns which the Romans worked.

The forest was dotted with monasteries in the middle ages, with some seven religious orders seeking solitude in the depths of these woods. At **Groenendael**, to the south of Brussels, the 14th-century mystic Jan van Ruysbroeck founded an Augustinian abbey, where he wrote most of his religious works. Cloître Rouge, also in the forest, was the priory into which the painter Hugo van der Goes retreated in about 1475. Here he completed several major works, including the great *Death of the Virgin* now in the Groeningemuseum in Bruges. In the 16th century, the forest was a favourite hunting ground of Charles V; many Flemish tapestries of the period, including one in Brussels' Musée Communal, depicted hunting scenes in the Forêt de Soignes.

On arriving at Tervuren's delightfully rural

station, where the tram terminates, we simply walk straight ahead down Leuvensesteenweg (the street names here revert to Flemish, for we have left the bilingual enclave of Brussels). Our destination is the **Koninklijk Museum voor Middenafrika** (Royal Museum of Central Africa) on the right.

The quiet village of Tervuren seems an unlikely setting for this museum, which was erected on the site of the Château de Tervuren. The old castle was destroyed by fire in 1879, at which time it was the home of Léopold II's sister, the unfortunate Charlotte. She had moved here in 1867, following the execution of her husband, the Emperor Maximilian of Mexico, whose death is movingly depicted in the famous painting by Manet. The loss of her husband left Charlotte deranged for the rest of her long life, much of which she spent talking to empty chairs.

After moving his unhappy sister to another royal castle, Léopold used what remained of the Château de Tervuren to house a collection of booty brought back from his private colony in the Congo. The present building was begun in 1904 by Charles Girault, the architect of the Petit Palais in Paris, but it was not completed until after Léopold's death.

Léopold held that his interest in the Congo was purely philanthropic, but many saw the venture as a brutal quest for profit. In an unusually vitriolic outburst, Mark Twain wrote that 'In fourteen years, Léopold has deliberately destroyed more lives than have suffered death in all the battlefields of this planet for the past thousand years.' And if this was not indictment enough, Joseph Conrad's novel *Heart of Darkness* was based on his experiences in the course of a horrifying journey through the Congo in 1890.

The museum contains a rich and exotic collection of masks and sculpture, together with plants, animals and even insects brought back from Central Africa. Some of the most interesting rooms are those devoted to European explorers in Central Africa. There are several relics of the American journalist, Henry Morton Stanley, who was employed by Léopold to explore the Congo. Look out for the battered old suitcase taken by Stanley on his African journeys, which still has a label attached to it by his wife Dolly, declaring imperiously, 'This Portmanteau belonged to H. M. Stanley. It was carried across Africa. It must never be removed from my Room and *never* on any account be used.' Equally unexpected are the objects connected with Dr Livingstone. We see the metal travelling case which the Scottish explorer took on his final, sad journey, and a handful of dry leaves plucked by a devoted admirer from the mpundu tree in Chitambo (now Zambia) beneath which his heart was buried. Another traveller removed part of the tree's trunk and preserved it like the relic of a medieval saint, prompting one to wonder what, if anything, remains of the tree in situ.

This room also contains several marvellous old maps of Central Africa, including one from Ortelius' *Theatrum orbis terrarum*, published in 1612. It is interesting to compare this with a British map published by John Cary in 1821, which marks a large blank area in the centre of Africa as 'Unknown Parts', even though these had been charted in great detail by Ortelius over two centuries earlier.

After exploring this odd and engaging collection, we can rest in the museum café, which occupies a lofty room looking onto the main courtyard. When the sun shines, we can sit out under white parasols drinking tea. Surrounded by tall ferns and African statues, we might almost have stumbled upon an outpost of the Belgian Congo.

VI. Anderlecht. Our final trip takes us west to Anderlecht, a former village which was swallowed up by the expansion of Brussels in the 19th century. Anderlecht has an interesting late gothic church and a small Béguinage, but the main reason for visiting this *commune* is the **Maison d'Erasme** at 31 Rue du Chapitre. To reach this house (which is closed on Tuesdays and Fridays) we should take metro line 1A to St Guidon, then make for the spire of the church, near which is the house we are looking for.

Maison d'Erasme is a misleading name, for it was in fact the chapter house of the nearby Eglise St Guidon. Erasmus stayed here for a mere five months in the summer of 1521 as the guest of his friend Pieter Wychman, a canon in St Guidon. Yet the house has become something of a shrine to Erasmus, prompted by a visit here in 1691 by William III, Stadholder of the Netherlands and King of England, accompanied by the Dutch diplomat Constantijn Huygens. In 1930 the house was purchased by the local council and opened as a museum.

Most of the building dates from 1515, as the four iron numerals attached to a wall reveal, although we enter by a small building erected in the 15th century. Tastefully restored in the style of the early 16th century, the Erasmus House is furnished with heavy oak chests, apothecary's vases and paintings in the disturbing style of the Antwerp Mannerists. There is also an *Adoration of the Magi* painted in about 1485 by Hieronymus Bosch (No. 236), which once hung in St Guidon.

The museum displays an extensive collection of portraits of Erasmus; many are facsimile copies of 16th-century works by artists such as Holbein and Metsys, but there are also less well known paintings by 19th-century romantics, and 20th-century ephemera, such as banknotes, theatre posters and caricatures featuring Erasmus. His portrait even appears on an L.N.E.R. poster advertising railway excursions to Cambridge, where Erasmus spent some unhappy months teaching theology and Greek. More surprising still, we see the figure of Erasmus at the far right of a painting of *The Judgement of Solomon* by Frans Francken the Younger (No. 258).

Erasmus relished having his portrait painted by the great artists of the day, and was clearly piqued when Albrecht Dürer abandoned a portrait begun in 1520. 'I would like to have my portrait painted by Dürer,' he wrote to Willibald Pirckheimer in 1525, 'for who would not wish to be painted by such a great artist. He began by making a charcoal sketch in Brussels, but he claims to have lost it long ago.' Dürer and Erasmus met several times in Brussels and Antwerp in 1520 and 1521, but their opposing attitudes to the vexing question of Luther appear to have soured their relationship. Dürer's diary entry of 17 May 1521 included a hysterical outburst against Erasmus: 'O Erasmus of Rotterdam, where do you wish to stand?' he asked in strongly Lutheran language.

'Hark, ye knight of Christ, ride off with Christ our Lord at your side, defend the truth, grasp the martyr's palm.' Erasmus, however, remained more level-headed about the claims of Lutheranism, writing in a letter to Ulrich von Hutten: 'If Christ were to grant me the strength, then I would elect to be a martyr, but I would not want to be a martyr for Luther.'

Despite their differences, Dürer eventually produced a portrait of Erasmus in 1526, apparently using the sketch which he once claimed to have lost. The woodcut portrait (No. 123 in the collection) now hangs in the study - a fastidious reconstruction of the room depicted by Dürer. The woodcut shows Erasmus sitting at his desk in winter, wearing three coats on top of one another, a hat pulled down over his ears, and an ink bottle held in his left hand to prevent the contents from freezing. Dürer seems to have had some misgivings about this portrait, for he included an apologetic inscription in Greek 'His works provide a better impression.' He also added - this time in Latin - the untruthful assertion: 'Painted from nature'. Erasmus, too, was unimpressed with the final result, commenting laconically 'Resemblance: none'. In a letter to Pirckheimer, he grumbled 'It is hardly surprising that the portrait is not a better likeness, since I am not the same person that I was five years ago.'

After exploring the garden, in which are a few fragments of local architecture, we have seen almost all that Anderlecht has to offer. The cafés hereabouts are disappointing; despite its name, the Darts Club Erasme opposite the museum does not look as if it seriously intends to tempt passing Erasmians within. Signposts behind the church may persuade us to explore Anderlecht's **Béguinage**, but this, too, is disappointing, apart from the striking view from its courtyard of the 19th-century spire of St Guidon. As for the church, its main attraction would appear to be the 11th-century tomb of St Guidon, who is revered locally as the patron saint of horses and cattle. Unfortunately, the church, which is sadly dilapidated, is seldom open, so we have little prospect of examining the tomb of St Guidon, or the 15th-century murals depicting the deeds for which he earned his renown.

The perfect café to conclude a visit to Brussels is situated back in town, opposite the Bourse. **Café Cirio** at 18 Rue de la Bourse opened its doors in 1886, four years before the explorer Henry Morton Stanley made a rousing speech in the Bourse in praise of Léopold II's development of the Congo. Cirio's interior recalls Georges Simenon's description of a Brussels café: 'It was as restful as a warm bath, this huge room hazy with smoke, full of the fumes of coffee and beer, where the chink of plates and glasses blended with the languorous strains of a Viennese waltz.' My favourite corner in Cirio is the back room, with its gleaming brass and its ancient glass cabinets filled with faded family photographs. It seems far removed from the world outside, as do the elderly ladies who quietly tipple Cirio's Italian white wine in the afternoon. The only complaint one might have is that the antiquated coin-operated eau-de-cologne dispensers in the toilets have long since ceased to function.

Leuven

Leuven

Duke Jan I of Brabant is a popular figure in Leuven for two reasons. In 1425 he founded Leuven University to revive the town's sagging economy; and he once issued a proclamation standing on top of a beer keg. He won the eternal admiration of students throughout the Low Countries, and many Dutch and Flemish university towns now boast a café Gambrinus (a corruption of Jan Primus) named in his honour.

Leuven University soon became one of the great seats of learning of medieval Europe. Many famous scholars stumbled to lectures along its bumpy cobbled streets, among them Erasmus, co-founder of one of Leuven's fifty colleges, and the heretical theologian Cornelius Jansen (who built an eccentric retreat in an abandoned tower left over from the old city wall). Charles V was the

most famous of the 6,000 students at the university in the early 16th century. He rewarded his former teacher, Adrian Florisz., by engineering his election to the papacy in 1522.

The modern Leuven University split into two in 1969 when, after prolonged clashes, the French-speakers were expelled, moving to a new campus at Louvain-la-Neuve and leaving Leuven to the Dutch-speakers.

Nowadays some 23,000 students of many nationalities swell the population of Leuven during term-time, jamming the narrow streets with their bicycles, and putting up complicated messages on doorbells of student houses. On Friday mornings, the town centre is further animated by a street market, with fresh fruit and vegetables in the Oude Markt, clothes and fabrics crammed into the narrow Parijsstraat, and *frites* stalls almost everywhere.

Wandering through the crowded streets on market day, it's difficult to imagine the town in ruins, as it was in August 1914, after the occupying German army set out to raze the town, burning 1,800 houses and reducing the world-famous university library in Naamsestraat to a smouldering ruin. If we stand in the Oude Markt and look up, we will see that almost all the restored houses have a small stone tablet with the date 1914 and the symbols of a sword and torch. The library was rebuilt in the 1920's with American funding in imitation Old Flemish style. The arcade facing the square is inscribed with the names of American donor colleges in ornate lettering.

Being a university town, Leuven has a multitude of cafés that make pleasant places to end the day. Gambrinus, built in the 1920's on the ruined Grote Markt, is the most traditional, with cut glass windows, gleaming brass coat hooks, and bucolic murals of frolicking cherubs. But I prefer the rambling, cluttered interior of Domus on Eikstraat, where you can sit at a carpet-covered table below a bust of Socrates and raise a glass of Stella Artois to Jan Primus.

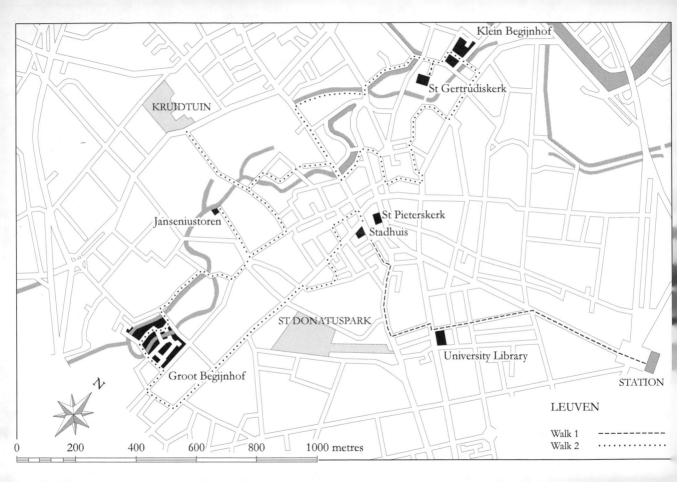

KLEIN BEGIJNHOF

St Gertrudiskerk

KRUIDTUIN

Janseniustoren

St Pieterskerk

Stadhuis

ST DONATUSPARK

University Library

Groot Begijnhof

STATION

LEUVEN

Walk 1 - - - - - -
Walk 2 · · · · · · · · ·

N

0   200   400   600   800   1000 metres

WALK 1

Gothic painting and architecture

Leuven can conveniently be visited in a day from Brussels or Antwerp, so our two walks are intended to fill a morning and an afternoon. On arriving at Leuven we may be disappointed by the town. Unlike the other Flemish cities we have visited, Leuven has neither a belfry nor a prominent church spire to guide us to the town centre. This is due to the *veen*, or marshy ground, on which the town is built, which prevented the construction of tall buildings. Yet Leuven does have a splendid gothic town hall and an impressive church, the Sint Pieterskerk. The aim of this walk, which will take about two hours, is to look at the town hall, and to explore the church, which contains many works of art, including two beautiful paintings by Dirk Bouts.

From the railway station, we walk straight ahead down Bondgenotenlaan. This street leads directly to the Sint Pieterskerk, but there is a more interesting way to approach the church, which is to turn left down Koning Léopold I Straat, and thence to a square dominated by the new university library. This replaces the old buildings destroyed by fire in 1914, and again in 1944, this time by Allied planes. The 1914 conflagration is vividly depicted in a bas relief on the front of the building, where we also see a curious Madonna wearing a Belgian First World War soldier's helmet. Built with American funds, the new library is designed in an ostentatious mixture of neo-baroque and neo-renaissance, its 85-metre high tower, built in spite of the marshy gound, modelled on a traditional Flemish belfry. The number 48, symbolising the states of the USA at the time of construction, is subtly incorporated into the building: each of the four clock faces is decorated with 12 stars, and the carillon contains 48 bells. The names of the universities and colleges that funded the rebuilding of the university are inscribed in flourishing calligraphy within the arcade.

On the far side of Herbert Hooverplein lies the Sint Donatuspark, a pleasant landscaped park with a small pond that is home to five shivering flamingoes. A lengthy stretch of the 12th-century town wall runs through this park, but we must leave this until later. For now our route takes us right down Tiensestraat, where we obtain a view of the magnificent gothic buttresses supporting the choir of Sint Pieters. We turn left then down Eikstraat for a splendid view of the eastern gable of the gothic town hall.

Built between 1439 and 1469, the **Stadhuis** is one of the glories of Brabant late gothic architecture. This exquisite building was begun by Sulpitius van Vorst, who originally envisaged a belfry to crown his work, a plan abandoned of course when it became apparent that the *veen* would not support such a towering edifice. Sulpitius died soon after work commenced, and it

had then to be supervised by Jan Keldermans the Younger from Mechelen. He too died before the completion of this monumental undertaking, and a third architect, Mathys de Layens had to be summoned in 1445 to finish the building off.

Despite these repeated setbacks, the town hall at Leuven is an exceedingly beautiful and well-proportioned building. Its basic design, like that of the Stadhuis of Bruges, resembles a gothic reliquary. And, as at Bruges, it is decorated with statues, pinnacles, and other delicate details. Yet Leuven's town hall is even more ornate, illustrating the intense delight in detail that is a feature of the Brabant late gothic style. The original design demanded some 282 niches, each to contain a statue. These niches rest on elaborately carved consoles, some decorated with little bunches of grapes, or oak leaves and acorns, others bearing curious scenes illustrating Biblical episodes or folk tales. Standing below the eastern gable we have just confronted, we can see several puzzling examples of late gothic sculpture. The consoles with Adam and Eve, the Expulsion from Paradise, and Hell, are all obvious enough, but what is the significance of the ship, the castle, or the bizarre scene in which one man is beating another with a jaw-bone, while a bemused fox looks out from its bolt-hole?

The exorbitant sculptural programme for the town hall had to be abandoned for financial reasons, with the unhappy result that the 282 niches remained empty until the mid-19th century. Finally, after much heated discussion, an ambitious plan was launched in 1852 to provide the town hall with some 236 statues. The figures chosen were drawn from Leuven's history, and included various Counts of Leuven and Dukes of Brabant, as well as humbler figures such as artists, architects, sculptors and scholars. If we stand on the terrace in front of the town hall, we will see the figure of Erasmus to the left of the doorway, and, further to the left, a figure in incongruous 18th-century garb. When the 19th-century sculptors had exhausted the list of distinguished forefathers, they resourcefully filled the remaining niches with figures representing institutions, virtues, and vices. We see the town hall here, photographed in all its new glory around 1900.

The **Sint Pieterskerk** opposite occupies a busy spot where the five main roads in Leuven converge. We enter by the south transept, squeezing past the foundations of a portal begun in 1497 but never completed. This unfinished work is but one of the many sad episodes in the history of Leuven's principal church. Built chiefly of white sandstone, it stands on the site of a romanesque basilica, and the same three artists who toiled on the Stadhuis were responsible for its present appearance. In 1425 Sulpitius van Vorst was put in charge of the construction of the choir, begun some fifteen years earlier. Upon his death in 1439 he was succeeded by Jan Keldermans the Younger, who saw the choir to completion. The transepts, begun by Keldermans, were gradually finished after his death by Mathys de Layens, and the nave was finally added towards the end of the 15th century.

The west front of the church should have been completed by three spires designed by Joos Metsys, brother of the Antwerp painter Quinten Metsys. The central spire was planned to reach a height of 170 metres, which would have outstripped by nine metres the spire of Ulm Cathedral, then the world's tallest structure. In 1497 the romanesque west front was demolished to allow work on the spires to begin, but this superlative project had to be abandoned in 1541 when it became apparent once again that the marshy subsoil provided a far from adequate foundation. All that remains to recall this ambitious project is an impressive stone model of the planned spires, made by Joos Metsys in about 1525 and now attached to the wall of the south transept.

These abandoned projects, together with the damage suffered in two world wars, have left the exterior of the church scarred. Yet the interior remains a very harmonious gothic space, the side walls in the nave looking almost like curtains because of the absence of capitals and other protrusions. The ornate late gothic rood screen separating the nave from the choir dates from 1488-90, and the majestic Calvary from about ten years later.

The only element that is not quite in harmony with this frail gothic interior is the heavy baroque pulpit. Like the one in Mechelen Cathedral, this came from a Norbertine abbey. It was carved by Jacob Berge in 1742 and depicts the sudden conversion of St Norbert. At the base we see a dramatic representation of Norbert being thrown from his horse by a bolt of forked lightning (which a cherub holds aloft), while a frightened squirrel scurries along the branch of a tree. The pulpit is surmounted by a vast canopy carved to resemble a sail, which several cherubs are desperately struggling to secure with lengths of rope.

It is worth visiting the little museum in the ambulatory, which contains an interesting collection of religious relics, paintings and sculpture. The first chapel contains a handsome recumbent effigy of Henry I, Duke of Brabant, who died in 1235. The effigies of his wife Matilda of Flanders, and daughter, Mary of Brabant, lie side by side in the fifteenth chapel of the ambulatory, on the opposite side of the choir. In the second chapel we come upon the damaged renaissance tomb of Michael Scribaen, a Leuven pharmacist, and his three wives. The sixth chapel contains the fine renaissance tomb of Jacobus Bogaerts, a

professor of medecine who died in 1520. Displayed in the cases opposite are the charred fragments of a splendid renaissance organ destroyed in 1944.

The eleventh chapel contains the *Martyrdom of Saint Erasmus*, painted by Dirk Bouts, whom we may remember from the *Judgement of Otto* now in the Musée des Beaux-Arts in Brussels but originally painted for the recently completed Stadhuis here in Leuven. In the *Saint Erasmus*, Bouts depicts the disembowelling of the martyr in a strangely clinical way. Erasmus' face appears quite unmoved as his intestines are slowly wound around a windlass. This peculiar - and unhistorical - method of martyrdom is the reason that Erasmus is venerated as the patron saint of sailors.

The fourteenth chapel contains Dirk Bouts' masterpiece, the *Triptych of the Last Supper*, painted in 1464-67 to hang in the Chapel of the Brotherhood of the Sacrament in Sint Pieters. The Last Supper is depicted in the central panel, the scene being set in a 15th-century Burgundian gothic interior, with views out to a garden at the rear, and through two side windows to a square

321

tentatively identified as Leuven's Grote Markt. Bouts depicts the moment when Christ blesses the Host and Chalice, conferring a ceremonial grandeur upon this scene by strategically placing a chimneypiece directly behind the figure of Christ so that he seems to be sitting on a throne. The chandelier above his head likewise serves to suggest a crown. A few of the disciples can be identified, such as Peter, to Christ's left, and John to his right. The four servants in the room wearing distinctive Burgundian dress were once believed to be portraits of Dirk Bouts himself (on the far right) and his sons, but a more plausible theory has recently been advanced that they are the Masters of the Brotherhood that commissioned the work.

The four side panels illustrate episodes from the Old Testament that were traditionally considered to prefigure the Last Supper. The top left panel shows Melchizedek offering bread and wine to Abraham outside the walls of Jerusalem. The panel below depicts the Passover, set by Bouts in a typical Burgundian gothic interior. The panel at the top right shows the Gathering of the Manna, the food that was miraculously sent from Heaven as Moses was leading the Israelites through the desert; the tiny drops of manna look almost like pearls. The final scene, at the bottom right, depicts Elijah who was saved from starvation in the desert when an angel appeared with food and drink.

When Baedeker wrote his 1905 guidebook, the middle panel was all that could be seen in Leuven. The side panels had been sold off to two separate collectors in Germany, and by 1905 the two top panels had found their way into the Alte Pinakothek in Munich, while the two bottom panels were in the Berlin picture gallery. The four were repatriated at the end of the First World War under the terms of the Treaty of Versailles. No record had been kept of their original positions, and at first the two Munich panels were placed one above the other on the left-hand side, while the Berlin panels were similarly placed opposite. This is the way the whole assembly appears in the photograph in Erwin Panofsky's *Early Netherlandish Painting*, but the present arrangement was proposed by the great art historian M. J.

Friedlaender, as it makes for a better alignment of the horizons in the two upper panels.

Perhaps the recurrent theme of food and drink in Bouts' five panels has turned our thoughts to lunch. On leaving the church, we find ourselves on **Grote Markt**, which in fact is neither *grote* nor a *markt*. It was originally the cemetery of Sint Pieterskerk, and so has none of the opulent dignity of the great squares in the other Flemish cities. But it does have a few cafés where we might eat simply. Gambrinus at No. 13 will serve us a sandwich and a good cup of coffee at a marble-topped table. Its handsome old interior lined with neo-renaissance panelling dates from 1921. The murals with bucolic Alpine scenes are older, having originally been painted in 1890 for the Café Suisse in Leuven.

As in many university towns, Leuven abounds in inexpensive restaurants, bistros and taverns. Muntstraat, a pleasant lane just behind the Stadhuis, has a variety of attractive places to eat. Mykene, at No. 44, is an informal, cosmopolitan restaurant with an interesting interior in which modern design is combined with an old renaissance arcade and a beamed roof. It is an ideal place for a simple Belgian lunch such as omelette and a glass of *De Koninck*, or steak with *frites* and a glass of wine.

The University and Begijnhof

Our second walk in Leuven begins at Grote Markt and follows a winding route through the old town. Our goal is the Begijnhof, one of the most delightful spots in Leuven, but we will also discover a number of less well-known curiosities along the way.

Café Gambrinus is as good a place to begin this walk as it was to end the last one. If we sit at a window table, we will again see that most of the houses on Grote Markt bear a small stone tablet with the symbols of sword and fire and the date 1914, revealing that they were destroyed in the conflagration in the First World War. A phoenix on top of one of the gables on Grote Markt makes the same point. Kortestraat leads from Gambrinus into Oude Markt, the old market-place. Rebuilt after 1914, this is now a pleasant square surrounded by bustling student cafés. Zeelstraat, on the left, leads up to the weathered Halle (cloth hall), best seen from the opposite side of Naamsestraat. Compared with the cloth halls at Bruges and Ypres, this one can disappoint, yet it has a remarkable history which is worth recounting. The original cloth hall was built between 1317 and 1345, all that now remains being the gothic ground floor. In 1432 a wing of the building was given to the recently-founded university to accommodate the faculties of theology, law and medicine. In 1676 the university acquired the remaining parts of the building and the cloth-workers moved to the baroque Dekenij behind the Stadhuis, part of which is now occupied by the tourist office (at Naamsestraat 1). In a fit of egregious bad taste, the university authorities decided in 1680 to add a baroque upper tier to the gothic cloth hall. The university library, with its incomparable collection of medieval manuscripts, was established in this most unsettling of buildings in 1724 but was totally destroyed by the Germans in 1914.

A short distance down Naamsestraat, we turn left up Standonckstraat to reach an attractive little square, **Hogeschoolplein**, created here in 1807-12. The east side of the square is dominated by the Pauscollege, founded in 1523 by Pope Adrian VI, the tutor of Charles V. This college was at first established in the Pope's former home, but it was rebuilt between 1776 and 1778 in a sober neoclassical style. We leave this square by turning right down St Michielsstraat, past the Maria Theresa College, founded by the Empress Maria Theresa in 1778 to accommodate graduates in theology who had not yet found a position.

Back on Naamsestraat, looking right we see the oldest university college, the **Heilig Geest College**, established in 1442. In 1790 this was rebuilt in the ubiquitous neoclassical style, and no trace now remains of the original building. Turn-

ing left down Naamsestraat, we pass the weathered **Sint Michielskerk**, a splendid baroque church designed in 1650 by the Jesuit Father Willem Hessius. The bold frontage with mock candelabra and trumpeting angels is by Jan van Steen, and is known locally as 'the altar without' because of its resemblance to a baroque altar.

We continue along Naamsestraat, past Koningscollege (King's College) at No. 59, founded by King Philip II of Spain in 1579, but rebuilt in a subdued neoclassical style in 1776-79. Further down, No. 61 was once the Norbertine college, jointly founded in 1571 by four abbeys, and rebuilt in 1755.

Number 70 is a classical dwelling known as the Residentie van Caverson; a passage beneath this house leads into an unexpected little park with an artificial bridge. This lies somewhat off our route, but it is a pleasing detour that offers a charming glimpse of red pantile roofs in the river valley below.

A few steps further down Naamsestraat, we come upon the most attractive of all the Leuven colleges at No. 80. Known as the **Van Dale**

College, it was founded in 1569 by Pieter van Dale, an eminent jurist and canon of Onze-Lieve-Vrouwekathedraal at Antwerp. It is a fine example of late gothic architecture, with alternating courses of pink brick and white sandstone. There is not a trace of anything 18th-century to mar the exquisite harmony of this college, apart from a small rococo chapel tucked away in a corner. The only incongruous feature is the renaissance portal bearing the date 1559 on the door jamb. This was rescued from another building by the university in 1971.

Opposite the Van Dale College stands a mysterious brick gothic house called the **Huis van 't Sestich**. This sadly neglected aristocratic townhouse dates from the 15th century and is built in a remarkable late gothic style, similar to the Gruuthuse gable overlooking the waterfront at Bruges. The letters LX at the top of the gable are a family monogram; the significance of the quatrefoils and Stars of David is more elusive.

We continue down this street until we come to an exquisite church standing atop a leafy hill close to the old city boundary. This is **Sint Kwin-tenskerk,** a curious blend of various styles of architecture. The oldest parts are the austere romanesque foundations of the west tower, dating from about 1200. The rest of this small church was built in the lofty style of Brabant gothic from 1440 or thereabouts to 1535. The tower was added in the 16th century and topped with a spire in 1900.

A cobbled lane called Sint Quintensberg descends from here to Sneppenberg, where we glimpse a little church partly concealed by a brick wall. This early 14th-century church, dedicated to Saint John the Baptist, is part of Leuven's **Groot Begijnhof**, founded in about 1230. A portal on Schapenstraat leads into the most beautiful Begijnhof in Flanders. It is almost a small town, for there are 62 houses, ten convents, a church, several squares with attractive water pumps (one photographed opposite), some shady arcades, and an extensive green. As we explore the cobbled lanes lined with handsome red-brick renaissance houses we catch tantalising glimpses of the River Dijle, which splits into two arms as it flows through the Begijnhof. The buildings

here were expertly restored in the 1960's by the university to provide student accommodation. One of the most interesting, however, was moved here from Parijsstraat. It is the remarkable baroque house at the end of Benedenstraat, which was rebuilt here in 1983. Dating from 1664, it has a row of eight sinister satyrs supporting the eaves, and a statue of St Nicholas.

Once we have explored this idyllic community, we can leave along Benedenstraat, then turn right along Redingenstraat, which follows an arm of the Dijle. On Schapenstraat we turn left and soon come upon the **Sint Antoniuskapel**, its exterior dating from 1617, though the interior is completely modern. To add to its strangeness, the chapel has been built into the hillside, so that we ascend a long flight of steps to reach the nave. Another flight of steps leads down into a gloomy crypt, where there is the tomb of Father Damien, a 19th-century Belgian missionary who worked among lepers.

Standing on the opposite side of the square is the **Hollandcollege**, a 16th-century townhouse in which a college was set up in 1617. If we walk through the gateway to the right of this college and down a bumpy cobbled lane we come upon two 12th-century towers on opposite banks of the River Dijle. In 1616 the theologian Cornelis Jansen, who founded the radical Catholic Jansenist movement in Leuven, built a retreat on top of the nearer of the two towers, which had long ceased to have any defensive function. Now known as the **Janseniustoren**, this secret scholarly retreat has recently been rescued and modernised, which I think adds to its eccentric appeal.

We now return to Pater Damiaanplein and turn left along Parijsstraat, then left along Minderbroedersstraat. If the day is at all decent, we can walk to the end of this long street and cross over to the **Kruidtuin**, a delightful botanical garden, where students and the elderly while away the day as the rest of the world goes its busy way.

If on the other hand the weather does not seem particularly inviting, we should turn right on Minderbroedersstraat along O. L. Vrouwstraat and once over the Dijle right into Sint Annastraat. After passing by the sadly decayed early gothic fabric of a Dominican church, we turn down Predikherenstraat through an old archway. To the left stands an imposing 16th-century town house in late gothic style. In 1538 Guy Morillon, secretary to Charles V, bought this house for his retirement, having lived in Leuven intermittently since 1531. Morillon was a friend and cautious supporter of Erasmus, and sent his sons to the Collegium Trilingue.

Predikherenstraat emerges on the busy Brusselsestraat, which we cross to continue along Koningin Astridlaan. We then turn right along Wandeling and thence into Mechelsestraat, a pleasant pedestrianised street leading to a small square with a statue of Erasmus. A likeable old-fashioned pharmacy occupies a fine rococo building known as *In de Ploegh* (At the Plough), at No. 5.

We turn left now down Schrijnmakersstraat, past an imposing neoclassical portal dated 1775. This was once the Drieux College, founded by a certain Michael Drieux in 1559, but it seems now to have been reduced to a garage. A similar fate has befallen the Collegium Trilingue, the scant remains of which can be seen in the Busleydengang, named after its founder, Hieronymus Busleyden. Busleydengang is a lane off the Vismarkt, which we reach by turning left along Vaartstraat, and then again left down Augustijnenstraat. A dilapidated renaissance portal marks the site of the Collegium. Erasmus first raised the idea of a college teaching Latin, Greek, and Hebrew during discussions in Mechelen with his friend. Indeed visitors to Mechelen can see the dining room in the Hof van Busleyden where Erasmus was entertained (described on page 220). Erasmus continued to take a keen interest in the development of the Collegium, which Busleyden had funded by a bequest in his will. It was this institution that inspired the French humanist Guillaume Bude to set up the Collège de France in 1529 on similar principles.

We leave this square on the north side along Karel van Lotharingenstraat, a crooked lane following the course of the 12th-century town wall. To prove the fact, there is a ruined turret in a garden just beyond No. 16. Back on Vaartstraat, we turn left past a row of brick warehouses, at No. 58, skilfully converted into apartments We are now entering the northern quarter of Leuven, where the giant Stella Artois brewery is based. Founded in the 18th century, it brews a famous lager which can be sampled at Café Gambrinus or in any other tavern in town. This is now a fascinating and yet forbidding industrial area, with sometimes incongruous elements such as the horse-drawn drays that stand outside the brewery's head office on Vaartstraat. Wandering once through this quarter, having searched in vain for a path to the summit of Keizersberg, I glanced inside one of the sheds and saw an enormous wooden beer barrel and a rustic inn, both looking quite out of place in this utilitarian environment.

At Vaartstraat 115, we turn left through a passage, then cross the River Dijle once more. We now cross Sluisstraat, where the familiar stone tablets with the fire and sword appear on the houses, a reminder of the extent of the destruction in 1914. Continuing straight ahead down Klein Begijnhof, a narrow lane overshadowed by the perimeter wall of the brewery, we turn a corner to discover a delightful and totally unexpected fragment of the 13th-century **Klein Begijnhof**. Looking down this lane of 17th- and 18th-century houses, we see the beautiful spire of the **Sint Gertrudiskerk**. This flamboyant addition was made to the 14th-century church in 1453, probably by Jan van Ruysbroeck, the architect of the spire of the Hôtel de Ville in Brussels.

Sint Gertrudis was once the church of an Augustinian abbey founded in 1204 by Duke Henry IV of Brabant. Fragments of this abbey can still be seen overlooking an overgrown courtyard behind the church. We reach this secret spot through a rococo portal. The Thierry Wing, straight ahead of us as we enter the courtyard, was assembled by Canon A. Thierry from fragments of buildings destroyed in the fire of 1914. Baroque portals and renaissance balustrades have been joined together in an ingenious fashion. In 1987 this immensely likeable building was converted into a row of eight houses, with the few modern details only increasing its bizarreness.

On leaving this delightful corner of Leuven, we turn left and, soon after crossing Mechelsestraat, left again down Halvestraat. This takes us once again along the River Dijle, which flows past the ruins of once-flourishing breweries and maltings. Keeping to the Dijle, we then follow Handbooghof, a quiet cobbled lane overlooked by a stretch of the 12th-century wall.

To return to Grote Markt, we turn left along Brusselsestraat, passing a beautiful 13th-century romanesque portal. This was once the entrance to a hospice, which may explain the odd faces carved on corbels, including a woman with her tongue sticking out as if she is about to be given some vile medieval medicine.

Once back at Grote Markt, our tour of Leuven is over. On our way back to the station, we might stop at Hortus (Bondgenotenlaan 124), an elegant tea room furnished in a heavy 19th-century style like an early painting by James Ensor, with mirrors, chandeliers, old paintings and ubiquitous ferns.

But possibly the proper place to end this little tour of Flemish cities is at Café Domus, on the corner of Tiensestraat and Eikstraat. This attractive, rambling café on several floors has a traditional Flemish interior, with ancient beams, creaking floorboards, and a miscellany of quaint objects, such as the bust of a philosopher and the figure of a knight leaning pensively on his sword. Sitting beneath a heavy iron lamp, sipping a coffee or a local beer, we might agree that this café is, as its Latin name suggests, home.

Perhaps the final word should come from Erasmus, who is connected in some way or other with almost all the cities we have explored. He met Thomas More in Bruges, discussed philosophy with Pieter Gilles in Antwerp, visited Hieronymus Busleyden at his splendid town house in Mechelen, stayed with his friend Pieter Wychman just outside Brussels, and taught his compassionate religious philosophy at Leuven. While living in Basel he still hoped to return to Leuven to live out his final years. His letters suggest that he felt at home in these cities more than anywhere else, perhaps sitting by a fireside on a cold night discussing classical philosophy or theology with a close friend. He even wrote to his friend Goclenius, Professor of Theology at the Collegium Trilingue, asking him to look out for a house in Leuven that he might buy for his retirement. It had to have a garden, he insisted. But Erasmus never made it back to Leuven. In his final letter, sent to Goclenius on 21 March 1536, he wrote wistfully: 'although I have many good friends in Basel, which was not the case in Freiburg, I would still, because of the religious controversies, prefer to end my life elsewhere. O, how I wish that Brabant was not so far away!'

Appendices

Flanders for Children

Children are reluctant travellers at the best of times and may well think that a trip to Flanders is not for them. Anxious parents for their part may worry that the only thing a child can do in Bruges is to fall into a canal. Yet Flanders offers ample opportunities to amuse a child, not the least being that the Flemish, like all Belgians, are besotted by cartoon books. The magic word Tintin may be all it takes to encourage a reluctant child. Add to that Lucky Luke and the Smurfs, and you can virtually sell a trip to Flanders as the next best thing to Eurodisney.

The Flemish have an almost Italian love of children. We will *never* be turned away from a café because we have children with us, nor will we ever have difficulty finding a restaurant where the children can eat plain chicken and chips. The coast is never far away and, if all else fails, we can make a trip to one of the four large theme parks that lie dotted around Flanders. The best is Belle-

waerde, outside Ypres, but Bobbejanland, near Antwerp, has its devoted fans, as does Walibi, near Brussels.

Bruges The first thing to do on arrival in Bruges is to take a boat tour of the canals, if possible from the embarkation point on Katelijnestraat. Even if it rains - or perhaps especially when it rains and the boatman has to pass out umbrellas - these trips in open-topped launches are immensely enjoyable. The main drawback, in my experience, is arguing with children who want to go on *again*. The other obvious activity for children is a jaunt on a horse-drawn carriage, the main pleasure perhaps being the look of rage on the face of the car driver stuck behing your slow-moving vehicle. On days when the weather looks trustworthy, I have sometimes rented a bicycle from a shop behind the belfry and headed off down the old canal to Damme, with one child on a back seat.

It is true that few children will have the temperament to enjoy a tour of the Groeninge-museum, but we might be able to strike a deal in which they get a day at the seaside, a mere fifteen minutes away by train, or a trip to the Boude-wijnpark, where they can watch dolphins leap out of the water, in return for which they solemnly promise not to touch the van Eyck paintings or throw themselves on the museum floor in a howling tantrum.

Ghent A boat trip on the Ghent canals is the main bait we can dangle before our children, but this time the boats have roofs, and so the prospect of rain holds no pleasure. A trip to the Graven-steen is the other attraction to mention. The children can explore the castle's medieval dungeons and battlements without the annoyance of a guide reciting dull dates. Most children are not likely to wait patiently while parents exam-ine the minute details on the Ghent altarpiece, but perhaps they can be led off to look at the tombs in the crypt. A final treat no child should be denied, unless they behaved really badly in the cathedral, is a trip for an ice cream to the splendid Salon Florian on the Voldersstraat.

Antwerp The zoo next to the main station in Antwerp has enough wildlife to keep children occupied for a day. It was built in the 19th century, when even the lamp-posts in Antwerp were designed to raise the city's standing in the world. Some of the buildings were destroyed in the war, but the splendid Elephant House is still there, as is the Greek temple in which turtles have their abode. The zoo is gradually introducing new attractions, the latest of which is an indoor trop-ical rain forest. It would be difficult to imagine somewhere better than this steamy jungle in which to spend a rainy afternoon.

Then there is the port. An elevated promenade runs along the Scheldt waterfront, making a good place for running or peering down on the Polish and Russian boats that occasionally tie up alongside. The maritime museum is on the water's edge, situated in an old castle. It has a good collection of model ships and a row of old boats on the quayside.

Brussels Mention of a trip to Brussels may cause children to dig in their heels, but you must tell them about the wonderful parks, such as the Bois de la Cambre, where we can cross to an island on a mechanical ferry *and* rent a rowing boat *and* go roller skating *and* buy Italian ice cream. If that doesn't lure them, we should promise a trip to the Parc de Wolvendael, reached on tram 91 or 92, where they can drive screaming miniature cars around a track and ride on ponies. That should earn us at least the time it needs to explore the old town on foot.

It is worth pointing out that Brussels has not one, but two children's museums. The Musée des Enfants at Rue du Bourgmestre 15 is the better of the two, but the quaint Musée du Jouet at Rue de l'Association 24 should not be ignored. Nor can any conscientious parent miss the opportunity offered for dinosaur spotting. The Musée de l'Institut Royal des Sciences Naturelles may have an atrocious name, no more welcoming in Dutch than French, but it owns a spectacular collection of dinosaurs, both genuine skeletons and snarling mechanical models. It also has whale skeletons, mock prehistoric caves and (I will leave you guessing on this one) a most intriguing staircase.

I have not mentioned the Cartoon Museum, as I half suspect that this is intended for nostalgic adults rather than children. The name - Centre Belge de la Bande Dessinée - makes it sound more like a government insitution, but presumably this reflects the serious Belgian approach to comic books. The museum occupies a handsome art nouveau department store designed by Victor Horta, not that any child will find this information important. The main points to recite are that children can touch some of the objects and indeed enter some of the interiors modelled on cartoon pictures. The guards, in my experience, tend to be tolerant of squeals and the occasional yelps.

Children sometimes respond well to the Musée des Beaux-Arts, particularly if the visit can be turned into an adventure. They might enjoy a tour, for example, that concentrated on paintings depicting children. There is a good number of children paintings to discover, such as the sad 16th-century painting of a girl holding a dead bird, and the baby whose mother is wiping his bottom in Jacob Jordaens' earthy *The King Drinks*. I wish I could offer children Pieter Bruegel the Elder's *Children's Games*, but that delightful painting was carted off to Vienna when the Hapsburgs ruled the region. We are left only with the children fighting in the mud in Pieter Bruegel the Younger's *Flemish Fair* opposite.

Tourist Information

Flanders lies at the heart of a dense network of trading routes dating back to the middle ages. These ancient arteries make it one of the most accessible regions in Europe. There are ferries and jetfoils from Ramsgate, in Kent, to Ostend and Zeebrugge; frequent flights to Zaventem airport, just outside Brussels, and rapid trains from Paris, Cologne, and Amsterdam, not to mention the sleek new Eurostar trains that, on a good day, nip from London Waterloo to the Gare du Midi in scarcely more than three hours.

Visitors arriving by plane can take the airport train to the Brussels stations of Gare du Nord and Gare Centrale, where connections can be made to any other Belgian city. Journey times are always pleasantly short in Belgium. Using Brussels as a base, we can be in Ghent or Antwerp in half an hour, or in Bruges within an hour of leaving Brussels.

Most of the walks described in this book are designed to keep us out of doors, but it can sometimes happen that torrential rain sweeps in from the North Sea, in which case it is comforting to know that, in addition to countless museums, Flanders is well supplied with cinemas, where the films are almost always screened in the original language.

The people of Flanders are normally friendly towards travellers and will make an effort to speak English if the traveller speaks no Dutch. We must, however, take care not to annoy toilet attendants, who expect a ten franc fee, and will pursue innocent offenders with a vengeance rarely seen in these parts since the Inquisition.

Public transport in Flanders is run by De Lijn. The system operates with magnetic tickets which can be stamped in the automatic machines on city trams and buses. In Brussels, however, the authority is Stib, and a different ticket is needed. Most other practical problems which might arise in the course of a trip can be solved by contacting the main Flemish tourist office at Rue Marché aux Herbes 61 in Brussels, tel. 02-5040 300. The staff are likely to speak English, not to mention Dutch, French and German.

The Dutch language. The language of Flanders is Dutch and not French. It is the same language as the Dutch speak in the Netherlands, even if Flemish Dutch sometimes strikes the Dutch as rather quaint and old-fashioned. A post office in Flanders is signposted *posterijen* whereas in the Netherlands it is simply indicated as *post*. A Dutch canal is a *gracht*, but in Flanders it is normally a *lei*, except in Bruges where it is a *rei*.

The Flemish, like the Welsh or the Catalans, are keen to defend their language, to such a degree that there are some villages where incoming residents must take a Dutch language test. It all seems very petty to the outsider, especially the bilingual signs in Brussels that say *taxis-taxi's*, yet the current situation has its roots in years of oppression. The Flemish have been treated by French-speakers as an inferior race since the late middle ages. The 19th-century industrialisation of Wallonia meant that the wealth of the country lay in the French region and those from Flanders were forced to learn French if they wanted a good job. Matters came to a head in the First World War when the officer class was in the habit of barking out orders in French to Flemish troops who understood not a word.

The situation changed after the last war, when Wallonia's old industries went into decline and the enconomy of Flanders began to boom. The Flemish, quite rightly, started to demand that Dutch be the official language in Flemish institutions. Absurd situations did arise, as when Leuven University split into two universities - French- and Dutch-speaking - and the library was simply divided down the middle. There was even a period in the 1970's when each university owned one half of a set of encyclopaedias.

The language riots are now a thing of the past, as Flanders has gained more or less everything it wants: its own government, a bilingual capital, classes in Dutch at the universities. Yet the Flemish are still slightly on the defensive, especially in the villages around Brussels where there is a very real threat of the Dutch language being swamped by commuters who prefer to speak French.

Ten years ago, most English-speakers would have considered learning Dutch a needless pursuit, but it is now quite useful to have at least a casual knowledge of the language. How else can you ever hope to pronounce the names of the Flemish fashion designers who are becoming better known - such as Anne Demeulemeester or Walter van Beirendonck? Not to mention order one of those delectable Flemish beers with names like Hoegaarden, Stropken and Dentergems?

One of the rewards of learning Dutch is to uncover a hoard of wonderful local proverbs, such as *hij heeft een klap van de molen gehad* (he has been walloped by a windmill). There is a fascinating Pieter Bruegel painting in Berlin in which dozens of these proverbs are depicted.

On first impression, many Dutch words look as though they were written by someone who had had *een klap van de molen*. Take the café Patersvaetje in the Blauwmoezelstraat in Antwerp.

How on earth do we get our tongues around such words? The secret is often to break down compound words into their component parts: Paters/vaetje and Blauw/moezel/straat. Once that is done, we will often begin to see a vague resemblance to English words: *pater* (father); *vaetje* (a vat or barrel); *blauw* (blue); *Moezel* (Moselle); *straat* (a street). Sometimes a slight reshuffling occurs, so that the English *the* becomes *het* in Dutch.

Pronunciation is not as big a problem as it might seem. The letter *g* is the hardest to master. Text books tend to tell you say it like the *ch* in loch, but many people find loch difficult enough to say. Other tips are to say *oo* in words like *brood* (bread) like the *oa* in toad. It will be a long slog before we can hope to discuss Flemish politics *in het Nederlands*, but surprisingly little effort is needed to make it less double Dutch.

Bruges
The Bruges tourist office (tel. 050 448 686) will be able to answer most practical questions prior to departure. Bruges (Brugge in Dutch) is 96 km

from Brussels and the train journey takes an hour. If we arrive at the railway station, we should either walk or take bus no. 2 (or another suitable bus) from the station to Markt. If travelling by car, we may need instructions from our hotel as to the best route to take once in town. As part of its new plan to deter cars, the city has recently opened two large, free car parks near the main station.

We should begin by heading to the medieval belfry. The tourist office is nearby, at Burg 11, where the medieval castle once stood. Even if we do not need any information, it is worth going inside to admire the 18th-century gilt leather wall hangings and ornate woodwork. The staff will supply a tourist map of Bruges for a few francs, or provide free leaflets listing restaurants and describing guided tours. They can also point us in the direction of the nearest bank with a currency-changing desk, though we may feel like making a short detour to cash our cheques in the building on Vlamingstraat where a bank has stood since the 15th century.

After seeing the results of the city's policy of discouraging cars, some may want to hire a bike to explore remote corners of Bruges. Eric Popelier runs a dependable and friendly rental shop just behind the Belfry, at Hallestraat 14. If we pick up a bike after breakfast, we can be in the pleasant canalside town of Damme for lunch.

There is a good bookshop on Markt, De Reyghere, which sells guidebooks, English novels and international newspapers. If it should start to rain, try looking up the programme of the Gulden Vlies cinema, at 32 Kuiperstraat, which may be the only cinema in the world located in a 15th-century building.

Ghent

The Ghent tourist office can be reached on 09-2665232. Ghent (Gent in Dutch and Gand in French) is 55 km from Brussels and 60 km from Antwerp. The train journey from Brussels, Bruges or Antwerp takes about half an hour. The main station in Ghent is St. Pieter's Station, built for the 1913 World Fair, and a longish hike from the town centre. I suggest taking tram no. 1 (or any other suitable tram) to Korenmarkt. The ride by tram gives an interesting first glimpse of the city as it rumbles along narrow cobbled streets. We might even want to stay on a few more stops, until the Gravensteen halt, to catch an impressive view of the canals. The tourist office is near the medieval belfry, in the basement of the town hall on Botermarkt. The staff are friendly and helpful, perhaps pleased that any tourist has chosen to visit Ghent rather than Bruges. They will provide a useful free brochure which has an excellent map of the city, but their help may still be needed to locate the Patershol quarter or the Sint Baafs Abdij.

Ghent is less of a tourist town than Bruges or Antwerp. Apart from the odd cluster of Japanese and German tourists gathered outside the cathedral, there are not that many foreign visitors. It is hard to find international newspapers, though the Fnac shop on Veldstraat has an excellent selection of English novels. The largest cinema in Ghent is Decascoop at Ter Plaeten 12, but many film enthusiasts prefer the intimacy of Studio Skoop on the leafy Sint-Annaplein. If I might steal a joke from Charles V, this Ghent cinema café is as snug as a *gant*.

Antwerp

The Antwerp tourist office can be reached on 03-232 0103. Antwerp (Antwerpen in Dutch and Anvers in French) is 48 km from Brussels and 60 km from Ghent. The journey by train from Brussels takes about half an hour. Arriving in Antwerp by train is an experience not to be missed. The spectacular architectural restoration of Centraal Station provides the perfect prelude to the city. After admiring the bombast, however, we may be perplexed as to what best to do next. A useful little tourist booth that once stood next to the station has been closed down. Some people will simply jump into a taxi, but I hope a few may be bold enough to take a city tram into town and thus get more of a feel of local life. The trams run through a tunnel under the station. The best stop to get off at is Groenplaats, a bustling square at the foot of the cathedral spire.

The Antwerp tourist office is not far away from the cathedral, at Grote Markt 15. We will probably need to call in for advice on the best way to reach the eccentric Cogels-Osylei quarter or where to find shops stocking Antwerp fashions.

While we are in the tourist office, we should hunt around among the brochures for a copy of the Cultural Bulletin, which lists some of the more highbrow cultural events in town. Ever since the city became a European Cultural Capital in 1993, the tourist department has taken care to provide travellers with a full list of artistic events. The main cinema is a modern multi-screen complex outside town. More charming cinemas, near the old town, include Cartoon's at Kaasstraat 4 and the Filmmuseum, which occupies a former royal palace at Meir 50.

Mechelen

The Mechelen tourist office can be reached on 015-297 655. Mechelen (Malines in French) is 28 km from Brussels, almost midway to Antwerp. The train takes 15 minutes from either city. The main train station is about ten minutes on foot from the town centre and the tourist office is located in the town hall on Grote Markt.

Brussels

The Brussels tourist office can be called on 02-513 8940. Brussels (Brussel to the Dutch and Bruxelles to the French) is 48 km from Antwerp and 96 km from Bruges. The train from Bruges takes an hour; Antwerp and Ghent are half an hour away, and Mechelen and Leuven just fifteen minutes. The city has three main stations, the most convenient of which is the Gare Centrale. High-speed trains from London and Paris stop only at the Gare du Midi, which is a mite too far from the city centre to walk. It takes a bit of an effort to make sense of the underground network, but once we have done so, it is a simple matter to catch an underground tram to the Bourse halt, close to Grand'Place.

The Brussels tourist office is located in a cramped office inside the town hall, on Grand'-Place. Visitors without a car will probably have to use a tram or metro at some time in Brussels, either to reach the Erasmus House or the Museum Park. Tickets are sold in metro stations and in some newsagents, either singly or in strips of ten. If in doubt about how to purchase or use the tickets it is best to check with one of the officials, as public transport inspectors are not known for their Bruegelian charms. Despite these cautions, the Brussels trams are an agreeable form of transport, particularly on routes 90 to 94, where new models have been introduced.

The trip out to Waterloo is one that vexes many tourists. It is a simple matter by car, but something of a logistic nightmare on public transport. We can catch a bus from Place Rouppe, which will take us to the very crossroads where the British army stood its ground, but we may have trouble catching the right bus back to Brussels. The Waterloo tourist office (tel. 02-354 9910), located next to Wellington's headquarters, is the most helpful source for battlefield pilgrims.

Guidebooks to Brussels, more detailed than this one, are on sale in W. H. Smith's bookshop, which has been at Boulevard Adolphe Max 71 for as long as anyone can remember. The fiction buyer takes great care always to have in stock a copy of Charlotte Brontë's *Villette*, that achingly romantic novel set in Brussels' aristocratic upper town. We might choose to read it while sipping a cup of Earl Grey tea in one of the city's outré tea rooms. They can be found within the Astoria, Conrad Hilton and Stanhope hotels, or dotted around the *communes* of Ixelles and Uccle.

Should it rain, we can retreat into one of the city's many cinemas, which tend to open their doors in the early afternoon. The Kinepolis complex offers many screens and perfect sound, but the more intimate cinemas of the old town, such as the Arenberg in the Galerie de la Reine, have a warmer atmosphere. The usherettes, however, can be quite brusque if you fail to tip. Even senior European diplomats are likely to be scolded if they fail to hand over twenty francs.

Leuven

The Leuven tourist office can be reached on 016 211 539. Leuven is 26 km from Brussels and the train takes about 15 minutes. The train station is about ten minutes on foot from the town centre. The tourist office is just behind the town hall, at Naamsestraat 1. The Super City Leuven cinema complex, with seven screens, is located near the station.

Choosing a Hotel

Bruges

It is hard in Bruges *not* to find a good hotel. In the past twenty years, dozens of small family-run hotels have opened, mostly located in old brick Gothic houses in the historic quarters. If asked to pick my favourite, I would be torn between choosing the **Egmond** at Minnewater 15 (tel. 050-341 445) and the **Ter Brughe** at Oost-Gistelhof 2 (tel. 050-340324). The Egmond is a white step-gabled house on the edge of the Minnewater with a lovely rambling Flemish interior. The Ter Brughe, in the merchants' quarter, is a brown gabled house overlooking a quiet canal. If the Ter Brughe turned out to be full, I would happily settle for the nearby **Europ** at Augustijnenrei 18 (tel. 050-337975), a canalside hotel with spacious bedrooms. Another option in the neighbourhood is the **Adornes** at Sint-Annarei 26 (tel. 050-341 336), a comfortable hotel located in a series of canalside brick houses. The **Ter Duinen** at Langerei 52 (tel. 050-330 437) is yet another old converted canalside house with elegant, if small bedrooms, well away from the tourist trail.

All of these hotels are moderately priced, but we might want to splash out on a superior hotel. The **Orangerie** at Kartuizerinnenstraat 10 (tel. 050 341649), located in a handsome 16th-century canalside house, is considered by many to be the best address, but I am fond of the **Oud Huis Amsterdam** at Spiegelrei 3 (tel. 050-341 810), an old trading house on a canal, furnished with 18th-century antiques. Or I might consider booking a room, if possible number 43, in **Die Swaene** at Steenhouwersdijk 1 (tel. 050-342 798). This charming old family hotel occupies a 15th-century house on a canal. Once, a few years ago, Die Swaene was voted one of Europe's most romantic hotels in a glossy magazine. They now offer 'Romeo and Juliet' weekends to maintain this reputation. If saving money is more important

than a romantic champagne breakfast in the morning, several inexpensive hotels are to be found overlooking the quiet Sint Gilliskerk. The **Jacobs** at Baliestraat 1 (tel. 050-339 831) and **De Pauw** at Sint-Gilliskerkhof 8 (tel. 050 337 118) are both perfectly adequate.

Ghent

I feel a certain loyalty towards the **St Jorishof** at Botermarkt 2 (tel. 09-224 2424), not only because it is the oldest hotel in Europe, nor even because of the easily remembered telephone number, but because its prices are reasonable, the rooms are comfortable and even the garage has a certain aged charm. Yet an hotel which opened up a couple of years ago may cause me to defect. It is the **Erasmus** at Poel 25 (tel. 09-224 2195). It may not be *quite* so old (the house was built in the 16th century), but it has a rambling old Flemish character. Each room is furnished in a different style, so we can choose between a garden view or an attic den. With an antique pram in the bedroom, breakfast in the garden and drinks in the cellar, I think I have found a place to linger for a while. There are, of course, other hotels, such as the elegant **Gravensteen** (tel. 09-225 1150), located in a handsome building opposite the castle. Even the modern **Ibis** (tel. 09-233 0000) and **Novotel** (tel. 09-224 2230) have good locations opposite the cathedral, but for sheeer local charm I think we must look to the older hotels.

Antwerp
Antwerp's most alluring hotel stands opposite the cathedral on the Handschoenmarkt. The **Villa Mozart** (tel. 03-231 3031) is small, friendly and comfortable. The location is ideal for those who like to roam around the old city after dark. Other hotels, often expensive, have opened recently in the old town. One new address is the **Hotel Rubens Grote Markt** (tel. 03-226 9582) at Oude Beurs 29. Situated in the heart of Renaissance Antwerp, it offers luxurious bedrooms, a garden and a splendid breakfast. The **Prinse** at Keizerstraat 63 (tel. 03-226 4050) is a quiet town house with elegant furnishings, located on one of the city's most handsome streets. For a cheaper night in Antwerp, the **Eden Hotel** at

Lange Herentalsestraat 25 (tel. 03-233 0608) is comfortable and convenient for the station.

Brussels
Despite its many charms, Brussels is still more of a business city than a tourist destination. During the conference season, rooms tend to be expensive, though many of the larger hotels are forced to slash their prices at weekends and during the summer months to woo customers. Several grand hotels can be found in the centre of town, clustered around Grand'Place and Place Rogier. The **Métropole** at Place de Brouckère 31 (tel. 02-217 2300) is the oldest hotel in town. Opened just over one hundred years ago, it is a splendid neo-renaissance confection designed by Alban Chambon with gilt mirrors and lofty ceilings. The more intimate **Amigo** at Rue de l'Amigo 1 (tel. 02-511 5910) is filled with antiques and tapestries to create the atmosphere of a British country house. Most of the bedrooms in the **New Siru Hotel** at Place Rogier 1 (tel. 02-217 7580) contain an original work of art by a Belgian artist. Roger Somville decorated room 408 with a voluptuous

nude female figure, and room 211 has four small granite rocks suspended above the bed. The artist originally intended to hang a giant slab of granite from the ceiling, but the management quietly said no. For a cheaper hotel try **La Madeleine** at Rue de la Montagne 20 (tel. 02-513 2973). Just off Grand'Place, it occupies two town houses whose rooms, though small, are perfectly comfortable. Other cheap hotels can be found in the Upper Town. The **Rembrandt** at Rue de la Concorde 42 (tel. 02-512 7139) is an attractive little hotel off Avenue Louise furnished with a few elegant antiques. Room 6 is my favourite. Further out, **Les Tourelles** at Avenue Winston Churchill 135 (tel. 02-344 0284) is a rather old-fashioned hotel occupying a quaint turreted building in Normandy style. Once a boarding school for girls, it still has a slight air of the Brussels institution for girls described in Charlotte Brontë's *Villette*. In other words, not the sort of place you roll in drunk after midnight.

Leuven

It used to be difficult to find a good hotel in Leuven, but there is now a **Holiday Inn Garden Court** at Tiensestraat 52 (tel. 016-290 770). Modern and convenient, it is the best that Leuven can offer.

Opening Times of Museums and Galleries

Bruges

Most museums and churches in Bruges are open every day. They tend to take a long lunch break, so that you need to time your visits carefully.

Museums: It pays to be at the **Groeningemuseum** (Dijver 12) as soon as it opens to avoid the crowds. The hours are April to September, 10-5.30; October to March, 10-12 and 2-4.30. The **Memlingmuseum** (Mariastraat 38) tends not to be so crowded, but watch out for the long lunch break. The hours are April to September, daily, 10-12 and 2-5.30; October to March, daily, 10-12.30 and (every day except Wednesday) 2-5. The **Gruuthusemuseum** (17 Dijver) and **Brangwynmuseum** (16 Dijver) are both open April to September, daily, 10-11.30 and 2-5.30. The little **Museum van het Brugse Vrije** on Burg, where you may well be the only visitor that day, is open daily, 10-12 and 1.30-5.

Churches: The **Heilig Bloed Basiliek** on Burg is open October to March, daily, 9.30 -12 and 2-6. For the rest of the year, it closes at 4 pm rather than 6 pm. **Onze-Lieve-Vrouwekerk** is open April to September, Monday to Saturday, 10-11.30 and 2.30-5, Sunday 2.30-5; October to March, Monday to Saturday, 10-11.30 and 3-4.30; Sunday 2.30-4.30. **St Salvatorskathedraal** has a complicated schedule of opening hours: April to September, Monday, Tuesday, Thursday, Friday, Saturday, 2-5, Sunday 3-5 (in July and August, it also opens 10-12 except on Wednesday and Sunday); October to March, Monday, Tuesday, Thursday, Friday, Saturday, 2-5. It is difficult to find the lovely **St Jacobskerk** open, but likely hours are 8.30-12, and, possibly, 2-5 in July and August. The **Jeruzalemkerk** (Peperstraat 3) is normally open daily 10-12 and 2-6.

Further sights: Those wanting to climb the **Belfry** should find the tower open April to September, daily, 10-5.15; October to March, daily, 10-11.45 and 1.30-4.15. The **Stadhuis** on Burg is open April to September, daily, 10-11.30 and 2-5.30; October to March, daily, 10-12 and 2-4.30. The courtyard of the **Hof van Bladelin** on Naaldenstraat can be visited, free of charge, April to September, Monday to Saturday, 9-12 and 2-6, Sunday 10-12 and 2-6. For the rest of the year, the gate is closed at 4 pm.

Ghent

Cathedral: Aim to visit the van Eyck altarpiece early in the day, before the little chapel in which it hangs becomes too crowded. The altarpiece is located in the **St Baafskathedraal**, which is open free of charge every day 7.30-7.15, except during Catholic services. You must buy a ticket to enter the van Eyck chapel and the crypt, open April to October, on Mondays to Saturdays, 9.30-12 and 2-6; Sundays and holidays 1-6; November to March, on Mondays to Saturdays, 10.30-12 and 2.30-4; Sundays and holidays 2-5.

Castle: The **Gravensteen** castle is open from April to September, 9-6. It closes one hour early between November and March.

Museums: The main city museums are closed on Mondays. You can visit the **Museum voor Schone Kunsten** (Citadelpark), the **Bijlokemuseum** (Godshuizenlaan 2) and the **Museum voor Sierkunst** (Jan Breydelstraat 5) Tuesday to Sunday, 9.30-5. The wistful **Museum voor Stenen Voorwerpen** (St Baafsabdij ruins, Gandastraat) is only open from April to October, the hours being 9.30-5. The **Museum voor Volkskunde** (Kraanlei 65), a sight not to be missed, is open April to October, Tuesday to Sunday, 9-12.30 and 1.30-5.30; November to March, Tuesday to Sunday, 10-12 and 1.30-5.

Antwerp

Bear in mind Victor Hugo's words: "Paintings in the churches, Rubens in the chapels; the city is literally overflowing with art." It is a mistake to try and see everything in one brief visit; choose two or three museums and perhaps one church, leaving the rest for another time.

Museums: Most museums in Antwerp are closed on Monday. The **Koninklijk Museum voor Schone Kunsten** (Leopold de Waelplaats) is open Tuesday to Friday, 10-5. The **Ruben-huis** (Wapper 9), **Museum Plantin-Moretus** (Vrijdagmarkt 22), **Steen** (Steenplein 1), **Vleeshuis** (Vleeshouwersstraat 38), **Museum Mayer van den Bergh** (Lange Gasthuisstraat 19), **Museum voor Hedendaagse Kunst** (Leuvenstraat 16), **Museum voor Fotografie** (Waalse Kaai 47) and **Rockoxhuis** (Keizerstraat 10) are open Tuesday to Sunday, 10-4.45.

Churches: Onze-Lieve-Vrouwekathedraal is open Monday to Friday 10-6, Saturday 10-3, Sunday 1-4 . **St Jacobskerk** (Lange Nieuwstraat 73) is open April to October, Monday to Saturday, 2-5; November to March, Monday to Saturday, 9-12. **St Carolus Borromeuskerk** on Hendrik Conscienceplein is open Monday, 11.30-12.30 and 2-4.30; Tuesday, 9.45-12.30 and 5.30-7; Wednesday and Thursday, 9.45-12.30 and 2 4.30; Friday 9.45-12.30 and 2-5.30; Saturday, 10-12.30 and 2.30-7.15; Sunday 9.30-12.45. **St Pauluskerk** on Veemarkt is open May to September, daily 2-5. **St Andrieskerk** opens May to September, Tuesday to Friday 2-5; October to April, Tuesday to Friday 9-12.

Further sights: The **Handelsbeurs** (Twaalfmaandenstraat) is open free of charge Monday to Friday, 7.30 am-7 pm. The courtyard of the **Oude Beurs** (Hofstraat 15) can be entered Monday to Friday, 9-12. The **Begijnhof** (Rodestraat 39) is open daily 9-5.

Mechelen
The **Hof van Busleyden** (Frederik de Merodestraat 65) is open Tuesday to Sunday 10-12 and 2-5.

Brussels
Museums in central Brussels: Museums in Brussels tend to close on Mondays. The royal museums in Brussels are open free of charge. The national art collection is found in two adjoining museums known as the **Musées Royaux des Beaux-Arts**. The Old Masters, such as Bruegel and Rubens, hang in the **Musée d'Art Ancien** (Rue de la Régence 3), open Tuesday to Sunday, 10-12 and 1-5. The modern art, including Magritte and Delvaux, is kept in the **Musée d'Art Moderne** (Place Royale 1), open Tuesday to Sunday, 10-1 and 2-5. The museum shop

and café stay open without a break. The **Musée de la Ville de Bruxelles** on Grand'Place is open Monday to Friday 10-5 (October to March closes one hour earlier), Saturday and Sunday 10-1. The **Centre Belge de la Bande Dessinée** (Rue des Sables 20), a museum devoted to Belgian comic books, is open Tuesday to Sunday 10-6.

The Museum Park: Three large museums are located in the Parc du Cinquantenaire, best reached by taking the metro to Mérode. A large collection of decorative art is displayed in the **Musées Royaux d'Art et d'Histoire**, open Tuesday to Friday 9.30-4.45, Saturday, Sunday and public holidays 10-4.45. The adjoining **Musée Royal de l'Armée** is open Tuesday to Sunday 9-12 and 1-4.45. The vintage car collection in **Autoworld** is open April to September, daily 10-6, October to March, daily 10-5.

Other museums: The **Musée Communale d'Ixelles** (Rue Jean van Volsem 71) is open Tuesday to Friday 1-5.30, Saturday and Sunday 10-5. The **Musée Wiertz** (Rue Vautier 62) is open Tuesday to Sunday 10-12 and 1-5. The museum sometimes closes at weekends. The **Musée Horta** (Rue Américaine 25) is open Tuesday to Sunday 2-5.30. The **Tour Japonaise** and the **Pavillon Chinois** (facing each other on Avenue Van Praet, best reached by taking tram 92 to Araucaria) are open Tuesday to Sunday 10-4.45. Both buildings, marvellous examples of Orientalism, are threatened with closure. It is wise to check with the tourist office before making a special journey. The **Maison d'Erasme** (Rue Chapitre 31, a short walk from Saint-Guidon metro station) is open Saturday, Sunday, Monday, Wednesday and Thursday 10-12, 2-5.

Churches: The **Cathédrale St Michel** is open 7-6. The **Eglise Notre-Dame du Sablon** is open 9-6. The **Eglise St Nicolas** is open Monday to Friday 7.30-6.30, Saturday 9-5.30 pm, Sunday 7.30 am-7.30 pm.

Further sights: The **Atomium** on the Boulevard du Centenaire (a short walk from Heysel metro stop) is open every day of the year, April to August 9-8, September to March 10-6. The **Chapelle de Nassau**, inside the Bibliothèque Royale, is open Monday to Saturday 12-5.

Leuven

The **St Pieterskerk**, where Dirk Bouts *Last Supper* hangs, is open Tuesday to Saturday 10-12, 2-5, Sunday 2-5. It is also open on Mondays from mid-March to mid-October, 10-12 and 2-5.

The Food and Beer of Flanders

Word is getting around. People are beginning to discover that Belgian cooking is quite possibly the best in the world. Tourists are coming home from trips to Antwerp or Brussels with tales of sublime and substantial meals eaten in Belgian restaurants - not just in the pricey Brussels restaurants, but even in plain bistros in the back streets of Zeebrugge, or in dockers' cafés in the port district of Antwerp. The art of eating well in Belgium goes back at least as far as the Burgundian middle ages, when lavish feasts were held in the ducal palaces of Brussels and Bruges. The delights of eating and drinking are reflected in the wedding feasts of Pieter Breughel and, even more, the banqueting scenes painted by the Antwerp artist Frans Snijders, such as the painting overleaf.

We do not need to search far to find good cooking in Belgium. There are excellent places in abundance, offering anything we might happen to need, be it a simple early morning *croissant* or a full six-course meal. The high quality of Belgian cooking raises the standard in every other type of eating place - Thai restaurants, pizzerias, Vietnamese market stalls, sandwich bars, station cafés and cake shops are all excellent. Even a humble aluminium *frites* stand in the middle of Antwerp docks has to maintain a certain standard, or the customers will soon head off somewhere else.

The beer culture in Belgium is equally sophisticated. There are hundreds of small breweries in Belgium where dedicated artisans produce old-fashioned ales. Almost every town in Belgium has its own brew, served in its own distinctive glass. The beer often has to be poured in a particular way, and even drunk in a particular manner. Whatever they drink, Belgians treat bottled beers

with the same devotion as the French regard good wines. We can usually find a good café or two in the main square, where the menu will perhaps list a dozen brews, or we might be fortunate enough to discover a specialised tavern down a back street where the owner will keep hundreds of different brews in stock, each variety with its own glass.

At other times we may find ourselves tempted by cake and coffee. Most cafés in Belgium serve excellent coffee, but we will probably only find cakes in a tea room. Belgian are particularly fond of waffles, of course, as well as chocolate cake, rice flan, or indeed anything offering a thousand calories per bite.

Then there are Belgian chocolates. Most Belgians like to pick up a little box of Leonidas now and again, but the most ardent chocolate eaters tend to favour the sophisticated Neuhaus or Godiva assortments. Others will swear by some tiny chocolate shop in a distant village, but we will probably be perfectly satisfied with a box picked up on the Grand'Place in Brussels.

Belgians like to tell you that French fries are in fact a Belgian invention. Whatever the truth of the story, Belgium is devoted to *frites*. We will probably find ourselves being served ample plates of Belgian chips in restaurants, but one can also pick up a portion at a little stall on a city square. On a cold winter day, when the wind howls across the plains of Flanders, nothing is quite so warming as a little cardboard box filled with plump, crisp *frites*. The national dish of mussels with *frites* accompanied by a Belgian beer, if taken in the right mood, is unsurpassable.

Bruges
To be honest, most of us would find it hard to resist a candlelit dining room with a view of a canal. Bruges can offer us some of the most romantic restaurants in Europe, where the food, if not the best in Belgium, is well above average. Twenty years ago, the ultimate address in Bruges was the **Duc de Bourgogne** at Huidenvetter-splein 12. It is still good, but not quite the best. Its neighbours, likewise good, but not remarkable, are **'t Bourgoensche Cruyce** at Wollestraat 41 and **'t Dreveken** at Huidenvettersplein 10. Locals

in search of good food would tend now to go a bit further from the centre, perhaps to **Pieter Pourbus**, in the street of the same name. Located in a house dating from 1561, this is the place to try fish, some of it landed in nearby Zeebrugge. The restaurant **Malpertuus** at Eiermarkt 9 is a good Flemish bistro, as is **'t Kutse** at Oude Burg 31. A few restaurants in Bruges have developed a cuisine based on beer, including **'t Paardje** at Langestraat 20, where we can try eels stewed in Rodenbach beer or frothy zabaglione flavoured with Brugse Tripel.

Bruges had some fifty breweries in the middle ages, but only two have survived. The Straffe Hendrik on Walplein is the better known, and has guided tours most of the year. The more interesting beers come out of the small De Gouden Boom brewery on Langestraat. Most cafés in Bruges sell Brugs Tarwebier, a tangy wheat brew made by De Gouden Boom, but it is more difficult to track down their superb Brugse Tripel, a strong ale served in a long glass. A small museum, open irregular hours, occupies the former malting house of the brewery. The distinctive reddish-brown Rodenbach beers, brewed near Bruges, are something of an acquired taste. Many Belgians consider Rodenbach the perfect beer to quench a thirst, but others find it just a bit too sour. We can sample a glass or two among the town's serious beer connoisseurs who gather in the café **'t Brugs Beertje** at Kemelstraat 5. The owner has some 300 beers in stock and runs a semi-serious weekly Belgian beer seminar in a back room.

Ghent

The waterfront restaurants in Ghent are as romantic as any in Bruges, and the food is often better. We might choose a window table at the **Graaf van Egmond** on the Sint-Michielsbrug for the spectacular view of Ghent's towers, or wander along the quays to the **Buikse Vol** at Kraanlei 17 to eat fish next to the waterside. We might even think about a meal in the **Sint Jorishof** at Botermarkt 2, if only for the experience of eating in the oldest hotel in Europe. The dining room dates back to the 13th century and the cooking follows the best classical traditions.

If we are in an exploring mood, we can wander down the cobbled lanes of the Patershol to investigate the new restaurants that have opened up here in recent years. Whether painted bright yellow or smothered in ivy, they are almost all good. We might try the **Blauw Zalm** at Vrouwebroerstraat 2 for its fish; **Le Petit Restaurant** at Rodekoningstraat 12 for its handsome interior; **Amadeus** at Plotersgracht 8 for simple spare ribs; or **Bij den Wijzen en de Zot** at Hertogstraat 8 for its refined Flemish cuisine.

The best place in Ghent to make a foray into Belgium's beer culture is **De Dulle Griet** at Vrijdagmarkt 50, where the beer menu runs to some 250 brews. A short wander across the square brings us to **Frituur Josef**, which has been dishing out crisp *frites* topped with a squirt of mayonnaise for the best part of a hundred years.

Antwerp

Fear not: there is no reason ever to go hungry in Antwerp. There are restaurants on every street and square. Some of the most attractive are found around the cathedral; in fact, a few small restaurants are built *onto* the cathedral. The most intriguing of these is **Het Vermoeide Model** (The Weary Sitter) at Lijnwaadmarkt 2, where we are led to our table through a warren of tiny rooms and creaking staircases. If this is not quite what we are seeking, we will find countless other good restaurants on the narrow cobbled streets nearby. **Pasta** at Oude Koornmarkt 32 is especially popular, so that to be sure of a table, we have to turn up soon after the cathedral clock strikes six. Not that we will starve if we cannot get into Pasta. We can try, for example, the **New Sir Anthony van Dyck** at Oude Koornmarkt 16. The owner of this distinguished Antwerp restaurant created quite a rumpus a few years ago by *sending back* his two Michelin stars, claiming that he wanted to create a less expensive, more imaginative cuisine. His gamble has paid off, and we may well find ourselves once again turned away, in which case we might wander into the warren of old alleys known as Vlaaikensgang, to a charming little bistro called **'t Hofke** (the alley entrance is at Oude Kornmarkt 16). If that too is full, we should look down Pelgrimstraat and Grote Pieter Potstraat. Something is sure to turn up.

We might be lucky enough to secure a table at Pottenburg at Minderboedersrui 38, a charming old bistro where local artists like to gather. But if we are looking for the bustling atmosphere of the new Antwerp, we should head southwards to **Hippodroom** at Léopold de Waelplaats 10, a frenetic multi-levelled modern restaurant with a splendid choice of unusual dishes.

A memorable ale called De Koninck is brewed in Antwerp. It is a dark, rich, old-fashioned beer, served in a chalice-shaped glass. Antwerp proudly claims to have well over two thousand drinking establishments, ranging from splendid old taverns to raucous seamen's dives. I could imagine an enjoyable *kroegentocht* that took in **Den Engel** at Grote Markt 3, the **Pelgrom** at Pelgrimstraat 15, **De Cluyse** at Oude Koornmarkt 26, and **Witzly Poetzly** at Blauwmoezelstraat 8. Flemish *frites* can be foundwithout too much searching to allay any sudden hunger pangs. Some people will tell you that the best are produced at a shop in the Hoogstraat, though I have heard a rumour that there is a stand somewhere in the depths of Antwerp's docks where the *frites* are the best in Belgium.

Mechelen

The best place to find lunch in Mechelen is in one of the cafés on the Grote Markt, such as the **Brasserie Royale** or **'t Voske**. The local beer is a rich, dark brew called Gouden Carolus, which can be sampled in one of the pleasant cafés on the Grote Markt, such as **In de Beer**. The name has nothing to do with beer; it means 'The Bear'.

Brussels

Where do we begin? Brussels had two thousand restaurants at the last count. Most tourists barely scratch the surface, finding something perfectly satisfactory in the warren of streets around Grand'Place. The Rue des Bouchers is lined entirely with restaurants, including old Brussels institutions such as **Aux Armes de Bruxelles** at Rue des Bouchers 13, and **Chez Léon** at Rue des Bouchers 18, the latter a famous mussel restaurant which now has branches all over northern

359

Europe. Other reliable restaurants in the neighbourhood include **Chez Jean** at Rue des Chapeliers 6, where waitresses of a certain age serve customers of a certain girth with thick steaks and huge helpings of *frites*. The **Brasserie de la Roue d'Or** at Rue des Chapeliers 26 is still very much a local brasserie, whereas **Falstaff** at Rue Henri Maus 25 tends to be full of tourists there to admire the art nouveau architecture rather than the food. A little out of the way, **La Manufacture** at Rue Notre-Dame du Sommeil 12 has a striking interior, once a leather factory. Even more off the beaten track is the typical Brussels bistro, **In 't Spinnekopke**, on the Place du Jardin aux Fleurs. We might find the name difficult, but it is a little easier than **Au Stekerlapatte** at Rue des Prêtres 4, another old bistro which produces excellent and inexpensive Brussels cooking. Anyone looking for fish in Brussels needs simply to head for the old fish market, where the best, or at least the most picturesque fish restaurants are to be found.

Once we head out of the centre, the possibilities are endless. The Sablon is surrounded by elegant, and expensive restaurants, and we can eat at half the price by walking down the hill into the Marolles, where some of the best bistros are located. A good place to try there is **L' Idiot du Village** at Rue Notre Seigneur 19. Further south, the commune of Ixelles, with its high number of artists and designers, has dozens of fashionable places. We can eat a hearty *jambonneau* in one such, the **Quincaillerie** at Rue du Page 45. This was once an ironmonger's, and the tiny rooms are still lined with the wooden drawers where nuts and bolts were stored. The **Old Inn** at Rue Washington 76 is a place to taste good Belgian cooking without paying an enormous bill.

Further out still, the leafy *commune* of Uccle is dotted with excellent restaurants, such as **Brasserie Georges** at Avenue Winston Churchill 259, near the Bois de la Cambre, and the historic inn **De Hoef** at Rue Edith Cavell 218. Another cluster of restaurants is found in the European Quarter, around the Rond-Point Schuman. Bustling at lunchtime, these places tend to be emptier in the evening. We find Greek, Spanish and Irish restaurants here, together with the wonderful **Rosticceria Fiorentina** at Rue Archimède 45.

The local beer of Brussels is a curious brew called Gueuze, fermented from microbes which flourish in the Senne valley and nowhere else in the world. Gueuze is brewed at the tiny Cantillon brewery at Rue Gheude 56, which sometimes runs guided tours. The best place in which to sample a glass of Gueuze is amid the faded grandeur of **A la Mort Subite** at Rue Montagne aux Herbes Potagères 7. Other old Brussels cafés, well worth a visit, are **Le Cirio** at Rue de la Bourse 18, a wonderful glittering café popular with elderly Belgians; **L'Imaige Nostre-Dame** in the Impasse des Cadeaux (off Rue du Marché aux Herbes 8), decorated in the style of an old Flemish inn, and, if you can find it, **La Bécasse**, an ancient establishment on two floors hidden down an alley at Rue Tabora 11. Everyone has their own favourite Brussels *friterie*, but most experts agree that it is hard to find better chips than those fried

Chez Antoine on Place Jourdan.

Leuven

Leuven is teeming with students who like to eat out in inexpensive brasseries, Vietnamese restaurants and pizzerias. The Oude Markt is surrounded by bustling restaurants which spill out onto the cobbled square at the first hint of spring. **Ming Dynasty** at number 9 is considered a good bet for traditional Chinese cooking. The more elegant **Belle Epoque** is a striking Art Nouveau restaurant at Bondgenotenlaan 94.

Leuven is the town where Stella Artois is brewed. Belgians claim it tastes better here than abroad, a claim we can check in any one of the town's many student cafés. The most attractive drinking place, popular with students and professors alike, is the rambling **Domus** in Tiensestraat, not far from the town hall. The café has its own small brewery next door, and the beer is fed into the café along a tangle of pipes.

Further Pleasures

I. Carillons

As we wander down a cobbled lane in Bruges or Ghent, we might suddenly become aware that the church bells are playing a familiar tune. It could be the opening bars of a Mozart symphony or possibly a Beatles' song. We should stop for a moment and listen, for this is a rare opportunity to hear a Flemish carillon concert.

The carillon was invented in the Flemish town of Oudenaarde in the 17th century. John Evelyn was so intrigued by one he heard in Amsterdam that he climbed the church tower to investigate 'whither the motion were from any extraordinary Engine.' He did not find any Engine, but a man sitting at an instrument resembling an organ: 'the hammers fastned with wyers, to several keyes, put into a frame 20 foote below the Bells, upon which he struck on the keys, and playd to admiration.'

Pity the poor carilloneur. He has to sit in a draughty little room high in the tower, which is furnished, if he is lucky, with a small electric heater. He may well, as Evelyn says, play to admiration, but he has no knowledge of this. All he can hear is the clattering of the wooden keys which he strikes with his fists and feet. It is no job for the faint-hearted. Every time he gives a concert, the carilloneur has to plod up several hundred stone steps, clutching his sheet music and perhaps a cup of coffee from a local café. In spite of these hardships, the little carillon school in Mechelen attracts eager young students from all over the world who study for four or five years and then wait patiently for a vacancy to come up as town carilloneur.

It is worth asking at the local tourist offices for details of carillon concerts in Bruges, Ghent, Mechelen, Antwerp and Leuven. Carillon concerts in Antwerp draw large crowds to the narrow lanes and the café terraces around the cathedral. The carillon hung in the north tower of the cathedral has 49 bells of different sizes, with a total weight of some 28 tons. The oldest bell was hoisted to the top of the tower in 1459 using a gigantic treadmill, but the majority of the carillon's bells were forged in 1658 in the Dutch town of Zutphen, by the famous Pieter Hemony. Concerts are normally held from mid-June to mid-September, on Mondays from 9-10 pm and on Fridays 11.30 am -12.30 pm. Those seeking the best acoustics should take up positions within the medieval alleys of the Vlaaikensgang, or in the courtyard of the Oude Beurs, though most local people are quite contented to sit with a beer at one of the café tables on Groenplaats or Grote Markt.

The carillon in Bruges hangs in the belfry above the Markt. The carilloneur has to climb 352 steps each time he gives a one-hour concert. From mid-June to September, the carillon is played on Mondays, Wednesdays and Saturdays, 9-10 pm and on Sundays 2.15-3 pm. The rest of the year, concerts can be heard on Sundays, Wednesdays and Saturdays, 2.15-3 pm.

The Belfry in Ghent houses a 52-bell carillon, of which 37 were cast in the Hemony workshop. The largest bell, named *Triomfante*, cracked in 1914 and had to be lowered to the square below, where it now sits on a patch of grass. Concerts take place in the summer months.

It is to the modest town of Mechelen that we must go to find out the secrets of the carillon. Mechelen is home to a famous carillon school, named in honour of the carilloneur Jef Denyn, which occupies a neat white rococo town house with geraniums tumbling out of window boxes. Two carillons, each with 49 bells, hang in the cathedral tower. The bells are played on Saturdays and Mondays, 11.30 am - 12.30 pm, on Sundays 3- 4 pm, and from June to mid-September on Mondays 8.30-9.30 pm. The best spot to stand, experts say, is in the alley called Straatje Zonder Einde. Students at the carillon school are taught on a small set of bells hung in the tower of the Hof van Busleyden, where they can bang away on the tinkly bells without the entire town hearing them hit C sharp instead of B flat.

The university town of Leuven has two carillons.

One hangs in the St Pieterskerk and is played every Saturday, 3- 4 pm. A second carillon which hangs in the tower of the university library is played during the university terms on Thursdays and Fridays, 6-6.45 pm.

II. Canal tours

A canal trip in Bruges *might* be an enjoyable experience. It depends on the number of people crammed into our boat and whether the rain holds off. One hundred years ago, as in our photograph, we might have had a boat to ourselves, but the aim these days is to pack in the maximum number of people. As well as being rather small, the motor launches have open tops to allow the craft to squeeze under the low medieval bridges. If it should start to rain, the boatman will distribute large striped umbrellas, but we may still end up chilled to the bone, as well as crushed. The boat trips leave from five different points on the Dijver canal. I tend to favour the company that runs from Katelijnestraat, though the commentary is virtually the same no matter which firm you choose. Bear in mind that the boatman expects a tip at the end of the tour, even if his bland commentary is rattled off like a catechism.

As we might expect, the boats in Ghent are more modern. The little fleet of vessels includes a few open-topped boats, but most are glass-roofed and look oddly like drifting greenhouses. The boats can be found moored on the Graslei from about Easter until the end of October.

In Antwerp, a fleet of large vessels run by the Flandria company lies moored next to the Steen. The ships regularly head off downstream on tours of the modern port. A certain interest in the logistics of container transportation is desirable if we are not to become bored.

III. Towers

Flemish craftsmen toiled throughout the middle ages on the construction of soaring Gothic spires, but many were left unfinished after war broke out or city finances ran dry. The traveller in Flanders now only rarely has the chance to climb a tower, and the opportunity when presented must be seized. The most rewarding climb is to the top of the Belfry in Bruges, the ascent of 366 steps relieved by various rooms of interest on the way. The view from the top inspired the poet Robert Southey to claim, 'from the Belfroy's height, no happier landscape may on earth be seen.'

It may be that the view from the spire of Antwerp's cathedral reveals an even happier landscape, but we cannot judge, as the tower is currently closed. Nor can we climb Mechelen's unfinished cathedral tower, except on certain Saturdays. We are in luck in Ghent, where the Belfry can be climbed, but only in the company of a guide. A lift will take us to the top of the Atomium in Brussels, where we have a panoramic, if bizarre view of a miniature Eiffel Tower and various other scaled-down buildings in the Mini Europe theme park.

IV. A Flanders library

Those who like to scour their local bookshops in search of travel literature may be disappointed by the poverty of books on Flanders or Belgium. This region of Europe, unlike Tuscany or Provence, does not excite many travel writers.

Baedeker's Belgium and Holland, published in Leipzig up until the Second World War, remains the best guide book ever written on the region. The maps are masterpieces of German cartography, though their usefulness is diminished by the pre-war convention of giving French names to Flemish streets. Long out of print, you may manage to dig out a tattered red-bound copy in an antiquarian bookshop, perhaps with some pages annotated by a previous owner in old faded ink.

The *Blue Guide to Belgium and Luxembourg* (London, A&C Black, 1993) began its long and useful career in 1920 as a guide to Belgium and the Western Front. Grieving mothers and forlorn widows used the Blue Guide to track down the graves of men killed in the Ypres Salient. The Blue Guide in later editions ossified into a rather rigid prose style, strong on dates but weak on atmosphere, though Bernard McDonagh's new edition has spiced up some sections of the text. The description of the Belgian Western Front is still one of the best accounts available in English.

Those with an interest in medieval Flemish painting can buy one of two hefty works by German art historians. Erwin Panofsky's two-volume *Early Netherlandish Painting* (New York, Harper & Row, 2 volumes, 1971) is a fascinating study of symbolism at work in the Master of Flémalle, the van Eycks and Roger van der Weyden. Max J. Friedlænder's *From Van Eyck to Bruegel: Early Netherlandish Painting* (New York, Phaidon, 1969) goes more deeply into the biographies of Flemish late gothic and early renaissance artists to explain their art. Those visiting Bruges may be tempted to buy Valentin Vermeersch's *The Flemish Primitives: Seven Masterworks, Seven Masters* (Bruges, Stichting Kunstboek, 1995), which describes in detail seven paintings in the Bruges museums. For those in Ghent who need the van Eyck Altarpiece explained, *The Complete Paintings of The Van Eycks* (London, Penguin Books, 1968) is a useful companion. For a more detailed account, you will find Peter Schmidt's *The Mystic Lamb* (Davidsfonds, 1995) in most Ghent bookshops.

One hundred years ago, travellers might have packed a copy of Georges Rodenbach's melancholy novella *Bruges-la-Morte* (first published 1892; reprinted London, Atlas Press, 1993) to read on the Ostend steamer. Set in a gloomy and fog-bound Bruges, and published with photographs of the city, it is the story of an Englishman who comes to Bruges to forget his dead wife. Less than one hundred pages long, Rodenbach's work brought literary-minded Europeans flocking to Bruges in search of the Quai du Rosaire and other locations mentioned in the novel. Even a century on, the tourist office still has to struggle hard to promote Bruges as *de*

Schone (the beautiful), rather than *la-Morte*.

Several classic English novels are set in Brussels - Charlotte Brontë's *Villette* and *The Professor*, and parts of William Makepeace Thackeray's *Vanity Fair*. The most famous modern Belgian novel is Hugo Claus' *The Sorrow of Belgium* (translation in Penguin, 1990), an epic and often amusing account of life in a small Flemish town during the German Occupation. The novel is teeming with eccentric nuns, corrupt priests and other wonderful Flemish characters.

Index

INDEX

371

Of course we're glad
28 million of you chose
to fly with us last year.
It must mean you like us.

Lufthansa

More than that,
you trust us.

PALLAS GUIDES
LANDSCAPE PEOPLE ART ARCHITECTURE

In our Pallas Guide series:

POLAND

This hefty item is a cultural treasure *Polish American Journal*

CZECH AND SLOVAK REPUBLICS

As carefully thought-out as an old Baedeker *Time Out*

WALES

Certainly the best book on the country *The New York Times*

A passionate and fabulously detailed book *The Rough Guide*

EAST ANGLIA

A stunningly good guide *Mail on Sunday*

Peter Sager is an unsung genius *Val Hennessy*

ANDALUCIA

The ideal companion we all dream of but rarely find *Irish Independent*

PALLAS GUIDES

LANDSCAPE PEOPLE ART ARCHITECTURE

Forthcoming

ISRAEL AND THE HOLY LAND

PAKISTAN   YEMEN

BAROQUE ROME   LONDON

TIBET   MALAYSIA   SRI LANKA

THE WEST COUNTRY

Excellent and in-depth - invaluable companions *Anderson's Travel Companion*
Travel books for the aficionado   *The Bookseller*
Thorough and thoroughly readable   *Griff Rhys-Jones, BBC1 Bookworm*
Superb *Traveller*

For more information, please contact
Pallas Athene, 59 Linden Gardens, London W2 4HJ

PALLAS GUIDES

LANDSCAPE PEOPLE ART ARCHITECTURE

Uniform with this volume:

VENICE FOR PLEASURE

J. G. Links

Not only the best guide-book to that city ever written, but
the best guide-book to *any* city ever written *Bernard Levin in The Times*

One of the most delightful and original guides ever written *Jan Morris*

MADRID OBSERVED

Michael Jacobs

He has a gift for finding exotic corners in a familiar city and of
resuscitating the forgotten with colourful intensity
Times Literary Supplement

One of the best current foreign writers on Spain   *Time Out*